Adobe
Premiere Pro
CC

JAN OZER

 Peachpit Press

Visual QuickStart Guide

Adobe Premiere Pro CC: Visual QuickStart Guide

Jan Ozer

Peachpit Press
www.peachpit.com
To report errors, please send a note to errata@peachpit.com
Peachpit Press is a division of Pearson Education

Project Editor: Nancy Peterson
Development Editor: Stephen Nathans-Kelly
Contributing Writer: Shawn Lam
Production Editor and Compositor: Danielle Foster
Technical Editor: Pamela Berry, Luisa Winters
Copyeditor: Scout Festa
Indexer: Jack Lewis
Interior Design: Peachpit Press
Cover Design: RHDG / Riezebos Holzbaur, Peachpit Press
Logo Design: MINE™ www.minesf.com

Notice of Rights

Notice of Liability

Trademarks

ISBN 13: 978-0-321-92954-9
ISBN 10:   0-321-92954-3

10 9 8 7 6 5 4 3 2 1

Printed and bound in the United States of America

Dedication

To my daughters, Elizabeth Whatley and Eleanor Rose, and my host daughters, Fran and Victoria. You all bring immeasurable joy to my life.

Contributing Author

Shawn Lam is a professionally accredited and multi-award-winning video producer and technical director. He has written over 50 articles for StreamingMediaProducer.com and its predecessor *EventDV Magazine*. His company, Shawn Lam Video Inc., specializes in corporate and event video production, including online video, video switching, webcasting, and video SEO. In addition to serving 5 terms as the President of the British Columbia Professional Videographers Association, Shawn has taught video production business at B.C.I.T and has spoken at several international video production conferences. Shawn lives in the Vancouver suburb of Port Coquiltam, with his wife and three kids and enjoys mountain biking, hiking, and going on adventures with his kids.

Table of Contents

Welcome to
Adobe Premiere Pro

Adobe Premiere Pro is the hub of the Adobe Creative Suite. It is an application through which input from After Effects, Illustrator, Photoshop, Prelude, Story, and other programs is integrated into a video production that can be shown anywhere from a mobile phone to a 3D theater metroplex. Lofty visions, but first you have to get comfortable with the program and learn where to find all the critical panels and controls. That's what you'll accomplish in this chapter.

You'll start with a quick tour of the interface and then an overview of Premiere Pro's non-linear editing workflow. Then you'll learn how to choose and customize Premiere Pro's workspaces and choose the most relevant preferences. The chapter concludes with a look at how to choose and customize keyboard shortcuts to streamline repetitive editing functions.

In This Chapter

Touring the Interface

Premiere Pro's interface has dozens of panels and hundreds of controls. To make these accessible without clutter, the program uses multiple tabbed panels configured into workspaces that you can customize. There are several key panels, so let's get acquainted with them first Ⓐ.

On the upper left is the Source Monitor, where you'll preview content before adding it into the project. Other tabs in this panel include the Effect Controls panel, where you'll customize the effects you add to your clips; the Audio Clip Mixer, where you can adjust the levels of audio files you add to your project; and the Metadata panel, where you view, search, enter, and edit clip metadata.

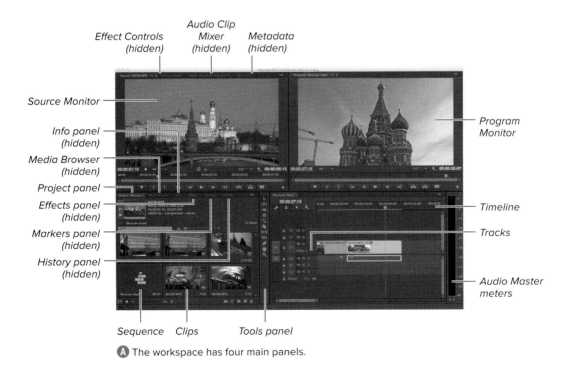

Ⓐ The workspace has four main panels.

On the bottom left are the building blocks that you'll use to build your movies. The figure shows the Project panel, which contains all source clips and sequences. Tabbed panels behind the Project panel include the Media Browser, where you can add clips to your project; the Info panel, which details the specs of each piece of content; the Effects panel, where you'll find transitions and effects; the Markers panel, which contains all markers added to the project; and the History panel, which displays a history of the last 32 edits made to the project. It's helpful to make the History panel visible when you need to accurately undo some edits.

On the bottom right is the Timeline, where you'll assemble the various audio, video, and still-image components of your project. On the top right is the Program Monitor, where you'll preview what you've produced in the Timeline. If you look closely at the bottom left of the Program Monitor, you'll see the timecode 00:00:27:16. You'll learn more about timecode later; what's critical here is that the timecode matches the time shown at the top left of the Timeline. This reinforces the point that the Program Monitor shows you what's being produced in the Timeline.

TIP Sometimes you'll accidentally close a tabbed panel. To reopen any panel, choose Window in the Premiere Pro menu. You'll see a list of panels, and you can scroll down and choose the desired panel.

The Premiere Pro Workflow

Premiere Pro is a non-linear editor. By way of background, video editing originally occurred on tape, and the only way to make a change in minute 29 of a 30-minute production was to start at the beginning, roll tape until that point, and make the change. With Premiere Pro, you simply fix the problem at minute 29 on the timeline and you're done.

Like all non-linear editors, Premiere Pro is non-destructive. You'll start most projects by capturing (from analog source media) or ingesting (from digital source media) lots of content. Then you'll cut the content into pieces, trimming frames here, splitting clips there, adding multiple filters and effects. Through all your edits, Premiere Pro never changes the original source footage— hence the non-destructive label.

Let's take a look at the various panels that you'll use to build projects in Premiere Pro.

■ Content ingest. You'll start by ingesting content into the project. The interface will differ depending upon whether your media is on tape or on fixed media. You'll learn both techniques in Chapter 3, "Importing Media." In the figure, you see an AVCHD video file already copied to a hard drive and in the process of being imported into the project from the Media Browser, which you can access via the keyboard shortcut Shift+8 .

Ⓐ Importing clips in the Media Browser.

■ View content. Once the content is imported, it appears in the Project panel (Shift+1). Double-clicking the content will load it in the Source Monitor (Shift+2) for a larger display **B**. In this panel, you can start the editing process by marking In points and Out points before adding the content to the Timeline. You'll learn all about this in Chapter 4, "Organizing and Viewing Clips."

■ Add clip to the timeline. You can add clips to the Timeline (Shift+3) from the Source Monitor or Project panel via keyboard shortcuts or by dragging, as shown **C**. You'll learn how to get clips to the timeline in Chapter 5, "Working With the Timeline." Then you'll learn how to edit your clips in the Timeline in Chapter 6, "Editing in the Timeline," and Chapter 7, "Advanced Timeline Techniques."

B Viewing a clip from the Project panel in the Source Monitor.

continues on next page

C Dragging a clip from the Source Monitor to the Timeline.

- Add effects, transitions, and Lumetri. Once on the Timeline, some clips will need color or brightness correction or other effects. You also may want to add transitions between clips or add Lumetri movie looks to your project. You access all of these elements in the Effects panel (Shift+7) . You'll learn how to add and customize these elements in Chapter 9, "Working with Video Effects," Chapter 10, "Working With Transitions," and Chapter 11, "Color and Brightness Correction."

D The Effects panel contains multiple elements that help polish your content.

- Customize effects and add motion-related effects in the Effect Controls panel (Shift+5) 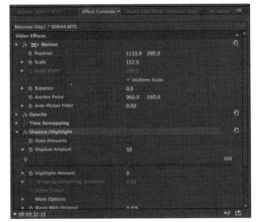. After you apply an effect, you can customize parameters in the Effect Controls panel. This panel also contains fixed effects applied to all video clips for motion (including position, scale, and rotation), opacity, and time remapping, as well as volume, channel volume, and panner adjustments for audio. You don't have to apply these fixed effects to customize these elements; you just have to customize the values. You'll learn how to adjust motion in Chapter 8, "Adding Motion to Clips."

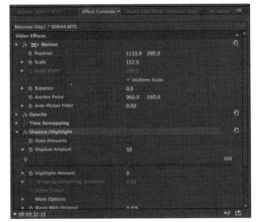

E The Effect Controls panel is where you'll customize and apply audio and video effects.

- Add titles. Titles are a critical component of any production, and Premiere Pro's Titler  offers a great mix of presets and text and design-primitive customization options. You'll learn how to create and customize titles in Chapter 14, "Working with Titles."

F Premiere Pro's excellent Titler.

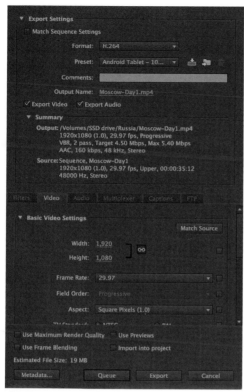

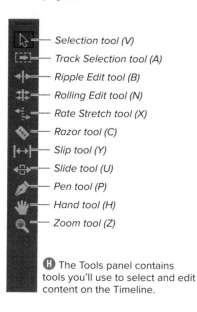

Render your project. Once you've finished work on the Timeline, you'll render your project for sharing with others. You'll use the Export Settings dialog ⒢ to render clips either directly from Premiere Pro or through the Adobe Media Encoder, which comes bundled with Premiere Pro and includes a range of useful presets, extensive customization options, and highly efficient parallel encoding. You'll learn how to use the Adobe Media Encoder in Chapter 16, "Publishing Your Video."

These are the basic workflow components common to most video projects. Other projects will employ features discussed in other chapters, such as Chapter 12, "Multi-Camera Editing," and Chapter 13, "Keying and Compositing."

Here are some other panels and interface components that you should know about.

Tools panel. Tools in this panel ⒣ control how you select content in the Timeline, the types of edits you'll perform in the Timeline, and other useful functions. For example, the Razor tool (C) makes it easy to split clips on the timeline, while the Track Selection tool (A) enables you to select all content on a track, which is useful when you need to shift it one way or the other in the Timeline. In Chapter 7, "Advanced Timeline Techniques," you'll learn about ripple, rolling, and slip edits.

continues on next page

⒢ The Export Settings dialog, which you'll use to render projects.

Selection tool (V)

Track Selection tool (A)

Ripple Edit tool (B)

Rolling Edit tool (N)

Rate Stretch tool (X)

Razor tool (C)

Slip tool (Y)

Slide tool (U)

Pen tool (P)

Hand tool (H)

Zoom tool (Z)

⒣ The Tools panel contains tools you'll use to select and edit content on the Timeline.

- The Info panel and Properties panel 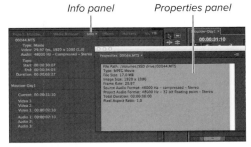 reveal complementary bits of information about a selected clip. The Info panel identifies some basic file information and the location of the clip in the project. The Properties panel, accessed by right-clicking the clip and choosing Properties, identifies format, total duration, and pixel aspect ratio. Probably most important is the file path to the clip, useful when you're trying to find the clip on your hard drive.

Info panel   Properties panel

I The Info panel and Properties panel are convenient for finding out useful details about your clips, including location.

- The History panel 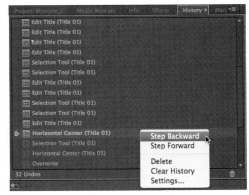 is a useful tool for precisely identifying the edits you'd like to undo. As you click each item in the list, Premiere Pro shows you the action that will be undone (plus all subsequent edits), a nice complement to the familiar keyboard shortcuts Command/Ctrl+Z for Undo and Command/Ctrl+Y for Redo, which Premiere Pro also supports. The History panel contains a configurable number of edits. The default is 32, and you can change this by right-clicking in the panel and choosing Settings.

J The History panel makes it easy to precisely undo previous editing steps.

TIP *Ingest* isn't just a fancy word for capture. Back when digital video editors first appeared, all video was analog and had to be converted to digital for editing. That analog-to-digital conversion was commonly known as capture. Now, virtually all video is shot in digital formats, so no conversion is necessary. Instead, the video is imported from the camera-based media to your hard drive, which is known as ingest. (The one exception is DV/HDV. Both are digital formats, so it's a digital-to-digital transfer, but because they're tape-based, the process is called capture.)

TIP As you've seen in some of these descriptions, Premiere Pro uses hot keys to switch among the major panels. You can see the shortcuts for each panel by choosing Window in the Premiere Pro menu, or you can experiment by holding down the Shift key and pressing numbers 1 through 9 on your keyboard.

TIP Use the buttons on the lower left of the Media Browser to change from List view to Thumbnail view, and use the slider adjacent to Icon view to make the icons larger and smaller. You'll find these same controls in the Project panel.

A Choosing a different workspace.

B Here's how you reset your workspace to its original layout.

C Click Yes to restore the workspace to its original layout.

Choosing Your Workspace

Editing involves many discrete functions and tasks, and Premiere Pro makes it simple to optimize the panels and windows in the user interface for these activities. Each custom arrangement is called a *Workspace*, and Premiere Pro comes with seven preset workspaces, which you can customize.

You can also reset any workspace back to the factory original (so to speak) or create additional custom workspaces.

To choose a workspace:

Choose Window > Workspace, and select the desired workspace **A**.

> **TIP** If you've been using Premiere Pro 5.5 or Final Cut Pro 7, the Editing (CS5.5) workspace will make you feel right at home; you'll find project content and effects on the upper left, just where you'd expect to see them.

To reset a workspace:

1. Choose Window > Workspace, and select the workspace to reset **A**.
2. Choose Window > Workspace > Reset Current Workspace **B**.
3. Click Yes in the Reset Workspace dialog **C**.

To save a custom workspace:

1. Arrange your workspace as desired.

2. Choose Window > Workspace > New Workspace . The New Workspace dialog opens.

3. Type the desired name in the Name field and click OK **E**.

TIP Import Workspace from Projects **A** works in this manner: If you want Premiere Pro to use the workspace saved with the project (and change the existing workspace when you load the project), make sure that Import Workspace from Projects is selected. If you want to keep the existing layout when you load an existing project, deselect Import Workspace from Projects.

TIP If you find yourself switching workspaces frequently, you can either use the keyboard shortcuts next to each workspace in the menu to load them, or choose Window > Options to open the Options window, which lets you easily switch between workspaces.

TIP Note the Delete Workspace option in the Window > Workspace menu. That's how you delete any workspaces that you've created.

D Choose New Workspace to save a new workspace.

E Enter the new name and click OK.

About Your Workspace

Premiere Pro's interface is made up of multiple elements and is infinitely configurable. If you want to work within the four major frames, you can; if you'd prefer to have dozens of windows or panels open simultaneously, you can do that as well.

Three concepts are essential to arranging your work: frames and panels; the components of a tab; and drop zones. Let's take a closer look.

The Premiere Pro interface is built around the concepts of frames and panels **A**. A frame is essentially a separate window in the interface, which can have one or more panels. In the default interface, there are four frames, but you can create as many frames as you would like, both within and outside the Premiere Pro interface.

Frames

Panels

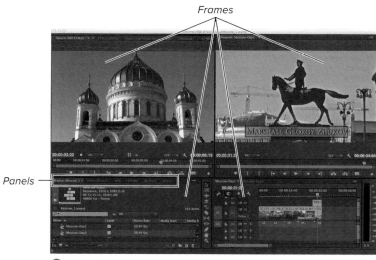

A Premiere Pro's interface is made up of panels and frames.

The panel tabs themselves have several subtle but powerful controls. On the extreme left is a textured "grab" area 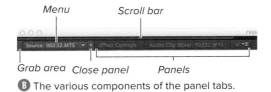. To move the panel, you have to grab that small textured area in the tab and drag the panel to the desired location.

Some panels, like the Source Monitor, can contain multiple elements. When there are multiple elements available, a menu will appear so you can choose among them. When you select a panel, an x appears on the right of the tab, and you can click it to close the panel.

If there are too many panels to display within the frame, a small scroll bar appears above the tabs; use the scroll bar to access hidden panels.

The final concept that you need to understand is drop zones. When you drag a panel into an existing frame, six faint drop zones appear around the selected frame. 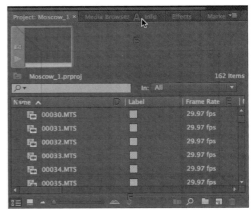 shows what happens when you drop the frame at the various locations. You can also drag the frame above the existing panel, which will create a window above all frames on that level.

If you experiment enough, you'll throw the interface completely out of whack. Just choose Window > Workspace > Reset Current Workspace to restore the workspace to its factory setting.

TIP Note that you can't undo interface adjustments, only actual edits to a project.

Menu — Scroll bar

Grab area — Close panel — Panels

B The various components of the panel tabs.

C Drop zones control panel and frame placement.

A *The panel will be added to the existing panels in the frame, with the tab located at the pointer location.*

B *The panel will open a frame above the selected frame.*

C *The panel will open a frame to the left of the selected frame.*

D *The panel will be added to the existing panels in the frame, positioned as the last tab on the right.*

E *The panel will open a frame to the right of the selected frame.*

F *The panel will open a frame beneath the selected frame.*

A Drag the scroll bar to reveal hidden panels in a frame.

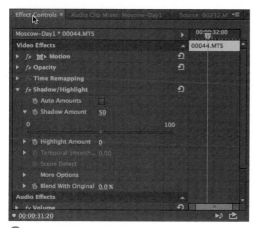
B Click the tab to open the panel in the frame.

C Click the Close icon to close the panel.

Customizing Your Workspace

With these basics, you should be able to make short work of these next few tasks.

To choose a different panel in a frame:

1. If the target panel isn't showing, drag the scroll bar **A** above the tabs to reveal it.

2. Click the panel tab to open the panel in the frame **B**.

To close a panel:

1. Click the panel that you wish to close **B**.

2. Click the Close icon on the right of the tab **C**.

To make a panel larger or smaller:

1. Hover your pointer over the edge that you'd like to adjust. Your pointer will convert to the double-arrow pointer 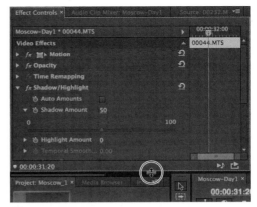.

2. Drag the edge in the desired direction 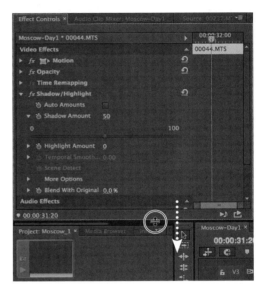.

To open a closed panel:

Choose Window in the Premiere Pro menu, and select the desired panel .

D The double-arrow pointer lets you adjust frame height and width.

E Making the Effect Controls panel taller to reveal more controls.

F You can open any panel from the Window menu.

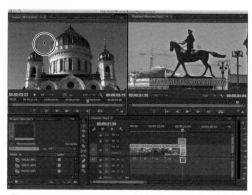

G Hover your pointer over a frame and then press the accent key (`) to maximize the frame.

H The maximized frame. Press the accent key (`) again to return the frame to its former position.

To maximize any frame:

1. Hover your pointer over the panel you wish to maximize **G**.

2. Press the accent key (`), which is to the left of the 1 key and directly above the Tab key on most keyboards. Premiere Pro maximizes the frame **H**.

3. To return the frame to its original position, press the accent key again.

TIP You can also maximize frames by choosing Window > Maximize Frame in the Premiere Pro menu.

Panel Menus

Each panel has a panel-specific menu that you can access by clicking the menu button in the upper-right corner **I** (controls vary by panel type). You'll be using these menus quite a bit when configuring the Source Monitor and Program Monitor later in the book.

I don't recommend using the Undock Panel and Undock Frame commands, because the results are counterintuitive. You're better off using the controls shown in the body of the chapter.

I Take a good look at how to open a panel menu, because you'll be working with them a lot.

To customize the buttons in the Source Monitor or Program Monitor:

1. Click the + button at the lower right of the Source Monitor or Program Monitor ⑂. The Button Editor opens.

2. Hover your pointer over any button to identify its function ⓚ.

3. To add a button to the interface, drag it down to the desired location in the transport control area ⓛ.

4. To remove buttons that you don't want, drag them upwards into the Button Editor and release the pointer ⓜ.

5 Click OK ⓜ to close the Button Editor. Premiere Pro saves the new configuration ⓝ.

TIP To reset the buttons to their default state, click the **Reset Layout** button.

TIP Note that you can remove the transport controls entirely by deselecting **Show Transport Controls** in the panel menu. Many professional editors who work exclusively via keyboard shortcuts do this to save screen real estate.

ⓙ Click the + button to open the Button Editor.

ⓚ The Button Editor's helpful tool tips identify button functions.

ⓛ Drag the button into the transport control area.

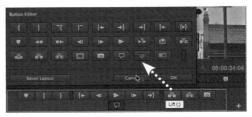

ⓜ Drag any buttons that you don't want back into the Button Editor.

ⓝ You've added the Closed Captioning Display button and removed the Lift and Extract buttons.

A This preference lets you control what happens upon program startup.

B These preferences control transition and still-image duration.

Setting Preferences

As you know from working with preferences in other programs, program preferences let you control key functions and operations within the program. While there are dozens of preferences, here you'll learn the most important ones, specifically those that relate to imported content and applied effects (General preferences), how frequently Premiere Pro saves backup copies of your project (Auto Save), where you store cached media associated with your projects (Media), and memory management (Memory). You'll learn about more-specific preferences in the editing-related sections.

All preferences are applied to future edits rather than prior ones. If you have a transition in a project that's 30 frames long and you then change the default transition duration to 15 frames, this doesn't change the duration of that 30-frame transition (or any other transitions already included in a project).

To open the preferences panel:

Choose Edit > Preferences (Windows) or Premiere Pro > Preferences (Mac OS). The Preferences panel opens, with the General tab selected.

To set General preferences:

1. To set the At Startup option, do one of the following:

   ▸ Choose Show Welcome Screen **A** to show the Welcome screen upon program startup.

   ▸ Choose Open Most Recent to open the most recent project upon startup.

2. Enter the default duration for video transitions in frames **B**.

continues on next page

3. Enter the default duration for audio transitions in seconds **B**.

4. Enter the default duration for still images (including titles) in frames **B**.

TIP A 1-second transition duration is good for general-purpose projects. When producing for the Internet, where long transitions might produce artifacts, you may want to shorten this to five to seven frames. Ditto for multi-camera projects, where transitions are typically used to smooth the switch from one camera to another rather than to produce a noticeable transition effect.

To set Auto Save preferences:

1. To access the Auto Save preferences, do one of the following:

> ▸ If the Preferences window is open, click the Auto Save tab.

> ▸ If the Preferences window is not open, choose Edit > Preferences > Auto Save (Windows) or Premiere Pro > Preferences > Auto Save (Mac OS).

The Preferences window opens to the Auto Save preferences **C**.

2. Enter how frequently Premiere Pro should auto-save your projects **C**.

3. Enter how many project versions Premiere Pro should retain **C**.

C These preferences control how frequently Premiere Pro auto-saves your projects and how many versions it retains.

Managing the Inevitable Crash

All programs crash, usually at the least opportune times. Since a lot can happen in 15 minutes—which is Premiere Pro's default auto save duration—and because it's absolutely heartbreaking to have to re-create these edits, I recommend a default auto save duration of five minutes 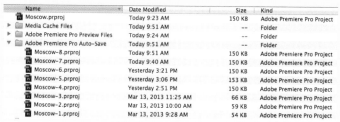. I also recommend saving each time you see the Auto Save message flit across the screen, just to be safe.

Premiere Pro stores the auto-saved projects in a subfolder, labeled Adobe Premiere Pro Auto-Save, that's located in the folder where you stored your project file ⒟. Premiere Pro will store as many versions as you've set in your preferences ⒞.

Let's review what happens when you crash. Premiere Pro will try to save your work in a recovered project, which you should save using a different name. Exit Premiere Pro (if necessary), reboot your system, run Premiere Pro again, and review the recovered project. If everything looks normal, it's probably OK to treat it as a normal project and carry on. I've never had a problem with a recovered project, though that doesn't mean you won't.

If the project looks corrupt in some way or you don't want to chance working with a recovered project, check the file creation times on the most recent auto-saved project and on the original project file. Open the most recent project and resume editing.

If you open an auto-saved project, it's best to save the project back into the original project folder. I typically don't overwrite the original project file, and then I name the auto-saved file something like Project-1.

Name	Date Modified	Size	Kind
Moscow.prproj	Today 9:23 AM	150 KB	Adobe Premiere Pro Project
▶ Media Cache Files	Today 9:51 AM	--	Folder
▶ Adobe Premiere Pro Preview Files	Today 9:24 AM	--	Folder
▼ Adobe Premiere Pro Auto-Save	Today 9:51 AM	--	Folder
Moscow-8.prproj	Today 9:51 AM	150 KB	Adobe Premiere Pro Project
Moscow-7.prproj	Today 9:40 AM	150 KB	Adobe Premiere Pro Project
Moscow-6.prproj	Yesterday 3:21 PM	150 KB	Adobe Premiere Pro Project
Moscow-5.prproj	Yesterday 3:06 PM	153 KB	Adobe Premiere Pro Project
Moscow-4.prproj	Yesterday 2:51 PM	150 KB	Adobe Premiere Pro Project
Moscow-3.prproj	Mar 13, 2013 11:25 AM	66 KB	Adobe Premiere Pro Project
Moscow-2.prproj	Mar 13, 2013 10:00 AM	59 KB	Adobe Premiere Pro Project
Moscow-1.prproj	Mar 13, 2013 9:28 AM	54 KB	Adobe Premiere Pro Project

⒟ The folder in which Premiere Pro stores the auto-saved project.

To set Media preferences:

1. To access the Media preferences, do one of the following:

   ▸ If the Preferences window is open, click the Media tab.

   ▸ If the Preferences window is not open, choose Edit > Preferences > Media (Windows) or Adobe Premiere Pro > Preferences > Media (Mac OS).

   The Preferences window opens to the Media preferences **E**.

E These preferences control where media files and their associated databases are stored.

Media Management 101

Even with the largest hard drives, media management can become a problem. If you're editing on a notebook, media management is absolutely essential.

There are four types of files associated with each project:

- Original media. This is the original media that you import into the project. Original media files almost always consume the most disk space of the four types of files, so it's important to know where they're stored so they can be easily deleted. I recommend creating a separate folder for each project, however large or small.

- Media cache files. When Premiere Pro imports video and audio in some formats, it creates unique versions of these files for faster preview and rendering. In particular, Premiere Pro creates .cfa auto files for most audio imported into a project. These files can be quite large—more than 1 GB for the audio associated with a one-hour HDV capture. You control the location of these files with the top preference in the Media preferences. I recommend locating these files in the same folder as your project so you can easily delete them when you're done with that project.

- Media cache database. When creating media cache files, Premiere Pro creates a database with links to the cached media files that it shares with Adobe Media Encoder, After Effects, and Encore, so that those programs can read from the same set of cached media files. These files are much smaller than the media cache files, and there's a convenient Clean button to remove them, so I recommend leaving them at the default location. Note that you can't remove these database files until after you delete the original media and media cache files.

- Preview files. When Premiere Pro renders prior to a preview, it creates and stores files in a folder named Adobe Premiere Pro Preview Files **D**, which is a subfolder of the project folder. You'll delete these files when you delete the project folder.

Each user's archive-related requirements are different. Some users archive each project, some don't. Either way, at some point after completing a project you'll have to remove the associated media files to make room for new projects. If you've followed the recommendations here, deleting the project folder and cleaning the database will remove all project files.

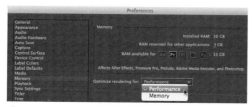

F These preferences control the allocation and optimization of memory.

2. Make sure the Save Media Cache files check box is unselected **E**.

3. Change the location of the media cache files by clicking the Browse button and navigating to the folder where your project files are stored **E**. Do not change the Media Cache Database setting.

4. After completing a project and deleting all original media and media cache files, click the Clean button to remove the database files associated with those media files.

To set Memory preferences:

1. To access the Memory preferences, do one of the following:

▸ If the Preferences window is open, click the Memory tab.

▸ If the Preferences window is not open, choose Edit > Preferences > Memory (Windows) or Adobe Premiere Pro > Preferences > Memory (Mac OS).

The Preferences window opens to the Memory preferences **F**.

2. If desired, increase or decrease the amount of RAM reserved for other applications **F**.

3. If you see a Low Memory warning, change the Optimize Rendering For preference to Memory **F**. Otherwise, use the default preference, which is to optimize rendering for performance.

TIP When you're working with high-resolution source files (either video or still image), Premiere Pro may run out of memory during rendering and present a Low Memory warning. In these cases, you should change the rendering optimization preference to Memory. Otherwise, use the default setting of Performance.

TIP Premiere Pro is a RAM-hungry program that works fastest and most reliably with lots of RAM. I recommend using the default memory allocation.

Working with Keyboard Shortcuts

As you get more experienced with editing with Premiere Pro, you'll start to use keyboard shortcuts like the spacebar to start and stop playback, or the backslash key (\) to show the entire project on the timeline. These keyboard shortcuts are much faster than the mouse-related equivalent, which is why Premiere Pro has shortcuts for most critical editing functions, allowing you to increase your editing speed.

Premiere Pro identifies the keyboard shortcuts via tool tips ⒶⒶ over most buttons and by showing them in menus ⒷⒷ. If you pay attention while editing, you'll quickly learn the shortcuts for your most common editing functions.

If you're coming to Premiere Pro from Final Cut Pro or Avid Media Composer, you can select a set of shortcuts used by those programs. This will help you feel right at home and become productive more quickly.

You can change Premiere Pro's keyboard shortcuts, or add shortcuts for editing activities for which Premiere Pro doesn't have an assigned shortcut. In this section, you'll learn how to choose and customize Premiere Pro's keyboard shortcuts.

To choose your keyboard shortcuts layout:

1. Choose Edit > Keyboard Shortcuts (Windows) or Adobe Premiere Pro > Keyboard Shortcuts (Mac OS). The Keyboard Shortcuts window opens Ⓒ.

2. Choose the desired layout from the Keyboard Layout Preset menu Ⓒ. Premiere Pro loads the preset.

Ⓐ Premiere Pro shows the keyboard shortcuts for most buttons in a tool tip. Playing and pausing video with the spacebar is one you'll use all the time.

Ⓑ Premiere Pro also shows keyboard shortcuts on menus. Here, you see that pressing Enter (Windows) or Return (Mac OS) renders the Timeline.

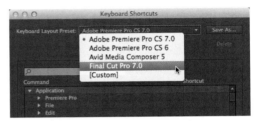

Ⓒ The Keyboard Shortcuts window, where you can choose a new layout or customize an existing layout.

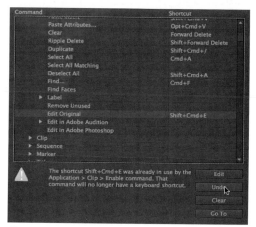

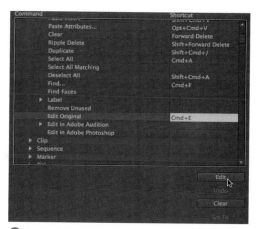

D Click the shortcut and then click Edit.

E This warning appears when the combination that you entered conflicts with an existing shortcut.

F Save the new custom keyboard layout.

G Enter the name and click Save.

To customize an existing keyboard shortcut:

1. With the Keyboard Shortcuts window open, click the command you wish to modify.

2. Double-click its Shortcut field, or click the Edit button in the lower-right corner of the Keyboard Shortcuts window D.

   The Shortcut field turns white.

3. Enter the new keyboard combination. If it conflicts with an existing combination, you'll see a warning message E.

4. Do one of the following:

   ▶ To revert to the old shortcut and restore the shortcut to the previous command, click Undo and repeat step 2 until you find a combination that doesn't conflict or that you wish to replace.

   ▶ To save the new preset layout, click Save As F. The Keyboard Layout Set dialog opens.

5. Type the name of the new preset in the Keyboard Layout Preset Name field G.

6. Click Save to save the new keyboard layout.

Managing Roaming Settings

If you frequently operate on multiple computers and like to customize your preferences
and keyboard settings, you're going to love
Premiere Pro's new Sync Settings feature.
Note that to take advantage of this feature
you'll need an Adobe Creative Cloud account
(basic membership is free).

It works like this: In the User Profile prefer-
ences , choose which types of preferences to upload to Creative Cloud, including
preferences/settings, workspace layouts, and
keyboard shortcuts. After choosing your preferences, upload them to your Creative Cloud
account. When you start work on a different
computer, log in to your account, and choose
File > User Profile > Download from Cloud to
download the user profile to that computer ⓘ.

When I looked at this feature in the beta software, the Mac and Windows versions were
completely different. On the Mac, the menu
option was Sync Settings, not User Profile.

I'm guessing that the interfaces will be
aligned before ship date, but I can't guaran-
tee that it will look like what you're seeing on
this page if you're editing on a Mac. While the
workflow should be very similar, the name of
the setting might be different. I apologize in
advance for any confusion.

Ⓗ Choosing which settings to store in Adobe
Creative Cloud.

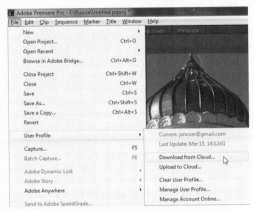

ⓘ Downloading settings to a new computer
(as it appears on Premiere Pro for Windows).

2

Setting Up Projects

Every time you produce a video in Premiere Pro, you'll produce it within a project file. However, project files do not contain the media that you import into the project; that would be too cumbersome. Rather, a project file is more like a file that points to your source files with instructions about which frames to include and exclude in the video that you're producing, which effects to apply, and where to apply them. If you copy a project file from your office workstation to your notebook for some weekend editing, you won't be able to get much done, because the content won't be there to edit.

Each project file has high-level settings for video capture, file storage, and performance. In this chapter, you'll learn how to create, save, and open project files, and adjust project settings. You'll also learn the proper way to move a project from one editing station to another so you can get that weekend editing done.

In This Chapter

Working with Projects

I was on a Southwest Airlines flight a few years ago, and the flight attendant started the safety chat about seatbelts with the line, "For those of you who haven't been in a car for the last 40 years, here's how you fasten a seatbelt." Well, for those of you who haven't created, saved, or opened a file on a Mac or Windows computer in the last 15 years, here's how you create, save, and open Premiere Pro project files (which have a .prproj extension, by the way).

Actually, it's not an exact parallel, because there are some important project settings that you'll want to set along the way—the kind of things that don't come up in most other applications. So, I'll try to speed through the stuff you know and focus on the aspects of project creation and management unique to Premiere Pro. Pay attention to the first exercise after this intro because I'll be walking through the critical project settings. You can change them later, but like anything else, it's better to get them right the first time.

To create a new project:

1. Do one of the following:

   ▶ In the Premiere Pro Welcome screen that appears when you start the application, choose New Project Ⓐ.

   ▶ With Premiere Pro running, choose File > New > Project Ⓑ.

   The New Project window opens Ⓒ. Here's where you'll select all project preferences. Note the two tabs near the top, one for General and the other for Scratch Disks. We'll get to scratch disks in a moment.

Ⓐ Creating a new project from the Welcome screen.

Ⓑ Creating a new project in the Premiere Pro menu.

Ⓒ Naming your project and choosing the location for the project file.

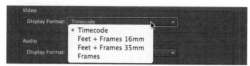

D Always choose GPU acceleration when it's available.

E Most projects will use the normal timecode.

F Most projects will use audio samples.

G Don't sweat this selection, as you can easily change it during capture.

H Go with the default settings here, and store all media in the same folder as the project file.

2. Type the name of the new project in the Name field **C**.

3. Click the Browse button, and choose the storage location for the new project file **C**.

4. Make sure you've selected the General tab, then click the Renderer menu **D** under Video Rendering and Playback, and, if it's available, choose Mercury Playback Engine GPU Acceleration (CUDA) (Windows) or Mercury Playback Engine GPU Acceleration (OpenCL) (Mac OS). See the sidebar "About the Mercury Playback Engine" for more details. If it's not available, you'll have to stay with Mercury Playback Engine Software Only.

5. Click the Video Display Format menu **E** and choose the desired format. For most projects, Timecode is the best option.

6. Click the Audio Display Format menu **F** and choose the desired format. For most projects, Audio Samples is the best option.

7. Click the Capture Format menu **G** and choose the desired format. Don't worry if you'll be using both DV and HDV, or neither; you can change this option when setting up for capture.

8. Click the Scratch Disks tab **H** to open those settings. Note that Premiere Pro shows the available disk space for each selected location.

continues on next page

9. I recommend storing all content types in the same folder as the project file, which is the default **H**.

10. Click OK on the bottom right of the New Project window to close the window and open your new project.

TIP If you're editing on a workstation, I recommend having a separate drive for your video projects, and saving each new project in a discrete folder off the root of that drive. Whenever you're working on a system with more than one drive, I recommend that you do *not* store your project files and content on the system drive.

About the Mercury Playback Engine

The Mercury Playback Engine is the collective name for the components in Premiere Pro that render and display previews from the Timeline. Briefly, the term *preview* refers to the ability to see how your effects look without actually rendering a file. As you would guess, the faster the preview, the more fluid the editing.

There are three components to the Mercury Playback Engine: 64-bit software, efficient multi-threading, and GPU acceleration. We'll discuss each in turn.

All versions of Premiere Pro CS7 are 64-bit programs, which can address much more memory than 32-bit applications. This is especially important when working with large source files. Of course, a 64-bit program can access more memory only if the memory exists in the system, and you should pack as much RAM into your editing station as you can afford.

The second component is efficient multi-threading, which means that Premiere Pro can access and use as many CPUs and CPU cores as are available on your computer. So you'll see a notice-able performance boost if you choose a 6-core CPU rather than a 2- or 4-core. If you edit on a dual-core notebook, you could be in for some significant delays.

The final component, GPU (graphics processing unit) acceleration, is the ability to use your graphics card to accelerate both preview and final rendering. In order to reap this benefit, you must have a supported graphics card in your computer. You can find a list of supported cards at www.adobe.com/products/premiere/tech-specs.html, but the short answer is that for most workstations, you need an NVIDIA card.

The performance difference that GPU acceleration affords depends upon the project type and source format. I absolutely beat this subject to death at bit.ly/AME_graphics, though the results you experience may differ a bit given that this testing was done with Premiere Pro CS5.5. The bottom line: If you're at all serious about editing, you'll want a card that provides GPU acceleration, and you'll want to make sure GPU acceleration is enabled in all projects.

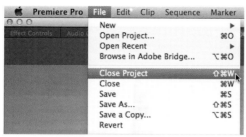

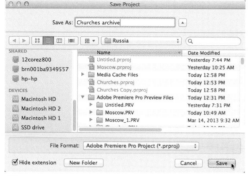

I Choose one of the options to save the project file.

J You know the drill: Type the name, choose the storage location, and click Save.

TIP If you choose File > Close, Premiere Pro closes whichever panel is open in the upper-left frame. Strange, but true.

TIP If you choose File > Revert, you'll revert to the last saved version of the current project, though you'll have to click Yes in the Revert dialog first.

TIP See the Chapter 1 section "To set Auto Save preferences" and the Chapter 1 sidebar "Managing the Inevitable Crash" to learn about Premiere Pro's Auto Save feature.

To save a project:

1. Do one of the following:

▸ Choose File > Close Project **I** (Control+Shift+W [Windows] or Command+Shift+W [Mac OS]). If you've made unsaved changes, Premiere Pro will ask if you want to save them. Whatever your answer, Premiere Pro will then close the project and open the Welcome screen.

▸ Choose File > Save **I** (Control+S [Windows] or Command+S [Mac OS]). Premiere Pro saves the project, and you can resume editing. This is a good keyboard shortcut to remember; whenever I see the Auto Save message flit across the screen, I save the project.

▸ Choose File > Save As **I** (Control+Shift+S [Windows] or Command+Shift+S [Mac OS]) to save the project under a different name and *start editing the new project*. Premiere Pro will open the Save Project dialog, where you can enter the name and storage location **J** (see step 2).

▸ Choose File > Save a Copy **I** (Control+Alt+S [Windows] or Command+Option+S [Mac OS]) to save the project under a different name and *resume editing the original project*, which is useful if you want to create an archival copy of the project. Premiere Pro will open the Save Project dialog, where you can choose the name and storage location for the project copy (see step 2).

2. If the Save Project dialog has opened **J**, type the project name in the Save As field, choose a storage location, and click Save to save the project file.

To open a project:

1. Do one of the following:

   ▸ In the Premiere Pro Welcome screen, click the target project **K**. Premiere Pro opens the project.

   ▸ Choose File > Open Project **L** (Control+O [Windows] or Command+O [Mac OS]). Premiere Pro opens a dialog in which you can navigate to, select, or open your project file (see step 2).

   ▸ Choose File > Open Recent **M** and choose the target project. Premiere Pro opens the project.

2. If the Open Project dialog has opened **N**, navigate to and select the project and click Open. Premiere Pro opens the project.

K Click the project in the Welcome screen to open it.

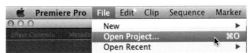

L Choose File > Open Project, then navigate to and open the project.

M A fast way to open a project you've recently edited.

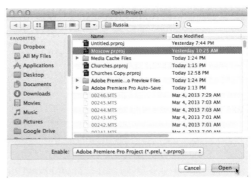

N Choose the target project and click Open.

Working with Missing and Offline Files

As mentioned at the start of the chapter, a project file is like a database charged with keeping track of all the content files and edits made in a project. If you move, delete, or change the name of a file that's been imported into Premiere Pro, Premiere Pro alerts you by opening the Link Media dialog A. The Link Media dialog also appears when you move, delete, or change the name of a file while editing, as well as when you move, delete, or change the name of a file imported into a project and later open that project.

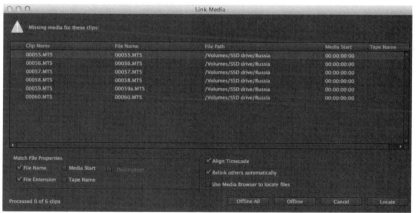

A The Link Media dialog allows you to link to missing media or treat it as offline.

How you respond to the dialog depends on what happened to the file and what your plans are for it. There are three scenarios covered in the following exercises. You can do any of the following:

- Locate the file right away, incorporating it back into the project and making the error message go away forever more.

- Treat the files as offline. Premiere Pro will create placeholders for the file (where it was used in the project) and post a big red "Media Offline" message in the Program Monitor and Timeline. You're free to either delete the files from the project or to later relink the placeholder to the actual media file. However, Premiere Pro will no longer prompt you with the Link Media dialog when you open the project. You know that the content is offline, and so does Premiere Pro.

- Procrastinate. You can put off a decision regarding the missing files. Premiere Pro will again create placeholders for the file (where it was used in the project) and post a big red "Media Offline" message in the Program Monitor. However, it will also prompt you with the Link Media dialog whenever you reload the project.

You can mix and match the first two options, locating and relinking some files and treating others as offline. But if you choose the procrastination option, it's applied to all missing files, and you'll have to deal with all of them the next time you open the project.

The following exercises assume that you've opened a project and are staring at the Link Media dialog.

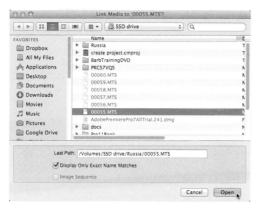

B The dialog you'll use to navigate to and select the missing files.

C Premiere Pro finds all missing files at that location and drops to the next missing file.

To immediately relink available files:

1. In the Link Media dialog **A**, choose the file to link and click the Locate button. The Link Media To dialog opens **B**.

2. Do one of the following:

   ▸ If the file has been moved (and the name has not changed), select the Display Only Exact Name Matches check box at the bottom of the Link Media To dialog. This makes the file easier to find.

   ▸ If the name of the file has changed, make sure the Display Only Exact Name Matches check box is unselected.

3. Navigate to and select the missing media file, and click Open. A check mark appears next to the file in the Link Media dialog **C**, and the file selection bar drops to the next missing file. If you left the "Relink others automatically" check box selected in the Link Media dialog, Premiere Pro will recover all missing files at the same location.

4. Repeat as necessary to relink all available files.

TIP If you prefer to use Premiere Pro's Media Browser to locate the missing file, select that check box in the Link Media dialog. I prefer the Link Media To dialog.

To treat one or more files as offline:

1. In the Link Media dialog, do one of the following:

   ▸ Click Offline All  🄳 to treat all files as offline. Premiere Pro will close the dialog, and all files will be shown as offline in Premiere Pro's 🄴 Project panel, Timeline, and Program Monitor.

   ▸ Choose a single file, and click Offline to make that file offline.

2. Either relink all subsequent files or treat them as offline. After you finish managing the last file in the Link Media dialog, Premiere Pro will close the dialog and open the project.

TIP Once the project is open, you can relink missing clips within the Project panel by right-clicking the missing clip and choosing Link Media 🄴, which opens the Link Media dialog.

To close the dialog and open the project:

In the Link Media dialog, click the Cancel button. The Link Media dialog closes, and all files appear as offline within the project. The next time you open the project, the Link Media dialog will reappear.

🄳 Treating all unlinked files or any single file as offline.

🄴 Here's what offline files look like in Premiere Pro. Open the Link Media dialog to relink them.

3

Importing Media

Premiere Pro can import an exceptionally wide range of audio, video, and still-image content in myriad ways. When doing so, there are three concepts to keep in mind. First, importing content into a project doesn't import it into the project file; you'll have to organize and manage your content independently from the project file.

Second, if you're working with file-based content, like footage from a DSLR or AVCHD camcorder, importing content into Premiere Pro doesn't transfer the file to your computer—Premiere Pro can edit content from any location without actually copying the content to your hard drive. So, the first step of working with file-based content is to copy it to your hard drive.

Finally, organization is key. When you're doing the copying, I recommend creating separate folders for the content within the same folder that you've stored your project file in. This makes the content easy to find while you're editing, and easy to find when you're archiving the project or deleting all content once you're done.

Import Options

Let's start with a quick list of the ways you can import content into your projects, some of which I'll detail later in the chapter, some of which I won't.

- **Media Browser.** Importing content from the Media Browser is great for file-based content that you'd like to preview before importing.

- **Capture panel.** Used when capturing video from a DV or HDV camcorder.

- **Dynamic Link.** Useful when integrating content from Adobe After Effects into your project.

- **Adobe Prelude.** A very useful utility when working with file-based video content, since it can copy content from your camcorder or camcorder media to your hard drive, and even transcode your media to a different format.

- **Adobe Bridge.** If you're used to Bridge from using it with other Creative Suite programs, you can also use it with Premiere Pro.

- **File > Import.** The old standby, useful for importing all types of content when you know exactly what you're looking for (that is, without previewing it) and where to find it.

- **Drag and drop.** You can drag any supported content type directly into the Project panel or Timeline from Windows Explorer (Windows) or File Manager (Mac OS) or from either operating system's Desktop.

When working with any of these techniques, keep in mind the concepts discussed in the intro: You're in charge of organizing your content for efficient use, archiving, and later deletion, which usually means making sure that all content is copied into the same folder that houses the project file, or a subfolder therein.

> **TIP** Premiere Pro can import an exceptionally broad range of native camera formats, from standard sources like DV, HDV, AVCHD, DSLR, MFX, and GFX to exotic formats like RED and ARRI ALEXA—which is a wonderful change if you're coming over from Apple Final Cut Pro 7 or X. So if you're concerned about whether Premiere Pro supports your camera, don't visit the website and check the specs—just try to import your content and see what happens. 99.9 percent of the time, Premiere Pro will import it without a problem.

> **TIP** Premiere Pro can import non–copy-protected VOB files from DVDs, making it a perfect tool for performing DVD-to-web conversions.

A What a properly preserved content folder looks like in the Media Browser.

B What the same content looks like in File Manager (Mac OS).

Ingesting File-based Content in the Media Browser

When working with file-based content, like video shot with an AVCHD camcorder or a DSLR, the so-called tapeless workflow has two components: copying the files from the original media onto your hard drive, and importing the files into Premiere Pro.

Sometimes you can just copy the media files themselves. However, with many media formats, particularly those that span a longer clip over multiple files, Premiere Pro relies on the metadata captured with video to properly import the files. With these formats, it's critical to copy all the metadata and content files into the folder structure that Premiere Pro expects, which varies from format to format.

For example, here you see a properly preserved content folder viewed in the Media Browser **A**, which shows a single video file and the associated metadata. The next image **B** shows the same content in File Manager, where you can see that it's actually made up of seven discrete files. Unless you copy all those files in the proper structure, Premiere Pro won't be able to properly identify and import the necessary files.

To simplify this task, Adobe has created a number of workflow guides for different camera formats, which you can access at http://tinyurl.com/workflowguides. I recommend checking this out before copying over your media in preparation for starting the editing process.

For the purposes of the following discussions, I'll assume that you've already copied the content to a sub-folder on your hard drive, preferably one that's located in the same folder as your project file.

To import file-based clips using the Media Browser:

1. Click the Media Browser tab to open the Media Browser (Shift+8) 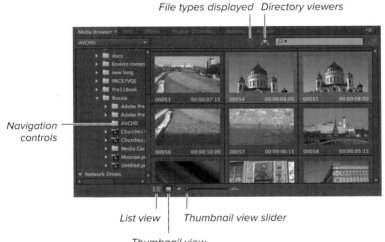.

2. If you wish to maximize the Media Browser, press the accent key (`) on the keyboard (to the left of the 1 key and directly above the Tab key).

3. Navigate to the folder that contains the content to import.

File types displayed   Directory viewers

Navigation controls

List view

Thumbnail view slider

Thumbnail view

C The most relevant controls in the Media Browser.

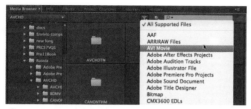

D Choose the proper directory viewer for the content (or choose File Directory for general-purpose content).

E Narrowing the search by file type (available only when File Directory is the viewer type).

F Dragging through the clip with the slider control.

G Hover your pointer over any non-selected clip to hover-scrub the clip.

4. To narrow the focus of your search, do one or more of the following:

▸ When importing file-based camcorder input copied to your hard drive, click the Directory Viewer **D** icon to make sure that the proper viewer is selected. If you're not getting a proper preview, check this setting.

▸ When importing general-purpose content, narrow your search by clicking the File Types Displayed **E** icon and choosing the desired format. Note that this option is available only when the Directory Viewer setting is set to File Directory.

▸ To search by filename, change the Media Browser to List view **C**. To search visually, choose Thumbnail view and drag the resize slider to the desired thumbnail size.

5. To preview the content, double-click a clip to play it in the Source Monitor, or click a clip and do one or more of the following:

▸ Press the L key to play the clip (or press L multiple times to fast-forward at faster speeds).

▸ Press the K key to stop playback.

▸ Press the J key to play the clip backwards (or press J multiple times to rewind at faster speeds).

▸ Drag the slider control beneath the selected clip to drag through the clip **F**.

For any clip that's not selected in the folder, hover your pointer over the video and, without clicking, drag through the clip **G** (called *hover scrub* in Premiere Pro-speak). Make sure Media Browser is the selected panel, or this won't work.

continues on next page

6. Select the clips to import using normal operating system conventions.

7. To import the clips, do one of the following:

- Right-click any selected clip and choose File > Import .

- In the Premiere Pro menu, choose File > Import from Media Browser 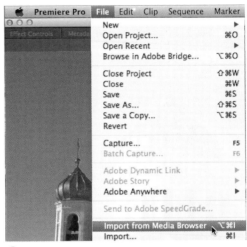.

- Drag the clips onto the Project tab and then down into the Project window . This one is a bit hard to follow, but it works.

- Drag the clips into the Timeline.

Premiere Pro imports the clips into the Project Window.

8. If you maximized the Media Browser in step 2, press the accent key (`) to minimize the Media Browser into its original frame.

TIP Note that Premiere Pro maximizes whichever panel your pointer is hovering over, not the selected panel.

TIP If you find hover scrub irritating, you can disable it in the Media Browser's panel menu, available by clicking the panel menu icon in the upper-right corner.

H Right-click and choose Import to import the selected clips.

I Or use the File > Import from Media Browser menu command.

J You can also drag the clips from the Media Browser to the Project tab and then down into the Project panel.

4-pin IEEE 1394 400

6-pin IEEE 1394 400

IEEE 1394 800

Ⓐ The three primary types of IEEE 1394 ports.

Importing from Tape-based Devices: Hardware

Many producers still shoot with HDV and DV camcorders, and in this section and the next, you'll learn how to connect an HDV/DV camcorder to your computer, configure Premiere Pro for capture, and capture video from these devices.

With the appropriate hardware, you can capture many different tape-based formats within the Premiere Pro capture interface. Unfortunately, the sheer number of camera and device permutations makes it impossible to document them all in this book. Once you install the hardware and connect the camera, however, the actual capture procedure should be very similar to the steps discussed here.

One of the reasons that DV and, later, HDV camcorders became so popular was that the IEEE 1394 interface required to transfer video from camcorder to computer came pre-installed on many computers, or could be added with a PCI card that cost under $20. For the purposes of this discussion, I'm assuming that you have an IEEE 1394 port (also known as FireWire) on your computer.

IEEE 1394 ports

There are multiple types of IEEE 1394 ports Ⓐ. The initial IEEE 1394 standard had a maximum speed of 400 megabits per second (Mbps), and was known as IEEE 1394 400. This standard was used for years by Windows and Mac computers alike, as well as all DV and HDV camcorders. As shown in Ⓐ, IEEE 1394 had two types of connectors: 6-pin and 4-pin.

Virtually all prosumer camcorders used the 4-pin connector, so any cable used for video acquisition had to have at least one 4-pin connector. Most desktop computers and workstations use 6-pin connectors, and most video producers worked on this class of machine, so the typical cable used by video producers was the 4-pin to 6-pin type . Though you can pay $20 or more for such a cable, if you shop wisely you can find them for under $5.

B The typical 4-pin to 6-pin IEEE 1394 cable.

As notebook computers became more powerful, many editors started producing on them as well. In the Windows world, your notebook probably has a 4-pin IEEE 1394 connector; if so, you need a 4-pin to 4-pin IEEE 1394 connector to capture HDV/DV video. They are less common, but you can still find them for under $12 if you shop around.

C A 6-pin IEEE 1394 400 to IEEE 1394 800 converter.

In 2002, IEEE 1394 800 was introduced, which ran at 800 Mbps. The target for this standard was primarily computer peripherals, and few, if any, camcorder vendors adopted it. However, in 2009, Apple started including IEEE 1394 800 ports on their Mac computers, which used a 9-pin connector A. IEEE 1394 is backward-compatible with slower connections, so this caused no serious compatibility issues, but traditional 4-pin and 6-pin cables no longer worked.

If you have a Mac with an IEEE 1394 connector, you have two options. You can buy a custom cable with a 9-pin 800 connector on one end and the required 4-pin or 6-pin 400 connector on the other. Or you can buy an adapter C that has a 6-pin 400 connector on one end and a 9-pin 800 connector on the other. They cost less than $5 each, so consider buying more than one; they're about the size of a USB key and are easily misplaced.

TIP Note that the key difference between a 6-pin and 4-pin IEEE1394 port is that the 6-pin connector carries power, so it can power an external device like a hard drive, while the 4-pin connector does not.

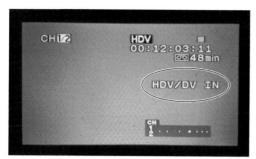

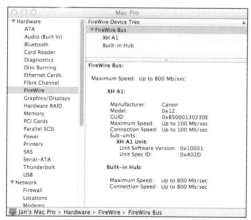

D It's a good sign when your camcorder sees the connection.

E Windows 7 sees my oldie-but-goodie Canon XH A1 in the Devices and Printers panel.

F As does my Mac.

Verifying the connection

Though connecting your camcorder to your computer and getting it recognized by Premiere Pro should be simple, it's often more complicated than you would expect. For this reason, it's useful to verify the hardware connection so you know that any problems are software-related.

Once you connect your camcorder and computer via the appropriate IEEE 1394 cable, you should see some indication in the camcorder screen **D**. If you don't see an indication like this, you've got a hardware issue, most likely a bad cable.

You can also check the connection on the computer side. On Windows 7, choose Start > Devices and Printers, and if the computer sees the camcorder, it will appear in that panel **E**. To see a similar confirmation on a Mac, click the Apple logo in the upper left, then choose About This Mac > More Info > System Report > FireWire **F**.

To connect your camcorder to your computer:

1. With computer and camcorder turned off, connect the IEEE 1394 cable to both computer and camcorder.

2. Turn on your computer.

3. Once your computer is fully booted, turn on your camcorder and set it to playback mode, which is often labeled VCR or Play mode.

4. Verify that your camcorder sees the connection by looking for "HDV/DV In" or an equivalent message on the screen **D**. (If the camcorder doesn't see the connection, you'll likely find a solution in the sidebar "Debugging Hardware Issues.")

5. Verify that your computer sees the connection. On Windows 7, choose Start > Devices and Printers, and see if the camcorder appears in the Devices panel **E**. On a Mac, click the Apple logo in the upper left, then choose About This Mac > More Info > System Report > FireWire **F**. (If the computer doesn't see the connection, see the sidebar "Debugging Hardware Issues.")

TIP 99.99 percent of the time, it's OK to connect your camcorder to your computer when both are on and running. But when both devices are running, there is a very small chance that power coming from the computer can damage the camcorder, which happened to me in 2005.

Debugging Hardware Issues

If the hardware connection cannot be verified by the camcorder, the computer, or both, it could be one or more of these issues:

- Faulty or improperly connected cable. Make sure the cable is firmly seated in both connections. If you have a spare cable, give it a try.

- Disabled IEEE 1394 connection. Make sure you haven't disabled your IEEE 1394 connection in the system BIOS.

- No card. Make sure that you have an IEEE 1394 card installed in your computer. Some computers come with the port but no adapter, which you have to buy and connect to the card.

- Bad card. If you have a spare IEEE 1394 card, try swapping it out.

- Bad FireWire connection on the camcorder. If all else fails, you could have a faulty FireWire connection on your camcorder. The only way to verify this is to send the camcorder in for repair.

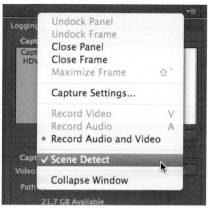

A Enabling Scene Detect during capture.

Importing from Tape-based Devices: Software

Once you get the hardware connected, the software side should be pretty straightforward. There are a couple of features that you may not be aware of, so let's touch on those.

First is device control. The IEEE 1394 cable that transfers video from camcorder to computer can also carry playback commands from the computer to the camcorder, allowing you to control the camcorder from the Premiere Pro capture interface—a nice convenience, and it enables advanced features like batch capture.

The second feature is scene detection. When you shoot either DV or HDV video, the camcorder records timecode on the tape, which includes time and date information. By analyzing the incoming timecode data, Premiere Pro can identify all the individual clips on the tape. If you enable Scene Detect in the Capture panel menu during capture **A**, Premiere Pro will capture each clip separately, which saves a lot of time over capturing all your shots in a single file and having to manually separate them.

We'll start our capture tutorial by establishing device control over the HDV camcorder connected to the computer. Then we'll step through the process of capturing HDV video and enabling scene detection.

To establish device control:

1. To open the Capture panel, choose File > Capture, or press F5. The Capture panel opens **B**.

2. In the upper-right corner of the Capture panel, click the Settings tab **C**.

3. Below the Capture Settings window, click the Edit button to open the Capture Settings dialog **C**.

4. From the Capture Format menu, choose the format that you're capturing **C**.

5. Click OK to close the Capture Settings dialog **C**.

6. On the bottom right of the Capture dialog, in the Device Control section, click the Device menu **D** and make sure that DV/HDV Device Control is selected.

7. On the bottom right of the Capture dialog, click the Options button **E**. The DV/HDV Device Control Settings dialog opens. If the dialog shows Online next to the Check Status button, you've established device control; click OK to close the dialog, and skip to the next section. Otherwise, proceed to step 8 (or see the sidebar "Debugging Software Issues").

B Premiere Pro's Capture dialog.

C Choosing the appropriate capture format.

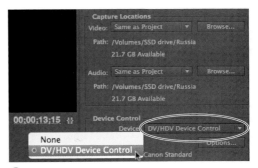

D Making sure that DV/HDV device control is enabled.

E Checking that the camera is online.

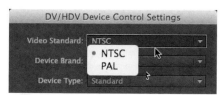

F Verifying that you've selected the proper video standard.

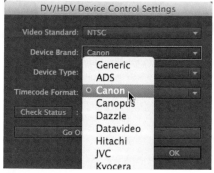
G Verifying that you've selected the proper device brand.

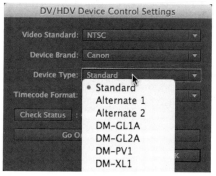
H Verifying that you've selected the proper device type.

8. In the DV/HDV Device Control Settings dialog, check that the proper video standard is selected **F** (NTSC for North America and Japan, PAL everywhere else). Click the Check Status button. If the camera shows as Online, you're done; if it shows as Offline, continue to the next step.

9. In the DV/HDV Device Control Settings dialog, check that the proper device brand is selected **G**. If your brand isn't listed, choose Generic. Click the Check Status button. If the camera shows as Online, you're done; if it shows as Offline, continue to the next step.

10. In the DV/HDV Device Control Settings dialog, check that the proper device type is selected **H**. If your type isn't listed, choose Standard. Click the Check Status button. If the camera shows as Online, you're done; if it shows as Offline, continue to the next step.

continues on next page

11. In the DV/HDV Device Control Settings dialog, check that the proper timecode format is selected 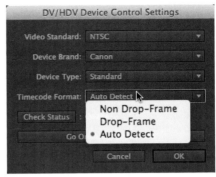. If you don't know, choose Auto Detect. Click the Check Status button. If the camera shows as Online, you're done; if it shows as Offline, continue to the next step.

12. In the DV/HDV Device Control Settings dialog, click Go Online for Device Info to open your default browser and navigate to a page on device compatibility (www.adobe.com/products/premiere/extend.html).

13. After trying any additional debugging steps listed on the Adobe website, click the Check Status button. If the camera shows as Online, you're done; if it shows as Offline, see the sidebar "Debugging Software Issues." When you've finished debugging, click OK to close the DV/HDV Device Control Settings dialog and return to the Capture panel.

TIP You'll learn about the differences between drop-frame and non–drop-frame timecode in Chapter 5.

① Verifying that you've selected the proper timecode format.

Debugging Software Issues

To be honest, I've never seen steps 8–13 resolve any software-related connection issues, but I had to list them for the sake of completeness. If both your computer and camcorder are seeing the connection and you still can't capture, it could be one or more of these issues:

- Wrong capture format. Return to step 4 and make sure that you've selected the right format.

- Camera set to wrong format. This is a funky one, but if the camcorder is set to record in one format (say, DV) and the tape you're playing back is HDV (and you're trying to record in HDV), Premiere Pro won't see the camcorder until you set it to record in HDV mode. This seems to happen a lot with Canon camcorders.

- Tape recorded over in wrong format. If you've recorded over a tape originally recorded in a different format, Premiere Pro may not see the format until you start playback on the camcorder. Let's say you originally recorded a tape in DV, and then recorded over it in HDV. When the tape is stopped, Premiere Pro may see the tape as DV, though once you start playback, Premiere Pro should recognize the HDV format. The solution is to start the tape rolling until Premiere Pro recognizes the format, and then capture manually.

Using Playback Controls in the Capture Panel

Once you've established device control, you can control playback using VCR-like controls in the Capture panel Ⓐ. This enables multiple functions, such as seeking to a specific time, single-file capture, and batch-capture of multiple scenes.

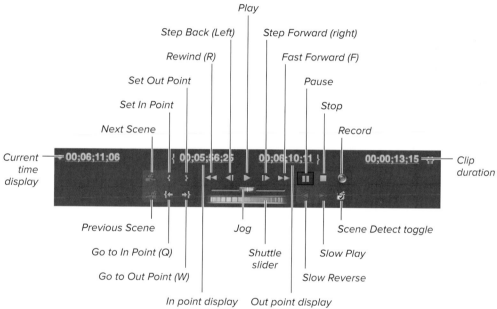

Ⓐ Once you establish device control, you can control playback with VCR-like controls.

To seek to a specific time on the tape:

1. In the lower-left corner of the Capture panel, click the timecode to make it active **B**.

2. Enter the desired timecode using only numbers (no colons or semicolons) and starting with the actual first number in the timecode. For example, to seek to 00;08;11;06, type 81106 **C** and press Enter (Windows) or Return (Mac OS).

   Premiere Pro cues the tape to the designated frame **D**.

TIP You can use this same procedure to seek to any point in the Timeline, or in the Source or Program Monitor, which is very useful.

TIP Premiere Pro has two transport modes: scan mode, which displays frames on the tape and is useful when trying to find a specific scene; and non-scan mode, which is much faster and is useful when you're trying rewind the tape or fast-forward to the end. If you click Play and then Fast Forward, you'll enter scan mode, and you'll be able to see all frames. If you press Stop and then Fast Forward, there won't be any preview, but the transport speed is much faster.

B The current time display is at the lower left.

C Enter the timecode without colons or semicolons.

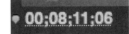

D Premiere Pro cues the tape to the specified timecode.

About Timecode

Timecode is pervasive in video production; it's in the video that you shoot with your camcorder, and it's on the Premiere Pro Timeline. You can use timecode to help capture video in the Capture panel.

So what is timecode? Timecode is the numerical representation of individual frames in a video file. Timecode is based on the number of frames per second captured in the video, and on the speed that the video plays back. In North America, the most commonly used timecode is 29.97 frames per second (fps), which is the NTSC standard that governed the original television playback. The PAL standard, 25 fps, applies to most of Europe.

Timecode identifies a frame's location in the format hours;minutes;seconds;frames. So a timecode of 00;06;11;06 means that the frame is located 6 minutes, 11 seconds, and 6 frames into the tape.

When you're shooting on tape, it's important to capture continuous timecode from start to finish. For example, if you're capturing to a new tape and you fast-forward beyond the existing timecode on the tape, your camcorder will restart the timecode, resulting in duplicated timecodes. In these instances, if you're batch-capturing or even seeking to a specific time on the tape, Premiere Pro has no way of knowing which of the duplicated timecodes you're actually designating.

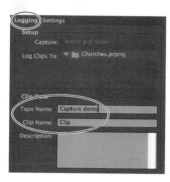

E Opening the Capture panel.

F Choosing the Logging panel, and entering the tape and clip names.

G Verifying the capture locations in the Settings tab.

H Enabling scene detection.

To capture audio and video using device control:

1. Choose File > Capture from the Premiere Pro menu (F5) to open the Capture panel **E**.

2. On the top right of the Capture panel, the Logging tab should be selected; if it is not, select it **F**.

3. In the Tape Name field, type the name of your tape **F**.

4. In the Clip Name field, type the clip name. If you capture multiple clips via scene detection, Premiere Pro will automatically increment the filenames.

5. On the top right of the Capture panel, click the Settings tab **G**.

6. Verify that the video will be stored in the desired capture location. You set these preferences during project creation, and the recommended and default setting is Same as Project, as shown **G**.

7. To enable scene detection, which is recommended, click the Scene Detect button **H**.

continues on next page

8. Using the transport controls beneath the capture preview, cue the tape to from 5–10 seconds before desired start of capture .

I Moving to the capture location.

9. Click the Record button (G) . Premiere Pro will start capturing audio and video. If you enabled scene detection, Premiere Pro will capture scenes as separate files.

J Click Record (G) to start capturing at that location.

10 To stop capture, click the Stop button (S) **K** or press the Esc key. The Save Captured Clip dialog opens **L**.

11. Type the desired information in the Save Captured Clip dialog, and click OK to close the dialog and return to the Capture panel.

K Click Stop (S) to stop capturing.

TIP When you're capturing from a digital source like DV or HDV, you have to capture both audio and video. If capturing analog, you can capture audio, video, or both via controls in the Capture panel menu **M**.

L Type the desired information, and click OK to return to the Capture panel.

Batch Capture in Premiere Pro

Premiere Pro can perform multiple-file batch capture when it has device control over the video camcorder or tape deck. The process is well explained in the Premiere Pro manual, in the section "Batch Capturing and Recapturing."

M Here's where you can choose to capture audio, video, or both when capturing from analog sources.

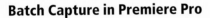

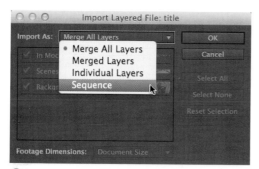

The import options for layered Photoshop files.

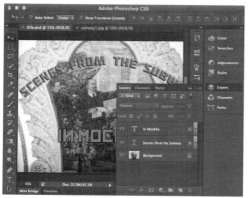

Ⓑ The three-layer file I'll be importing.

Ⓒ Importing using Merge All Layers creates a flattened PSD file with all layers.

Working with Adobe Photoshop Files

Tools in the Adobe Creative Suite are designed for integrated use, and the integration of Photoshop and Premiere Pro is a great example. You can import Photoshop files into Premiere Pro with layers intact, if desired, even if the Photoshop files contain videos or animations. Transparent regions in the Photoshop files are imported as an alpha channel, so you can overlay them on other tracks to create a title or logo effect with minimal effort.

You can also create Photoshop files in Premiere Pro, ensuring the perfect size and aspect ratio. In this section, you'll learn both operations.

Importing layered Photoshop files into Premiere Pro

A quick look at the options available in the Import Layered File dialog Ⓐ will add clarity to the following tasks. There are four import options (the results shown are for a three-layer Photoshop file Ⓑ comprising a background image and two text elements).

- Merge All Layers Ⓒ. This merges all layers into a single flattened PSD file during import. Use this if you want to import all layers but don't need to adjust any of them separately in Premiere Pro.

continues on next page

- Merged Layers  **D**. This allows you to select layers for merging into a single flattened PSD file during import. It's useful if you have a master PSD file with multiple layers that you need to customize during import (like a lower-third title with four names) but for which you don't need to adjust any layers separately in Premiere Pro.

D Here I imported only the text layers using the Merged Layers option.

- Individual Layers **E**. This allows you to select layers for importing as separate PSD files, stored in a separate bin. This is useful when you want to deploy the selected layers separately after importing them into Premiere Pro.

E Here I imported the layers individually by using the Individual Layers option. Note that the imported files are stored in a separate bin.

- Sequence **F**. This allows you to select layers for importing as separate PSD files, consolidated in a Premiere Pro sequence and stored in a separate bin. This is useful when you want to use the stacked layers together in a sequence once imported into Premiere Pro. Note that the resolution of the new sequence will match that of the original Photoshop file. If that resolution matches your project resolution, as in instances where you created a Photoshop file in Premiere Pro to use as a title, this option works well. However, if the imported sequence resolution does not match your project file (as when working with digital pictures) or at least use the same 16:9 or 4:3 aspect ratio, it may be cumbersome to import the sequence created during import into an existing project. In these instances, Individual Layers is probably the better option.

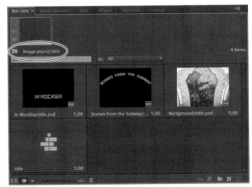

F Here I imported the layers individually and created a sequence using the Sequence option. Note that the resulting files are stored in a separate bin.

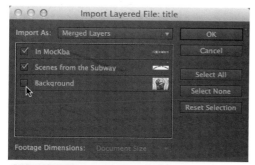

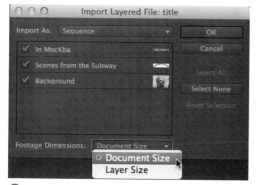

If you choose any option but Merge All Layers, you'll choose the layers to import by using simple check boxes .

G Choose which layers to import using these check boxes.

If you choose either Individual Layers or Sequence, you can choose to import the content as Document Size **H**, which imports the selected layers at the resolution of the original Photoshop file, or Layer Size, which imports the selected layers at their actual frame size in the Photoshop document. In my tests, the Document Size option reproduced the look of the original Photoshop file more closely than did Layer Size, so Document Size should be your default option.

H The Document Size option generally produces better results.

Note that neither option matches the resolution of the imported Photoshop content to the actual project resolution. That, of course, relates in part to the fact that projects have no native resolution, because resolution is set when creating a sequence, and projects can have multiple sequences. The bottom line is that there is no way to use the Import Layered File dialog to import Photoshop images at a specific project- or sequence-related resolution.

TIP You can set still-image duration in the General Preferences dialog, accessible by choosing Edit > Preferences > General (Windows) or Premiere Pro > Preferences > General (Mac OS). On that same Preferences tab, you can also choose whether images are automatically scaled to frame size (the Default Scale to Frame Size check box) or displayed at native resolution. You'll learn more about the latter option in Chapter 4.

TIP Premiere Pro supports most but not all of Photoshop's layer-related blending modes. For this reason, it's better to start simple and test Premiere Pro's ability to successfully preserve these elements than to complete an exotic composition in Photoshop and just hope for the best.

TIP All text files are imported as graphics, so you can't edit them with Premiere Pro's Titler utility. However, you can always edit the original files in Photoshop by right-clicking the file and choosing Edit in Adobe Photoshop. All saved changes will immediately flow back into your Premiere Pro project.

To import layered Photoshop files into Premiere Pro:

1. Click the Media Browser tab (Shift+8) to open the Media Browser 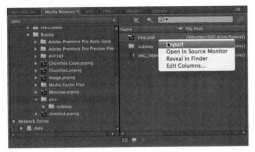.

2. On the navigational panel on the left of the Media Browser, select the folder containing the Photoshop file ❶.

3. In the content panel on the right of the Media Browser, right-click the Photoshop file and choose Import ❶.

   The Import Layered File dialog opens.

4. In the Import As menu, choose the desired import option ❶.

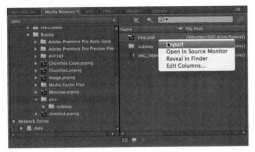

❶ Navigating to and importing the layered PSD file in the Media Browser.

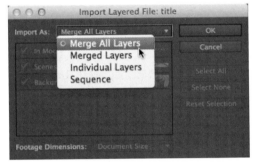

❶ Choose the desired import option.

Working with Images in Premiere Pro

Here are some thoughts to consider when preparing images for importing into Premiere Pro.

First, while larger images generally produce higher quality, they can also slow Premiere Pro down. So for more efficient editing, you should scale images down as much as possible.

That said, images should be as least as large as the sequence you intend to use them in; as with video, scaling images to higher resolutions causes pixelation and quality loss.

If you intend to add pan-and-zoom effects to the image, the image should be sufficiently large to be at no more than 100% of resolution at the maximum zoom. For example, if you're working on a 1080p sequence (1920 x 1080 resolution) and plan to zoom in to the image to 200% resolution, the image should have a resolution of at least 3840 x 2160. A higher resolution adds no quality and could slow Premiere Pro down; a lower resolution could introduce pixelation at maximum zoom.

Importing using the Merge All Layers option to produce a single flattened PSD file.

Choosing the layers to import.

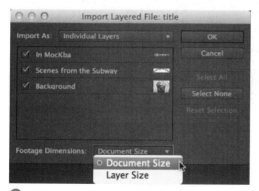

Choosing the footage dimensions (Document Size is generally preferred).

5. If you selected Merge All Layers, click OK; Premiere Pro imports all layers of the file as a single flattened PSD file . If you selected any of the three other options, select the layers to import .

6. If you selected Merged Layers in step 4, click OK . Premiere Pro imports the selected layers of the file as a single flattened PSD file.

   If you selected either Individual Layers or Sequence in step 4, in the Footage Dimensions menu choose either Document Size or Layer Size . Document Size is generally the preferred option.

7. Click OK . Premiere Pro imports the selected layers using the selected options.

TIP You can perform the same procedure using the File > Import command, though you won't have the same search or preview functions as are available in the Media Browser.

To create a Photoshop file in Premiere Pro:

1. Choose File > New > Photoshop file  **N**. The New Photoshop File dialog opens **O**, deriving the video settings from the sequence then open in the Timeline.

2. If desired, change the width and height for the new Photoshop file **O**.

3. If desired, change the timebase for the new Photoshop file **P**.

4. If desired, change the pixel aspect ratio for the new Photoshop file **Q**.

N Start here to create a new Photoshop file.

O Enter the desired width and height.

Importing Adobe Illustrator Images

You can import an Adobe Illustrator still-image file directly into a Premiere Pro project. Premiere Pro converts path-based Illustrator art into the pixel-based image format used by Premiere Pro, a process known as rasterization. Premiere Pro automatically anti-aliases, or smooths, edges of the Illustrator art. Premiere Pro also converts all empty areas into an alpha channel, so that empty areas become transparent.

If you want to define the dimensions of the Illustrator art when it is rasterized, use Illustrator to set crop marks in the Illustrator file. For information about setting crop marks, see Illustrator Help.

Even though the layers in Illustrator are merged in Premiere Pro, you can edit the layers by selecting the clip and choosing Edit > Edit Original.

— From the Premiere Pro Help file

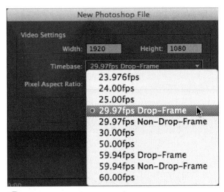

P Choose the desired timebase.

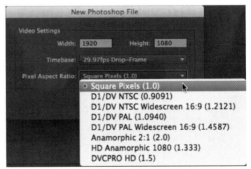

Q Choose the desired pixel aspect ratio.

 Click OK to close the dialog.

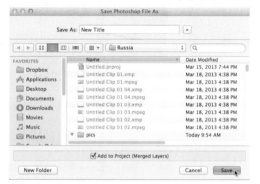

 Choose a name and storage location for the new file, and click Save.

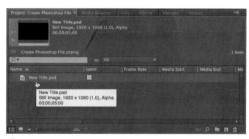

 Meet your new Photoshop file.

 To view your sequence settings, right-click the sequence in the Project panel and choose Sequence Settings.

5. Click OK to close the dialog . The Save Photoshop File As dialog opens .

6. Enter the filename and choose the storage location, and click Save to save the file . Premiere Pro creates the new file (which you can see in the Project panel) and opens the file in Photoshop if it's installed on your system.

TIP As noted in these tasks, in many instances the parameters of the new Photoshop file should match the sequence that you intend to use it in. To view the settings for that sequence, right-click the sequence in the Project panel and choose Sequence Settings .

Importing Files from Your Hard Disk

Although you can use the simple File > Import command to import content into Premiere Pro, the Media Browser is the preferred tool and has the better preview capabilities. That said, if you know which file you're looking for and exactly where it is, the Import command is fast and convenient.

Of course, if you know the location of the file you're looking for and you happen to have it open in Windows Explorer (Windows) or File Manager (Mac OS), drag-and-drop is another fast way to load the content into Premiere Pro. In this section, I'll demonstrate both techniques.

To import files using the Import dialog:

1. Do one of the following:

   ▸ Choose File > Import, or press Control+I (Windows) or Command+I (Mac OS) .

   ▸ Right-click in the Project panel and choose Import **B**.

   ▸ Double-click on an empty space in the Project panel.

   The Import dialog opens **C**.

2. Choose one or more files to import **C**.

3. Click Open (Windows) or Import (Mac OS) to import the files **C**.

   Premiere Pro imports the files and adds them to the Project panel.

> **TIP** Note that with the Windows Import dialog (not shown), you can use a file type dialog to limit your searches to specific file types. This option is not available on the Mac.

A Importing files using the Import dialog.

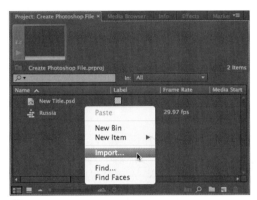

B Accessing the Import dialog by right-clicking in the Project panel.

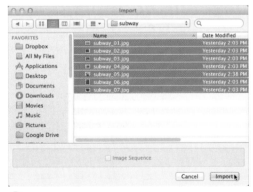

C You know the drill here: Choose the files and click Import (Mac OS) or Open (Windows).

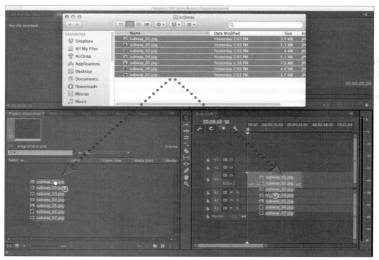

D Choose the files to add to the project in either File Manager (Mac OS, shown) or Windows Explorer.

To import files using drag and drop:

1. Locate and select the files to import in Windows Explorer (Windows) or File Manager (Mac OS) **D**.

2. Do one of the following:

   ▸ Drag the files into the Project panel **E**. Premiere Pro adds the files to the project.

   ▸ Drag the files directly into a Timeline sequence **E**. Premiere Pro inserts the files sequentially into the Timeline and adds them to the Project panel.

   TIP Not to beat a dead horse, but make sure you consider the content management side of things when importing files. It's usually best to copy the files into the same folder as the project file (or a sub-folder therein) before importing them, so they aren't inadvertently deleted from other folders. You can intentionally delete them once the project is complete.

E Drag the files into the Project panel or onto a sequence in the Timeline.

Importing Content from Premiere Pro Projects

As your portfolio of Premiere Pro-produced projects propagates, you'll likely find yourself wishing to utilize content from past projects in your current projects. Fortunately, Premiere Pro makes that simple, allowing you to scan through any existing project on your system and import content, sequences, titles, or the project itself.

There are two workflows for importing content from previous projects. Using the Import dialog, you can choose a project file and import either the entire project or any selected sequence from that project. If you import the entire project, you import all content and sequences from the project; if you import a sequence, you import all content used in that sequence, and the sequence itself.

In the Media Browser (the workflow I demonstrate here), you can choose a project file and import the entire project, any sequence, or any discrete piece of content from that project. You can also use the Media Browser's File Types Displayed option to quickly find Premiere Pro project files in crowded folders.

Working with Final Cut Pro and Avid Media Composer Project Files

If you're a Final Cut Pro or Avid Media Composer editor coming over to Premiere Pro, welcome. Adobe welcomes you too, with lots of excellent content on making the transition, and also on how to load projects from these editors into Premiere Pro (and how to load keyboard shortcut presets for either program, as you learned in Chapter 1). You can find these resources on a web page titled "Premiere Pro CS6 resources for Final Cut Pro and Avid Media Composer users," at http://bit.ly/switcher_pp.

A Navigating to the proper folder in the Media Browser.

B Choosing to show only Premiere Pro project files.

C Double-click the desired project file...

D ...to fire up the Dynamic Link server...

E ...which displays all content and sequences in the selected project. Select one or more elements, right-click, and choose Import.

To import content from Premiere Pro projects:

1. Click the Media Browser tab (Shift+8) to open the Media Browser **A**.

2. On the navigational panel on the left of the Media Browser, select the folder containing the Premiere Pro project file **A**.

3. If desired, click the File Types Displayed icon and choose Adobe Premiere Pro Projects **B**.

4. In the Media Browser content window, double-click the desired project file **C**.

   The Media Browser runs Adobe Dynamic Link **D** and displays (in essence) a view of the content sitting in the Project panel of the selected project file **E**. If desired, you can double-click any file to preview it in the Source Monitor.

continues on next page

5. Right-click the selected file or files and choose Import.

Premiere Pro imports the selected files and inserts them in the Project panel 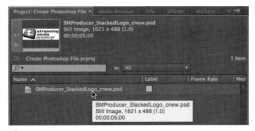.

TIP **G** shows the screen you would see when importing a sequence using the Import dialog. You can import any sequence, but not specific content. You also can't preview sequences, as you can with the Media Browser, which is why the Media Browser is the preferred tool for this operation.

TIP You can use this same workflow to import After Effects compositions into Premiere Pro. Just choose an After Effects project rather than a Premiere Pro project, and the compositions available for import will appear in the Media Browser's content window. See the discussion of Dynamic Link later in this chapter.

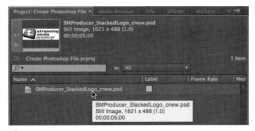

F The selected file in the Project panel.

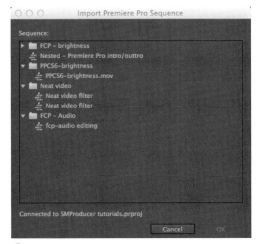

G Your options when importing sequences via the Import dialog.

Generating Media with Adobe Premiere Pro

When you import project elements into Premiere Pro, you'll often have a need for a still image or a video to serve as background for other content. Premiere Pro can create these and other media types for you.

Premiere Pro can create the following media types:

- Bars and tone. Used when your SD video is destined for broadcast and needs the output calibration.

- Black video. Useful as a background for videos and other elements.

- Closed captions. Used to add captions to a sequence.

- Color matte. Useful as a background for still images.

- HD bars and tone. Used when your HD video is destined for broadcast and needs the output calibration.

- Universal counting leader. Useful when creating film output from a sequence, as it lets the projectionist verify that audio and video are present and synchronized (also required by some TV stations that still require tape delivery).

- Transparent video. Useful when applying to an entire sequence an effect that generates its own content (such as the Timecode effect).

The general workflow for creating all media types is similar: You choose the type, choose the resolution and a few other parameters, and click OK. Premiere Pro generates the content and inserts it in the Project panel.

Working with Dynamic Link

Most video projects involve multiple content types—audio, video, and still images—produced in multiple forms—video, animation, DVD. To facilitate these projects, the Adobe Creative Suite offers separate programs with interfaces and toolsets optimized for particular media or tasks: Photoshop for images, Audition for audio, After Effects for animations and complicated compositions, Premiere Pro for video and overall integration, Encore for DVD, and Adobe Media Encoder for everything else.

Of course, working with multiple programs complicates production if there isn't an efficient way to integrate their operation. You've already explored Premiere Pro's ability to import Photoshop files and to re-edit them quickly and easily via the Edit in Photoshop command. Later, you'll explore the ability to send audio files to Audition for editing, with all saved changes automatically updated in Premiere Pro.

These "edit original" functions involve sending the asset from Premiere Pro to the other program, editing and saving them therein, and then re-importing the new file back into Premiere Pro. This happens transparently to you—as soon as the file is saved it's automatically re-imported—but that's the workflow. This works well because the rendering of still images and audio is nearly instantaneous.

With some types of projects, most notably After Effects compositions and Premiere Pro sequences, rendering can take minutes if not hours. So the edit original style doesn't work. For these, Adobe designed Dynamic Link.

As you learned in Chapter 2, sequences are the essential building blocks for Premiere Pro. While these exist within a project, you build your videos in a sequence. In After Effects, compositions serve the same function.

Dynamic Link allows you to import unrendered Premiere Pro sequences into After Effects and Encore, where they appear pretty much as regular videos. It also lets you utilize unrendered After Effects compositions in Premiere Pro and Encore. If you spot any necessary changes, you simply open the relevant program and make the necessary changes, which are dynamically updated wherever the sequences or compositions are deployed. No time-consuming rendering is required until you're ready to produce the final video or DVD.

Dynamic Link works in multiple ways. For example, you can use the procedure discussed in "Importing Content from Premiere Pro Projects" to import After Effects compositions into a Premiere Pro project. The Media Browser even has an After Effects filter (accessed via the File Types Displayed icon) to show only After Effects projects. Double-click the project, and the compositions available for import will appear.

Since this is the import chapter, I'll demonstrate how to create an After Effects composition to import into Adobe Premiere Pro.

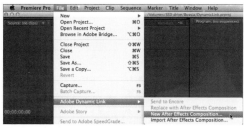

A The first step in creating an After Effects composition.

B Entering width and height in the New After Effects Comp dialog.

To create an After Effects composition:

1. Choose File > Adobe Dynamic Link > New After Effects Composition **A**. The New After Effects Comp dialog opens.

2. Enter the width and height for the new composition **B**. This should generally match the sequence that you intend to import the composition into.

continues on next page

Working with Adobe Prelude

Adobe Prelude is a standalone application that comes with Adobe Creative Cloud as well as with the Master Collection and Production Premium Creative Suites. It's a totally killer product for anyone working with file-based video content.

Prelude lets you quickly sort through the stored clips, adding markers and In and Out points, and letting you sequence the clips into a "rough cut" of your final video. When you're done, you can save your file-based clips from your camera media to multiple locations on your hard disk or LAN and send a copy of the rough cut and source clips to Premiere Pro so you can continue editing there.

It is particularly useful for those producers who shoot multiple short clips to assemble into a final production, as compared to event shooters who might shoot a 60-minute event straight through. But whatever type of shooter you are, if you're shooting on file-based media, Prelude is worth a look.

3. Choose the timebase for the new composition . This should generally match the sequence that you intend to import the composition into.

4. Choose the pixel aspect ratio for the new composition . This should generally match the sequence that you intend to import the composition into.

5. Click OK to close the New After Effects Comp dialog 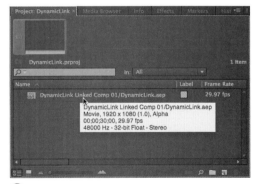. Premiere Pro runs After Effects, which opens the Save As dialog .

6. Choose the name and storage location for the new composition, and click Save .

   After Effects saves the composition, and Premiere Pro imports the new composition into the Project panel .

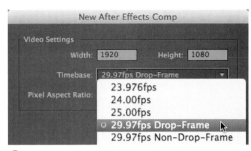

C Choosing the timebase.

D Choosing the pixel aspect ratio.

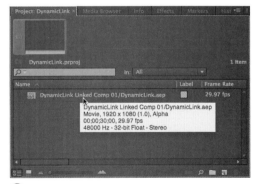

E Closing the New After Effects Comp dialog.

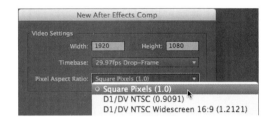

G The new composition in the Project panel.

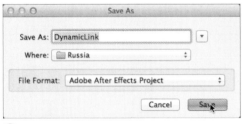

F Naming and saving the new After Effects composition.

Organizing and Viewing Clips

So you've captured, ingested, and imported your clips into your project, and there they are, quite the mess, staring at you from the Project panel, begging for order. Don't be daunted; in this chapter you'll learn how to organize and manage your source clips, view them in the Source Monitor, and get them ready for inclusion into your projects. You'll also learn how to create sequences, the building blocks of video projects.

While this organizational stuff sounds boring, efficient content management can shave minutes, if not hours, from total project time. Nothing is more frustrating than spending minutes looking through your project bin for that one video or picture you know is there, and nothing is more subtly disturbing than a messy project bin.

We can't control the neatness of our kids' bedrooms or what happens in our nations' capitals, but by golly, we can organize and maintain a squeaky-clean Project panel that streamlines and simplifies an entire project. You with me? Let's get started.

In This Chapter

Working in the Project Panel

Rousing intro notwithstanding, if you've spent time organizing files on your hard drive with Windows Explorer or the Mac's File Manager, you'll find most of these concepts very familiar; Adobe made a good decision in not trying to re-invent this particular wheel. So it's all about creating bins (rather than folders), moving content into those bins, choosing column heads for sorting, and the like. There are some media-specific elements, and you'll need to see how all this works within the Premiere Pro interface, but we're not breaking much new ground here.

Let's take a quick flyover of the Project panel and its elements Ⓐ. The bin/sub-bin organization should look familiar, as should the metadata columns you can use to sort content in the bin. Just a note: I created the organization shown in the Project panel; every project starts with a clean slate, with no bins or other structure.

Beneath the Preview area is the Find box, which allows you to search for content in the Project panel and within any metadata associated with any clip. You'll find this field in many Premiere Pro panels that contain content, including effects and transitions panels, and it can be an exceptionally fast way to find exactly what you're looking for.

On the bottom left of the Project panel, you see buttons that control the display. There are two modes, List view and Icon view, and the Project panel is currently in List view. Icon view shows larger thumbnails of the content and is very useful during the early stages of a project, when you're identifying the most relevant bits of content to include in a video.

Note the panel menu in the upper-right corner; click it to reveal the three configuration options that you can enable and disable from that menu: Preview Area, Thumbnails, and Hover Scrub. The Preview Area is the little preview window in the upper-left corner. While the window itself is too small to show much (and a quick double-click on the content opens it in the Source Monitor), the content description to the right of the preview window is often invaluable, so I typically leave this open. The Thumbnails option toggles the little display to the left of the content in the Project panel—it's not currently selected, so you see content-specific buttons to the left of content; when it is selected, you see a tiny thumbnail of the content itself. The default setting enables thumbnails in Icon view and disables them in List view, and that's how I typically leave it. Finally, Hover Scrub is a preview function available in Icon view that I'll cover in more detail later in this chapter.

On the bottom right are other controls that I'll review in more detail in this chapter, including the Automate to Sequence button, a great way to create a rough cut of your project. The Find button opens a Find dialog that you can use if the Find box bears no fruit. The New Bin button is a one-click way to create a new bin (though I prefer the right-click command), and Clear is what it looks like, a fast way to delete selected content.

Which leaves the New Item button, a nondescript button that's one of the most powerful, frequently used tools on the panel. Intrigued? How's that for creating tension in an otherwise dry narrative?

OK, hold your applause until the end. As you'll learn, you can drag any piece of content onto the New Item button and create a sequence that perfectly matches the content. Unsure if you shot at 30p or 60i but need a sequence to match? No problem—just drag the imported content onto the New Item button, and Premiere Pro will take care of it. I use this button to create virtually all my sequences.

Well, that's the flyover. Let's get down to our detailed tasks.

TIP You can maximize the display of the Project panel by clicking it to make it active (or pressing Shift+1) and then pressing the accent key (`), which is to the left of the 1 key and directly above the Tab key on most keyboards. Restore the workspace by pressing the accent key again.

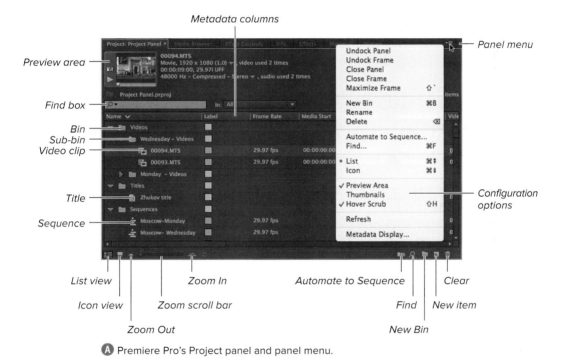

A Premiere Pro's Project panel and panel menu.

Project Panel Basics

There are some tasks that you'll perform irrespective of whether you're in List view or Icon view.

To open and close the Preview Area:

From the panel menu in the upper-right corner, select Preview Area 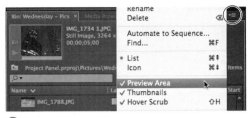 to open the Preview Area; deselect Preview Area  to close the Preview Area.

TIP I typically leave the Preview Area open (at least in List view), primarily because the clip detail **C** displayed next to the window is really helpful.

A Preview Area open.

B Preview Area closed.

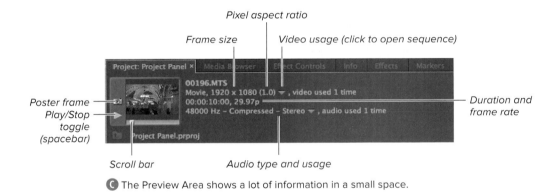

Pixel aspect ratio

Frame size

Video usage (click to open sequence)

Poster frame
Play/Stop toggle (spacebar)

Duration and frame rate

Scroll bar

Audio type and usage

C The Preview Area shows a lot of information in a small space.

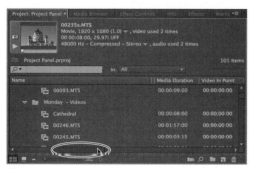

D Use this scroll bar to see more clips.

E Use this scroll bar to see more columns in List view.

To navigate in the Project panel:

1. To navigate vertically in the Project panel (and see more clips), use the scroll bar on the right side **D** to scroll up or down.

2. To navigate horizontally in the Project panel (and see more columns when in List view), use the scroll bar on the bottom **E** to scroll to the left or right. Note that Premiere Pro keeps the clip names on the left as you scroll to the right.

TIP When the Project panel is selected, you can use the scroll wheel on your mouse to vertically scroll through the contents.

Clip Management in the Project Panel

There are a number of housekeeping functions available in the Project panel that you probably already know how to do.

A Dragging to select clips in the Project panel.

To select and deselect clips in the Project panel:

1. To select a clip or clips, do one of the following:

   ▶ Click a clip.

   ▶ Shift-click adjacent clips.

   ▶ Control-click (Windows) or Command-Click (Mac OS) non-adjacent clips.

   ▶ Drag to select adjacent clips A.

   ▶ Press Control+A (Windows) or Command+A (Mac OS) to select all files in the panel.

   ▶ Choose Edit > Select All to select all clips.

2. To deselect a selected clip or clips, do one of the following:

   ▶ Click any open space in the Project panel.

   ▶ Choose Edit > Deselect All.

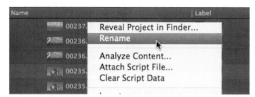

B The right-click command for renaming a clip.

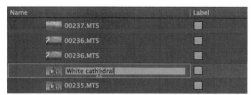

C Type the new name.

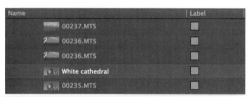

D The renamed clip.

E Click the clip to select it.

F The familiar menu command for copying.

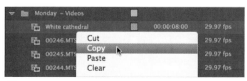

G Right-clicking to copy.

To rename a clip:

1. Click the clip to select it, and do one of the following:

   ▸ Right-click the clip and choose Rename **B**.

   ▸ Click the text area to the right of the thumbnail to make it active.

   ▸ Press the Tab key to make the text active.

   ▸ Press Enter/Return.

2. Type the new name **C**, and do one of the following:

   ▸ Press the Enter key.

   ▸ Click anywhere else in the Premiere Pro interface.

   Premiere Pro renames the clip **D**.

TIP If you've sorted the content in the Project panel by file name, Premiere Pro will immediately move the renamed clip to its proper location. This may cause the clip to leave the viewing window.

To copy and paste a clip:

1. Click the clip to select it **E**.

2. To copy the clip, do one of the following:

   ▸ Choose Edit > Copy **F**.

   ▸ Right-click and choose Copy **G**.

   ▸ Press Control+C (Windows) or Command+C (Mac OS).

continues on next page

3. Navigate to the bin  you want to paste the clip into, and do one of the following:

- Choose Edit > Paste 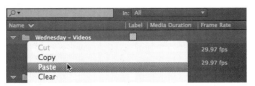.
- Right-click and Choose Paste .
- Press Control+V (Windows) or Command+V (Mac OS).

Premiere Pro pastes the clip in the target bin .

TIP To copy a file into the same bin, it's easier to choose Edit > Duplicate (or right-click and choose Duplicate) **L**, which creates another clip in the same bin and appends Copy to the file name.

TIP To delete a clip in one bin and paste it into another, use the Cut and Paste commands, with Cut available in the Edit menu or via right-clicking. Or, you can simply drag the clip from one bin to another.

H Choose the bin to paste the file into.

I The familiar menu command for pasting.

J Right-clicking to paste.

K The pasted file in the target bin.

L The Duplicate command.

Choose the file to delete.

You can delete a file in the menu.

Or you can delete it via right-click commands.

Or you can use the Clear button.

Clear (Delete)

To delete a clip:

1. Click the clip to select it .

2. Do one of the following:

   ▸ Choose Edit > Clear .

   ▸ Right-click and choose Clear .

   ▸ In the lower-right corner of the Project panel, click the Clear button .

   ▸ Press the Backspace (Windows) or Delete (Mac OS) key.

   Premiere Pro deletes the clip.

TIP Premiere Pro won't delete clips included in a sequence without warning you and asking you to confirm the action.

Metadata and the Project Panel

Metadata is usually a binary concept with most producers: It's either almost totally irrelevant or the most important aspect of the entire production. But it's also a little like the old parable of the blind men and the elephant: Your view will vary depending on which part of the elephant you touch.

Briefly, metadata is data stored about a clip. It can come from many sources, including scripts, video cameras, and manual input. For larger producers, metadata controls workflows and helps automate distribution, which is why it's absolutely critical to monetizing video. For many smaller producers, the only relevant aspect of metadata is the role it plays in the Project panel.

Specifically, you choose the columns that display in the Project panel by using the metadata panel that is accessed via the panel menu. You'll learn how to open that panel and choose metadata fields in the section "Working in List View."

Finding Clips in the Project Panel

Premiere Pro offers two options for searching for clips: the Find box and the Find dialog. Of the two, the Find box is faster and more convenient, while the Find dialog is more functional. Both work similarly: You type in your search data and Premiere Pro displays files that meet your criteria in the Project panel.

Ⓐ Choosing which fields to search.

To find clips via the Find box:

1. On the top left of the Project panel, click the In menu and choose one of the following Ⓐ:

   ▸ All, to search all clip-related metadata.

   ▸ Visible, to search only the metadata that is currently visible in the Project panel.

   ▸ Text Transcript, to search only in the Speech to Text metadata field (essentially a dialogue search).

   Most of time, you'll be searching for clips that you've specifically named, so All is the best option, though Visible would provide identical results.

2. Next, do one of the following:

   ▸ Click the Find box in the Project panel.

   ▸ Click to select the Project panel, and press Shift+F.

   This activates the Find box so you can start typing search characters therein.

3. Type the term to search for 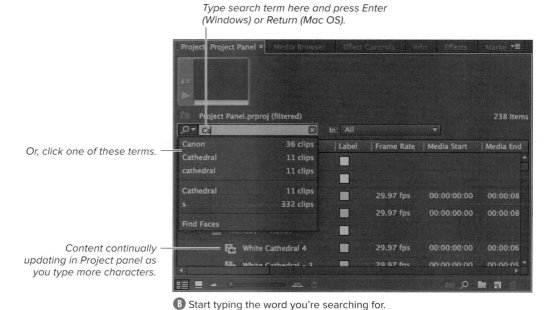. Note that the search is a live search, so Premiere Pro continually refines the results with the letters that you type, displaying the matching files in the Project panel. Premiere Pro also shows a list of matching terms, in the magnifying glass drop-down menu, that you can click to speed your search.

continues on next page

Type search term here and press Enter (Windows) or Return (Mac OS).

Or, click one of these terms.

Content continually updating in Project panel as you type more characters.

Ⓑ Start typing the word you're searching for.

4. To finalize the search and close the magnifying glass drop-down, do one of the following:

- ▸ Press Enter (Windows) or return (Mac OS).
- ▸ Click one of the search terms in the magnifying glass drop-down.
- ▸ Click anywhere outside the drop-down.

Premiere Pro displays clips that match your search parameters in the Project panel 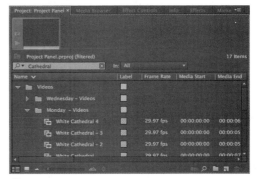.

5. Click the Close button  to end the search and show all assets in the Project panel.

C Premiere Pro shows the matching clips in the Project panel.

D Click the Close button to delete the search term and show all clips in the Project panel.

TIP Note that Premiere Pro retains previous searches, so you can easily search for them by clicking the magnifying glass icon in the Find box **E**.

TIP If you were searching for content and later noticed that many of your clips appeared to be missing, it's probably because you forgot to click the Close button and remove the search term. In all search panels (transitions, effects, and the like), the typed text will remain until deleted, and the only content that will appear is content that matches the search term.

E You can easily re-search for content by choosing a term from the drop-down.

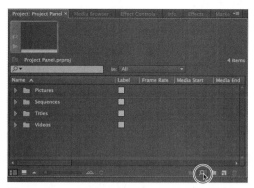

F Click the Find button to open the Find dialog.

G Choose the first metadata field to search.

H Choose the desired search operand.

I Enter the search term.

To find clips via the Find dialog:

1. To open the Find dialog, do one of the following:

   ▸ On the bottom right of the Project panel, click the Find button F.

   ▸ Press Control+F (Windows) or Command+F (Mac OS).

   The Find dialog opens.

2. From the Column menu, choose a metadata field to search G.

3. From the Operator menu, choose a search condition H.

4. In the Find What field, type the search term I.

continues on next page

5. If desired, repeat steps 2–4 for the second column **J**.

6. From the Match menu **K**, choose one of the following:

   ▸ All, to find content that matches *both* criteria.

   ▸ Any, to find content that matches *either* criterion.

7. If desired, select the Case Sensitive check box **L** to make your searches case-sensitive.

8. Click Find **M** to find content that matches the search parameters.

   Premiere Pro displays the clip in the Project panel. Note that in the Find dialog, Premiere Pro highlights only the first clip that meets your criteria, not all clips that meet your criteria.

9. To find additional clips that meet your criteria, click Find again.

10. When your search is complete, click Done **M** to close the Find dialog.

TIP If you have only one criterion to search for, the Find box is the faster and easier approach, because it opens all matching content in the Project panel, rather than making you search for each item one by one.

TIP Note that you do not need to have the selected metadata fields open in the Project panel to search for them in the Find dialog. For example, the Media Type metadata field is not currently selected in the Project panel, but Premiere Pro still finds the content.

J Define the second search term, if desired.

K Choose your matching criteria.

L Choose whether to make the search case-sensitive.

First clip to meet search criteria

M Click Find to find the first item that meets your search criteria. Repeat as necessary.

A You can create a bin this way.

B Or you can create it this way (or via a keyboard shortcut).

C However you do it, here it is.

Organizing Your Content with Bins

Bins are the major organizational element available in the Premiere Pro Project panel. Most of the basic operations relating to bins are similar to those you would use working with folders in Windows Explorer or File Manager (Mac OS), so the steps in these tasks should look familiar.

To create a bin:

To create a bin, do one of the following:

- Choose File > New > Bin A.

- On the bottom right of the Project panel, click the New Bin button B.

- Press Control+B (Windows) or Command+B (Mac OS).

Premiere Pro creates a new bin in the Project panel. Names are sequential, starting with Bin 01 C.

TIP Note that if you have the bin sorted by the Name field, the new bin will be sorted alphabetically and may appear outside the Project panel viewing area. Just use the vertical scroll bar on the right to see the new bin.

TIP It's most efficient to rename the bin right after you create it. See the next task.

To name the bin:

1. Click the bin to select it 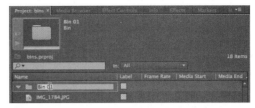 (if it's not already selected).

2. Do one of the following:

   ▸ Click the text area to the right of the bin to make it active .

   ▸ Press the Tab key to make the text area active.

   ▸ Press Enter/Return.

3. Type the desired name **E**.

4. Do either of the following:

   ▸ Press the Enter (Windows) or Return (Mac OS) key.

   ▸ Click anywhere else in the Premiere Pro interface.

   Premiere Pro renames the bin **F**.

D Click the text area to make it active.

E Type the new name.

F The bin shifted down because of the sorting preferences in the Project panel.

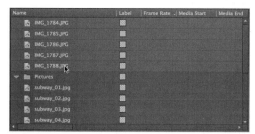

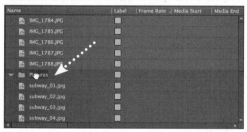

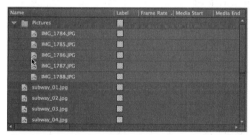

G Select the clips to move into the bin.

H Drag the clips in.

I There they are, in the bin.

To move clips into a bin:

1. Select the clips you'd like to move **G**.

2. Drag them into the bin **H**.

    Premiere Pro moves the clips into the bin **I**.

TIP Reverse the procedure to remove clips from a bin, or to move clips from bin to bin. Just select and drag to the desired location.

To hide and reveal bin contents:

1. To reveal the hidden contents of a bin, click the triangle next to the bin name **J**.

2. To hide the revealed contents of a bin, click the triangle next to the bin name **K**.

TIP See the next section for more about opening and displaying bin contents.

J Click the triangle to open the bin.

K Click it again to close the bin.

Working with Bin-Related Preferences

Premiere Pro can open bins three different ways, as shown in the bin-related preferences  in the General tab of the Preferences panel. When you double-click a bin **B** in the Project panel, one of the following happens:

- Open in Place opens the bin and makes it the sole content in the Project panel **C**. To navigate to the Project panel, click the Navigate Upward button **D**. Note that the text next to the button shows your bin/sub-bin location within the Project panel. This is the mode that I use most, since I don't like the clutter that results from the two alternatives.

A The three preferences for opening bins.

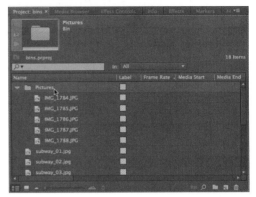

B Our starting point. We want to open the Pictures bin.

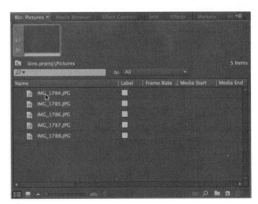

C Open in Place opens the bin in the Project window, making it the sole visible occupant.

D Navigate back to the Project panel with this button.

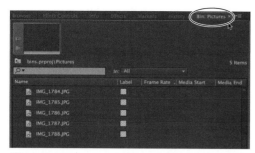

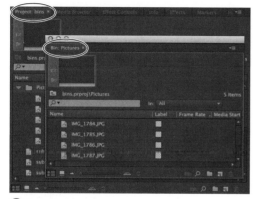

E Shockingly, choosing Open New Tab opens the bin in a new tab.

F Open in New Window is useful for moving content from one bin to another.

- Open New Tab opens the bin in a separate tab in the same frame as the Project panel **E**.

- Open in New Window opens the bin in a floating window **F**. This mode is useful when moving contents from one bin to another.

To set bin-related preferences:

1. Choose Edit > Preferences > General (Windows) or Premiere Pro > Preferences > General (Mac OS). Premiere Pro opens the Preferences panel to the General tab **G**.

2. From the Double-click menu, choose the desired option **G**.

3. From the + Ctrl (Windows) or + Cmd (Mac OS) menu, choose the desired option **H**.

4. From the + Alt (Windows) or + Opt (Mac OS) menu, choose the desired option **I**.

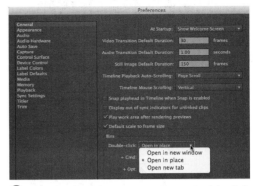

G Choosing what happens when you double-click a bin.

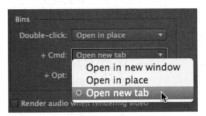

H Choosing what happens when you Control-click (Windows) or Command-click (Mac OS) a bin.

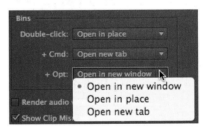

I Choosing what happens when you Alt-click (Windows) or Option-click (Mac OS) a bin.

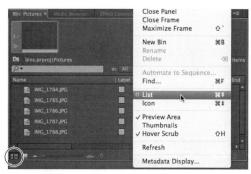

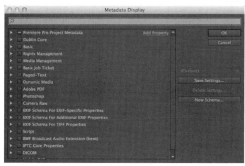

A Two ways to enter List view.

B Opening the Metadata Display dialog. Note the columns in the Project panel, because they are about to change.

C The categories in the dialog.

Working in List View

List view lets you easily sort your content according to categories that you can select and order as you desire. Features and capabilities in this view will come in handy during the organizational phase of your projects.

You choose the columns in the Project panel by choosing items in the Metadata Display dialog. For example, one of the columns I find essential is the Media Type column, which lets you sort content by type. Someone at Adobe doesn't share this view, so it's not one of the default columns in the Project panel. Fortunately, Adobe has made these columns configurable.

To enter List view:

To enter List view, do one of the following:

- On the lower left of the Project panel, click the List View button **A**.

- Click the panel menu and choose List **A**.

- Press Control+Page Up (Windows) or Command+Page Up (Mac OS).

Premiere Pro switches to List view.

To choose the columns displayed in List view:

1. In the upper-right corner of the Project panel, click the panel menu and choose Metadata Display **B**. Premiere Pro opens the Metadata Display **C** dialog, which includes multiple metadata categories.

continues on next page

2. To select all items in a category, select the check box next to the category name **D**.

3. To open a category, click the triangle next to the category **E**.

4. Select check boxes to select individual items within a category **F**.

5. Click OK **F** to close the Metadata Display dialog and apply the selected schema.

Premiere Pro updates the columns to the new schema **G**.

TIP Note that on the right side of the Metadata Display dialog are controls for saving and managing different display schemas **H**.

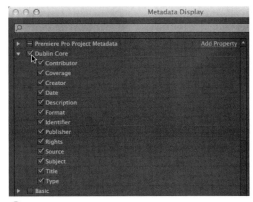

D Select a category's check box to include all items within that category.

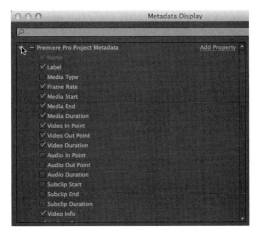

E Click the triangle next to a category to open that category.

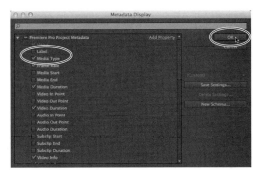

F Choose the categories that you want to include and exclude. Among other changes, I've added Media Type and removed Label.

G The fruits of our labors—now we can sort by media type!

H Note the controls on the right for saving and managing metadata schemas.

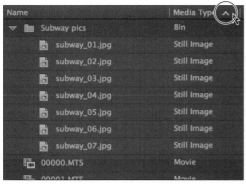

I Click the column head. The triangle displays the sort order, ascending or descending.

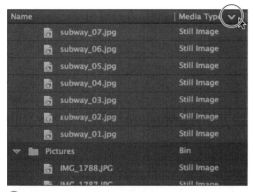

J Click the column head again to reverse the sort order.

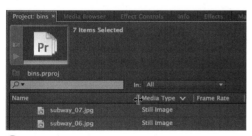

K Note the column resize pointer.

To sort by a column:

1. Click the column head to select it **I**. Premiere Pro will immediately display the current sort order—either ascending or descending—via a small triangle on the column head.

2. To change the sort order, click the column head again **J**. Premiere Pro reverses the order.

To adjust column width:

1. Hover your pointer over the right edge of the column until the column resize pointer appears **K**.

2. Drag the column to the left **L** or right.

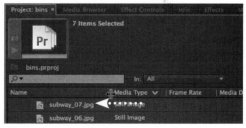

L Once the pointer appears, drag in either direction. Here, I'm making the Name column smaller.

To adjust column order:

1. Click the target column to select it .

2. Drag it to the desired location. Note that as you start to drag, Premiere Pro places a blue line over the column that you're shifting 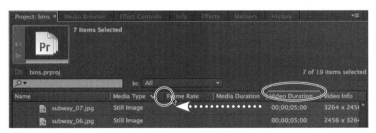. A blue indicator will appear in the space where the column will be inserted.

3. When you get to the desired location, release the pointer . Premiere Pro shifts the column to the selected location.

Ⓜ Click the column you wish to move.

Ⓝ Drag it to the new location and release the pointer.

Ⓞ Premiere Pro inserts the column at the desired location.

A Choose either of these options to enter Icon view (or use the keyboard shortcut).

Working in Icon View

Whereas List view is good for fast sorting of content, Icon view is best for quickly viewing your content to see exactly what you're working with. Icon view offers two modes for viewing the content of source clips.

When you choose a clip, a scroll bar appears, which you can use to drag through the clip—you can even set In and Out points. When you later add the clip to a sequence, these In and Out points mark the portion of the clip actually included in the video, giving you a head start on the editing process.

With unselected clips, you can use a technique called hover scrub to scrub through the content. Combined, the two modes simplify the task of viewing and prepping your imported footage.

Let's spend a few moments working with the features and controls in Icon view.

To enter and customize Icon view:

1. To enter Icon view, do one of the following:

   ▸ On the lower left of the Project panel, click the Icon view button Ⓐ.

   ▸ Click the panel menu and choose Icon Ⓐ.

   ▸ Press Control+Page Down (Windows) or Command+Page Down (Mac OS).

   Premiere Pro switches to Icon view.

continues on next page

2. If desired, click the panel menu 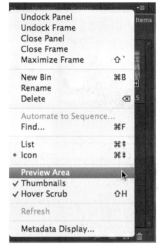 and do the following:

  ▸ Deselect Preview Area to make room for the icons.

  ▸ Select Thumbnails to show thumbnails.

  ▸ Select Hover Scrub to enable the hover scrub function.

The screens on the following tasks assume that you made these selections.

3. To adjust icon size, do one or both of the following:

  ▸ On the bottom left of the Project panel **C** click the Zoom Out or Zoom In buttons.

  ▸ Drag the zoom scroll bar.

4. Click the Sort Icons button **C** adjacent to the Zoom In button and choose the desired option **D**. The screens in the following tasks assume that User Order is selected.

> **TIP** When selecting sort order with the Sort Icons button, you would first choose the meta-data field to sort by. The Ascending Order and Descending Order menu options then become live, and you can adjust sort order accordingly.

B Here are the options I work with in Icon view.

Sort Icons button

Zoom scroll bar

C Adjust icon size with these controls (and note the Sort Icons button).

D Use these options to sort the icons.

E Use the scroll bar to drag through the clip.

F Navigate to the desired In point.

To preview clips in Icon view:

1. Click the clip to select it. A scroll bar with playhead control appears beneath it **E**.

2. To navigate through the clip, do one or more of the following:

   - Click the orange scroll bar beneath the clip at any point. The playhead moves to that point.

   - Drag the playhead **E**.

   - Play the clip with keyboard shortcuts:

     - Press the spacebar to start or stop playback.

     - Press J to rewind the clip; press J again to rewind faster. Stop the rewind by pressing K or the spacebar.

     - Press L to play the clip; press L again to accelerate. Stop playback by pressing K or the spacebar.

   TIP Note that these keyboard shortcuts work in all viewing situations in Premiere Pro. They may be overkill in the Project panel, but they are incredibly important keyboard shortcuts to learn.

   TIP To change the default frame showing for a clip in Icon view, move to the desired frame, right-click the clip, and choose Set Poster frame. Or, press Shift+P (Windows) or Command+P (Mac OS) to set the poster frame.

To mark In and Out points:

1. Using one of the techniques in the previous task, navigate to the desired In point (that is, where you want your clip to start playing once it is in the project) **F**.

continues on next page

2. To select the In point, choose Marker > Mark In (or press I) **G**. Premiere Pro sets the In point, which you should see reflected in the orange scroll bar beneath the clip **H**.

3. Using one of the techniques in the previous task, navigate to the desired Out point (that is, where you want your clip to stop playing) **H**.

4. To select the Out point, choose Marker > Mark Out (or press O) **I**. Premiere Pro sets the Out point, which you should see reflected in the orange scroll bar **J**.

TIP Give yourself plenty of leeway when marking In and Out points at this stage of the project, though you can access the full clip once it's on the Timeline. In other words, mark the In point two or three seconds before the actual In point, and the Out point two or three seconds after the actual Out point, to allow for transitions and other adjustments.

TIP Like all Premiere Pro edits, marking In and Out points is non-destructive; Premiere Pro doesn't touch your source clips.

G Set the In point with this menu command or by pressing I.

Portion excluded by in point selection　　　*Desired Out point*

H Navigate to the desired Out point.

I Set the Out point with this menu command or by pressing O.

J The trimmed clip, ready for inclusion in the project. Note how the duration changes from 8:00 seconds in **F** to 4:10 here.

 The black waveform icon means the clip has linked audio.

 Orange icons indicate that the clip has been used in a sequence.

 Click the icon to see where you've used the clip, and click the sequence to open that sequence in the Timeline.

To view clips with hover scrub:

1. Select the Project panel by clicking the panel or pressing Shift+1.

2. Move your mouse left to right over any unselected clip. Do not click and select the clip.

   Notice that Premiere Pro displays the contents of the clip as you move your mouse. The left edge of the clip represents the start, and the right edge represents the end. Moving left to right lets you quickly scroll through the entire clip.

To view clip usage information:

1. Hover your pointer over (but do not click) any unselected clip in the Project panel. If the clip contains linked audio, a black waveform will appear .

2. If the audio and/or video component of the clip has been used in a sequence, orange icons will appear on the bottom right. Hover your pointer over either icon to see how many times that component has been used .

3. Click either icon to see which sequences the clip as been added to, and their location . Click the sequence, and Premiere Pro will open that sequence in the Timeline.

Viewing Clips in the Source Monitor

The basic function of the Source Monitor is to display content from your project so you can watch the footage at full resolution and choose In and Out points. But there's a lot going on in a small space. As you'll see, there are ten different views 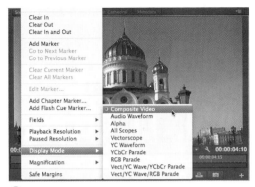 in the Source Monitor (and Program Monitor), which you'll use for chromakeying, color correction, and the like.

You can view all types of content in the Source Monitor, with different views for audio and video/images. You can load multiple clips into the Source Monitor and switch between them, and, of course, you can customize the Program Monitor (check out the section "To customize the buttons in the Source Monitor or Program Monitor" in Chapter 1).

To navigate to the Source Monitor keyboard shortcuts, press Shift+2. Once you're there, you can maximize the display of the Source Monitor by clicking the panel to make it active and then pressing the accent key (`), which is to the left of the 1 key and directly above the Tab key on most keyboards. Restore the workspace by pressing the same key again. You'll want to do that a lot to see your HD clips in their full glory.

To view clips in the Source Monitor:

1. To load a single clip in the Source Monitor, do one of the following:

    ▸ Double-click the clip.

    ▸ Drag the clip into the Source Monitor 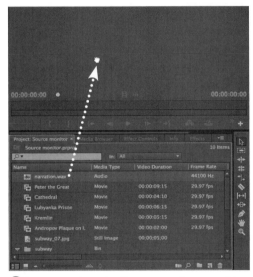.

    Premiere Pro loads the clip in the Source Monitor **C**. Since narration.wav is an audio clip, it appears as a waveform in the Source Monitor.

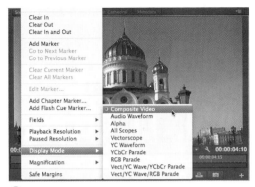

A The different views of the Source Monitor.

B Drag a clip from the Project panel to open it in the Source Monitor.

C Audio clips appear as waveforms.

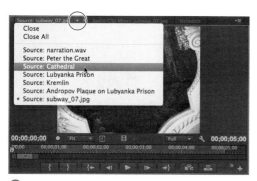

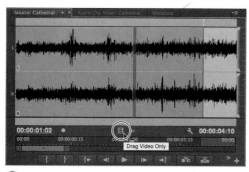

D Use the Source menu to switch between and close clips.

E To view the audio component of a clip, click the Drag Audio Only button.

F To view the video portion, click the Drag Video Only button.

2. To load multiple clips into the Source Monitor, select them in the Project panel and drag them into the Source Monitor.

3. To switch between clips in the Source Monitor, click the triangle to the right of the current clip's name on the Source tab to open the Source menu, and then choose the desired clip **D**. The Source Monitor switches to that clip **E**.

4. To display the audio component of a video clip, click the Drag Audio Only **E** button beneath the preview area in the Source Monitor. The Source Monitor shifts to waveform view to display the audio component **F**. To switch back, click the Drag Video Only button.

5. To close the current clip in the Source Monitor, open the Source menu and choose Close **D**.

6. To close all the clips in the Source Monitor, open the Source menu and choose Close All **D**.

TIP The Source Monitor can display clips from the Project panel and from sequences open in the Timeline. In the Source menu **G**, clips opened from the Project panel will be listed by name. Clips opened from a sequence will show the sequence name, the name of the clip, and the location of the clip in the sequence.

G Clips opened from a sequence will show the sequence name, the clip name, and the clip location in the sequence.

Controlling Playback in the Source Monitor

Let's face it: In this digital age, most 5-year-olds can work the basic playback controls in the Source Monitor. But editing video requires a degree of precision unnecessary for *Barney* DVDs or YouTube clips, and keyboard shortcuts can really save you time when you're in a hurry. Invest a few minutes here learning Premiere Pro's playback controls and their associated shortcuts, and you'll make up that time in short order.

There's a lot happening in the Source Monitor A; let's look at it section by section. Immediately below the preview window are two timecodes and a time ruler. The timecode on the left is the playhead location; the timecode on the right is the total clip duration.

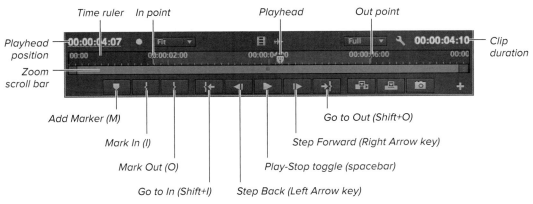

Time ruler   In point   Playhead   Out point

Playhead position 00:00:04:07 ● Fit ▼ 🗒 ╫ Full ▼ 🔧 00:00:04:10 — Clip duration

Zoom scroll bar

Add Marker (M)

Mark In (I)

Mark Out (O)

Go to In (Shift+I)   Step Back (Left Arrow key)

Go to Out (Shift+O)

Step Forward (Right Arrow key)

Play-Stop toggle (spacebar)

A Playback and related controls in the Source Monitor.

The time ruler beneath the timecodes represents the duration of the clip. The playhead is at whatever position is currently showing in the Source Monitor. The playhead is a key concept in editing, and you'll see one practically every time you view a clip in Premiere Pro.

If you've been working through this chapter, you'll recall this clip as 00055.MTS, since renamed Cathedral. Earlier, in the Icon view of the Project panel, we marked its In and Out points. Now that the clip is loaded in the Source Monitor, these markers appear in the time ruler, with the selected portion of the clip in light gray and the excluded portions in darker gray. As you'll learn later, you can use the zoom scroll bar to zoom in to regions of the clip, which is useful when you want to isolate short regions of a longer clip.

Beneath the zoom scroll bar are various controls for marking clips in and out and for playing the clip back. Most of the playback controls should look familiar, but note the Step Back and Step Forward buttons, which you'll use a lot, though the Left Arrow key and Right Arrow key shortcuts

for moving through the video frame by frame are useful and easy to remember. The spacebar toggle for play/stop is absolutely essential.

Premiere Pro has shortcuts for most playback actions—even some that you can't perform via mouse commands. Here's a short list that you may find helpful.

- Remember the J, K, and L keys. J plays the clip in reverse, and pressing it multiple times increases rewind speed. K (or the spacebar) stops playback.

- L plays the clip, and pressing it multiple times increases fast-forward speed. K (or the spacebar) stops playback.

- Pressing Shift+J rewinds in slow motion at about 10 percent speed (so three frames per second instead of 30). Pressing J accelerates rewind speed. K (or the spacebar) stops playback.

- Pressing Shift+L plays in slow motion at about 10 percent speed (so three frames per second instead of 30). Pressing L accelerates playback. K (or the spacebar) stops playback.

Configuring the Source Monitor

The Source Monitor panel includes a number of configuration options that you need to be aware of. Let's walk through them.

Note that you can access many of the Source Monitor settings from two locations : the panel menu (in the upper-right corner of the Source Monitor) and the wrench-like Settings button (on the right, just above the time ruler). You can also access most of these controls by right-clicking in the Source Monitor. In these tasks, I'll refer to the Settings button for simplicity.

A Most settings discussed in the following tasks can be accessed through the Settings button and the panel menu.

Working with safe zones

Safe zones exist for two reasons. First, the outer 10–15 percent of a video (called *over-scan*) was typically not viewable on analog television sets **B**. Though modern digital displays like LCDs and plasma screens don't share this problem, to ensure that your complete title is viewable on all sets, place it within the *title-safe* zone. Though you have a bit more leeway with your actual footage, when shooting your video you should ensure that the critical action happens in the *action-safe* zone.

The second reason is that some 16:9 videos have their outer edges cut off when displayed on 4:3 devices, so that only the "center cut" is shown. If your video might be displayed on older 4:3 TV sets, make sure that your titles are within the 4:3 title-safe zone and that your critical action is within the 4:3 action-safe zone.

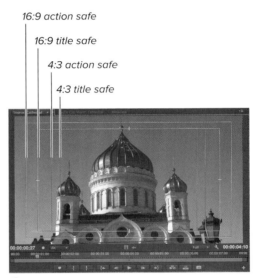

16:9 action safe

16:9 title safe

4:3 action safe

4:3 title safe

B Mind these safe zones when shooting or editing for television display.

C Turn safe zones on and off using the Safe Margins menu option.

D Change the dimensions of the safe zones here.

If you're editing strictly for web distribution or other non-TV display, you can disable safe zones. If your video will be displayed on TV sets, either via broadcast, DVD, Blu-ray, or another mechanism, and you want to make sure your action and titles can be fully seen by all viewers, you should enable and mind the safe zones when shooting and editing.

To enable and disable safe zones:

1. To enable safe zones, click the Settings button to open the Settings menu and select Safe Margins **C** (a check mark should appear next to it).

2. To disable safe zones, click the Settings button to open the Settings menu and select Safe Margins (the check mark disappears).

> **TIP** Change the dimensions of the safe zones in the Project Settings dialog **D**, accessed by choosing **File > Project Settings**.

> **TIP** Many camcorders have safe zone settings that you can enable in the viewfinder. If you're shooting for television display, check for them on your camera gear.

Changing the magnification level

When you load a clip into the Source Monitor, Premiere Pro fits the entire clip into the display. When you're working with HD footage, this typically means that the video is scaled down by a significant degree. This works well for most editing functions, but sometimes you need to see the entire video, pixel for pixel, or even zoom in to 200% or more.

To customize playback resolution in the Source Monitor:

1. Click the Select Zoom Level drop-down **E** and choose the desired setting **F**.

2. Premiere Pro switches to that setting **G**. Use scroll bars around the frame to navigate to the desired region.

TIP Any magnification adjustments made via these controls are for display only and won't affect the magnification of your footage in the sequence.

Adjusting display quality

When you're previewing video in the Source Monitor, sometimes real-time playback is more important than the quality of the pixels. Depending on the source of your video footage and the power of your computer and graphics card, playing back full-resolution HD footage may not be possible. For this reason, Premiere Pro lets you adjust the resolution of video during playback.

If preview is slower than full frame rate on your workstation, you may want to lower the display resolution to achieve full-frame-rate playback. Note that you can tell when you're dropping frames by enabling the Dropped Frame Indicator in the Source Monitor and Program Monitor.

E Click the Select Zoom Level drop-down.

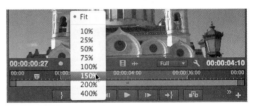

F Choose a zoom level.

G Use the scroll bars at the bottom and right to navigate around the frame.

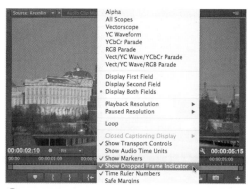

H Enabling the Dropped Frame Indicator.

I You'll know there's a problem when the ball turns orange. Hover your pointer over the ball to get more details.

47 Frames Dropped During Playback

J Click here to adjust playback resolution.

Select Playback Resolution

K Choose the desired resolution.

You can also adjust the display resolution when playback is paused, though since there are no playback constraints, Full (100%) is almost always the recommended setting.

To enable and disable the Dropped Frame Indicator:

1. To enable the Dropped Frame Indicator, click the Settings button to open the Settings menu and select Show Dropped Frame Indicator so that the check mark appears **H**. The Dropped Frame Indicator appears **I**. (Note that this screenshot shows the Program Monitor.)

2. To disable the Dropped Frame Indicator, click the Settings button to open the Settings menu and select Show Dropped Frame Indicator so that the check mark disappears **H**.

To adjust the playback resolution:

Do one of the following:

- Click the Select Playback Resolution drop-down **J** on the Source Monitor and choose the desired resolution **K**.

continues on next page

- Click the Settings button in the Source Monitor window, and choose Playback Resolution and the desired resolution ①.

Premiere Pro adjusts the playback resolution.

TIP Depending on the size and configuration of your Source Monitor, you may not notice any change at all. For example, if you're editing on a notebook with the Source Monitor at a fraction of the size of the original HD video, playback may appear exactly the same, though the load on the computer will be much lower.

To adjust the paused resolution:

Click the Settings button in the Source Monitor window, and choose Paused Resolution and the desired resolution ⑩.

Premiere Pro adjusts the paused resolution.

① You can also set playback resolution in the Settings menu.

⑩ Adjusting paused resolution in the Settings menu.

Working with interlaced footage

As you probably know, the "frames" we see in interlaced footage are made up of two fields. With high-motion footage, when both fields are showing, this can often result in double images (also called venetian-blind, or slicing, artifacts) .

Sometimes you may want to see these double images—for example, when you're debugging a rendering issue and want to verify that the source footage is interlaced. Most of the time, however, you'll probably want these artifacts to disappear. Here's how you control the display of interlaced footage.

To control the appearance of interlaced footage:

1. Click the Settings button to open the Settings menu ⓞ.

2. Choose one of the following:

   ▸ Display First Field, to display the first of the two interlaced fields that make up the frame.

   ▸ Display Second Field, to display the second field.

   ▸ Display Both Fields, to display both fields.

   Premiere Pro adjusts to the selected setting ⓟ (in this case, Display First Field).

TIP If your goal is to make the double images and artifacts disappear, there's no difference between displaying the first or second field.

ⓝ Both fields are showing in this interlaced frame.

ⓞ Choosing Display First Field to eliminate the double image.

ⓟ Displaying the first field only, so the double image is gone.

Working with Clips in the Source Monitor

Now that you've got the Source Monitor configured, let's focus on tasks you'll perform in the Source Monitor. Much of this relates to inserting markers and choosing In and Out points.

You'll insert markers to identify points that you may use later during editing. For example, you may need to sync clips for multicam editing via markers, or mark the location for the insertion of a DVD chapter marker. Markers inserted in the Source Monitor remain with the clip once it's inserted into the sequence.

As we've discussed, a clip's In point is where playback will start once the clip is added to a sequence. All frames before the In point will be ignored. Similarly, the Out point is the place where playback will stop, with all subsequent frames ignored. You can insert In and Out points in the Project panel in Icon view, or in the Source Monitor.

You may need to zoom in to a clip by using the zoom scroll bar. For example, you may choose a marker location or In and Out points with reference to a clip's audio waveform. In such instances, it's much easier to find the appropriate location by zooming in to the clip.

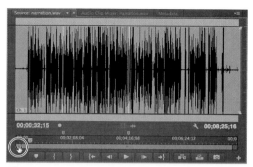

A Grab the edge of the zoom scroll bar.

B Drag the edge inward to see more detail. Note the additional detail in the waveform and how the timecodes reflect this.

C Drag the zoom scroll bar to the desired location in the file.

To adjust the detail shown in the Source Monitor:

1. Just beneath the time ruler in the Source Monitor, grab one edge of the zoom scroll bar A. Your pointer converts to a two-headed pointer.

2. Do one of the following:

   ▸ To see more detail, drag the edge inward B.

   ▸ To see less detail, drag the edge outward.

   Premiere Pro adjusts the amount of detail shown in the Source Monitor.

3. If necessary, drag the zoom scroll bar to the desired location C.

Working with audio in the Source panel

As long as we're looking at an audio waveform, let's examine several audio-specific adjustments in the Source Monitor. In addition to displaying the time ruler in traditional video timecode, the Source Monitor can display the time ruler in audio time units, which provides 48,000 discrete edit points in this 48 KHz audio file—much greater precision than the 29.97 edit points available using video timecode. In addition to scaling horizontally into the waveform, as you just learned, you can scale vertically to provide a closer look at the file in the Source Monitor.

D shows a stereo audio file in the Source Monitor—in this case, the audio component of the Cathedral clip you've seen throughout this chapter. As you can see, the Source Monitor looks more like a traditional timeline, showing the entire file and its In and Out points. Note the vertical zoom scroll bars on the right; you'll learn to use those in a moment.

Playhead

In point button

Out point button

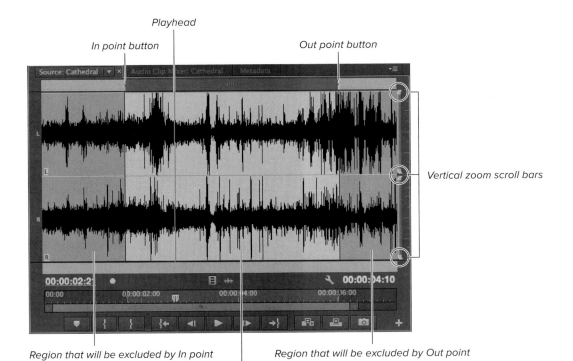

Vertical zoom scroll bars

Region that will be excluded by In point

Region that will be excluded by Out point

Region that will be included in the project

D The Source Monitor showing a stereo audio file.

E Changing to audio time units.

F The time ruler and timecodes showing audio time units.

To enable and disable audio time units:

1. To enable audio time units, click the Settings button to open the Settings menu and choose Show Audio Time Units (so that the check mark appears) **E**. The Source Monitor changes to audio time units **F**.

2. To return to video timecode, click the Settings button to open the Settings menu and choose Show Audio Time Units so the check mark disappears **E**.

TIP To get a feel for the additional editing precision that audio time units provide, enable audio time units and press the Right Arrow key to move through the clip. With video timecode and 29.97 fps video, it takes 30 presses to move one second of video. With audio time units and 48 KHz audio, it would take 48,000 presses (good luck with that).

To zoom vertically into a clip in the Source Monitor:

1. On the right side of the Source Monitor, grab one edge of the vertical zoom scroll bar .

2. Do one of the following:
   - ▸ To see more detail, drag the edge inward ⒣.
   - ▸ To see less detail, drag the edge outward.

   Premiere Pro adjusts the amount of detail shown in the Source Monitor.

Ⓖ Grab the edge of the vertical zoom scroll bar.

Working with markers in the Source Monitor

Markers inserted in the Source Monitor can be used for various purposes, including syncing clips for multicam editing. Note that markers inserted into clips from the Project panel are called clip markers, whereas markers inserted into a sequence are called sequence markers.

To insert markers in the Source Monitor:

1. Drag the playhead to the desired location for the marker ⒤.

Ⓗ Drag inward to see more detail. Note the additional detail in the waveform.

Ⓘ Drag the playhead to the desired marker location.

J Click the Add Marker button to add a marker.

*Time ruler   Marker on current
marker indicator   frame indicator*

K Two marker indicators, one showing the marker above the time ruler, the other indicating that the current frame contains a marker.

L Note the marker indicator inside a clip added to the Timeline. Markers inserted in a sequence (sequence markers) appear above the Timeline.

2. Do one of the following:

- ▸ Click the Add Marker button **J**.
- ▸ Press the M key.
- ▸ Right-click and choose Add Marker.
- ▸ Choose Marker > Add Marker.

Premiere Pro inserts a marker at that location **K**. Note the marker icon directly above the time ruler, indicating that there is a marker at that location. The larger marker above and to the left tells you that there is a marker on the current frame. The marker will appear in the Timeline once the clip is included in a sequence **L**.

TIP Note that you can add a marker while a clip is playing by clicking the Add Marker button or pressing the M key.

TIP To add an explanation to a marker, right-click the marker and choose Edit. The Marker dialog opens, and you can name the marker, add comments, or convert the marker to a chapter marker, a web link, or a Flash cue point.

To move markers in the Source Monitor:

1. Grab the marker **M**.

2. Drag it to the new location **N**.

> **TIP** Note the options available by right-clicking **O** or by choosing Marker in Premiere Pro's main menu.

Setting In and Out points

When you import a clip into a project and then drag it into a sequence, Premiere Pro adds the entire clip to the sequence, from the first frame to the last. Typically, however, you'll want only a segment of each source clip included in a sequence. Although you can edit out the unneeded sections of a clip on the Timeline, it's usually faster and more efficient to do this in the Source Monitor.

You'll use In and Out points to accomplish this. Specifically, mark the In point at the first frame of the video you want included in the sequence and the Out point at the last frame you want included in the video. All frames before the In point and after the Out point are simply excluded from the sequence.

In and Out points also allow you to create subclips: essentially, short segments of a longer clip that look and act like independent clips imported into your project. There is more on subclips in the next section.

M To move a marker, just grab it and...

N ...drag it to the new location.

O Navigational and housekeeping options.

Navigate to the desired In point.

Click the Mark In button, or press I.

Navigate to the desired Out point.

Click the Mark Out button, or press O.

To adjust either the In Point or the Out Point, drag the marker to the desired location.

To set In and Out points:

1. Drag the playhead to the desired In point .

2. Do one of the following:
   ▸ Click the Mark In button .
   ▸ Press I.

   Premiere Pro sets the In point .

3. Drag the playhead to the desired Out point .

4. Do one of the following:
   ▸ Click the Mark Out button .
   ▸ Press O.

   Premiere Pro sets the Out point and shades the region between the In point and the Out point .

TIP You can move the In point or Out point by hovering your pointer over either marker until it becomes the trim head icon and dragging the edge to the desired location.

TIP You can move the entire selected region without affecting its duration by clicking the In/Out Grip (the textured area in the center of the marked region) and dragging it to the desired location .

TIP For clips with both video and audio components, the In and Out points mark all tracks.

You can drag the entire selected region by grabbing the textured area in the marked region.

Working with Subclips

Subclips are sections of imported clips that you want to edit separately in a project. Once you've created a subclip, it looks and acts much like a regular imported clip, and you can edit it the same way.

Here's an example. At the end of a 29-second long pan of Red Square, I shot about five good seconds of Saint Basil's Cathedral. I wanted to isolate the segment for later use in a short video on churches in Moscow. The best way to accomplish this was to create a subclip of this short segment.

One nomenclature-related note: The clip from which a subclip is created is referred to as the *master clip*.

To create a subclip:

1. Mark the In point and Out point of the target section in the master clip .

2. Do one of the following:
   - ▸ Right-click in the Source Monitor and choose Make Subclip **B**.
   - ▸ Choose Clip > Make Subclip.
   - ▸ Press Control+U (Windows) or Command+U (Mac OS).

   Premiere Pro opens the Make Subclip dialog **C**.

Ⓐ I want to create a subclip from the final 4:21 of the Red Square video.

Ⓑ Right-click, and choose Make Subclip.

Ⓒ Naming the clip in the Make Subclip dialog.

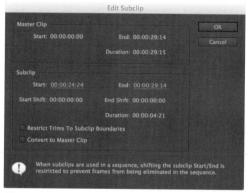

D The subclip in the Project panel, where it looks and acts just like a regular imported clip.

E Edit the subclip in this dialog.

3. Deselect the Restrict Trims to Subclip Boundaries check box C. This will allow you to access all frames in the master clip in any subsequent edit.

4. Type the name of the subclip in the Name field C.

5. Click OK to save the subclip C.

   Premiere Pro saves the subclip in the Project panel D. Note that the duration, 4:21, matches the selected region shown in A.

6. To edit the subclip, right-click the subclip in the Project panel and choose Edit Subclip; the Edit Subclip dialog opens E. You can extend the clip in either direction by adjusting the Start and End values, or you can convert the subclip to a master clip, which is essentially a duplicate of the master clip from which the subclip was derived.

TIP When creating a subclip, Premiere Pro does not create a separate source file on your hard disk, just pointers to the original master clip. Obviously, if you delete the master clip, the subclip won't have any content.

Choosing Display Modes

In addition to the composite video and audio waveform modes that you've seen throughout this chapter, both the Source Monitor and Program Monitor have other modes  that you access via the Settings menu. For the most part, they are analysis modes that are useful when adjusting clip color and brightness. You'll learn more about several of them in Chapter 11.

Ⓐ Changing modes via the Settings menu.

Here's a quick description of each mode.

- Composite Video: Displays the video in normal mode. This is the primary mode that you'll use in the Source Monitor and Program Monitor.

- Audio Waveform: Displays the audio waveform; it's useful when working with audio files.

- Alpha: Displays the transparency of a video file or image. You'll work with transparency in Chapter 13.

- All Scopes Ⓑ: Displays a waveform monitor, vectorscope, YCbCr parade, and RGB parade.

- Vectorscope: Displays a vectorscope, which measures a clip's color characteristics. This scope was very useful for working with analog cameras but has dropped in importance with digital gear.

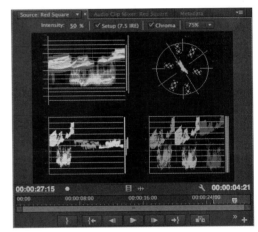

Ⓑ All the available scopes in one panel.

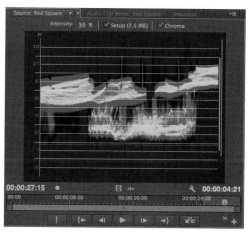

C The waveform monitor, a critical scope for adjusting brightness and contrast.

- YC Waveform C: The primary scope for adjusting the brightness and contrast of a clip. You'll learn all about it in Chapter 11.

- YCbCr Parade: A waveform monitor that displays the Y, Cb, and Cr components of the video separately, in IRE.

- RGB Parade: A waveform monitor that displays the R (red), G (green), and B (blue) components of the video separately.

- Vect/YC Wave/YCbCr Parade: Displays a waveform monitor, vectorscope, and YCbCr parade.

- Vect/YC Wave/RGB Parade: Displays a waveform monitor, vectorscope, and RGB parade.

To choose a different display mode:

1. Click the Settings button to open the Settings menu, and choose the desired display mode A.

2. To return to Composite Video, click the Settings button to open the Settings menu and choose Composite Video A.

Modifying Clip Properties and Interpreting Footage

There are a lot of calculations and computations going on under the hood in Premiere Pro, and one of the most complicated is the interpretation of source footage. Specifically, the myriad types of source footage (HDV, AVCHD, DSLR, PNG, JPEG, TIF, and so on) have an equally varied schema of frame rates, aspect ratios, field orders, and transparency values.

The vast majority of the time, when you import disparate footage into Premiere Pro, the program knows how to interpret the footage correctly. But every once in a while, you'll see an image that just looks wrong . The place to investigate is the Interpret Footage dialog 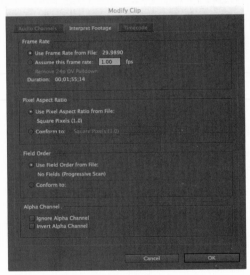, accessed by right-clicking the clip and choosing Modify > Interpret Footage.

As you can see, the dialog is designed to address these four problems:

- Frame Rate: If your footage appears faster or slower than the true frame rate, select the "Assume this frame rate" option and enter the true frames per second (fps) . There are no hard-and-fast rules here; you just need to experiment until the footage looks right.

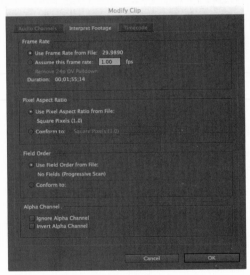

E The Interpret Footage dialog.

D This clip has a distorted aspect ratio.

F Adjusting the frame rate.

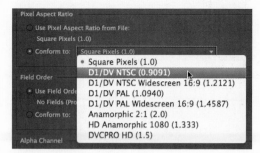

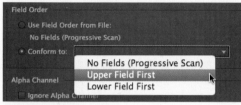

G Adjusting the aspect ratio.

H Adjusting the field order.

I Changing the default alpha channel settings.

■ **Pixel Aspect Ratio:** This is the problem shown in D and is by far the most common problem you'll address in this dialog. In the Pixel Aspect Ratio area, select the "Conform to" option and choose the correct aspect ratio from the menu G. Again, you may have to experiment with several settings to fix the problem.

■ **Field Order:** These problems tend to manifest as jittery footage (either on the Timeline or after rendering) or as footage with funky slicing artifacts. In the Field Order area, select the "Conform to" option and choose the proper field order from the menu H.

■ **Alpha Channel:** Problems here almost always occur with logos, titles, and other synthetic footage rather than actual video clips, and arise when the wrong portion of an image is transparent. You can attempt to address the problem by choosing one of the two check boxes I.

Again, you won't see problems like these very often, but when you do, making these adjustments in the Interpret Footage dialog will typically resolve them quickly.

TIP Often you won't notice you have a problem until you include the clip in a sequence. Wherever you find the problem, the solution is the same: Select the clip in the project bin and adjust as described here. All changes should flow through to wherever you've used the clip.

Working with Metadata

We looked at metadata before as it related to choosing columns to display in the Project panel. Now let's take a deeper look at Premiere Pro's Metadata panel.

Your use of this panel will depend largely upon the type of projects that you produce. If you're producing events like ballets, sports, or webcasts, you may never look at metadata at all. But if you're producing movies or other content built from hundreds of source clips, or content that has long-term archival value, metadata is critical to being able to find and monetize your video.

Before getting started, let's briefly discuss the two types of metadata managed by Premiere Pro, clip-based and file-based. Clip-based metadata is stored only in Premiere Pro project files and can't be seen in other programs.

File-based metadata is stored in the file itself (or in a sidecar file if the file doesn't support direct embedding) via Premiere Pro's support for the Extensible Metadata Platform (XMP). Metadata entered in these fields can be seen by other programs.

The Metadata panel also contains fields for speech analysis (see the sidebar in this section).

To enter data in the Metadata panel:

1. Click a clip in the Project panel Ⓐ.
2. Click the Metadata tab Ⓑ to open the panel, or choose Window > Metadata if the tab isn't available. The Metadata panel opens. You'll see three categories of metadata: Clip, File (powered by XMP), and Speech Analysis.

Ⓐ Choose the clip.

Ⓑ Click the Metadata tab. Or choose Window > Metadata if the panel isn't open (or you can't find it).

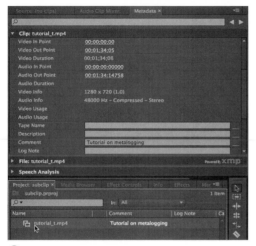

C Opening and navigating to the target fields.

D Type the desired data and click Enter (Windows) or Return (Mac OS).

E Metadata makes it simple to find clips.

3. Click the triangle C to the left of each category to view subcategories and fields. Use the scroll bar on the right to navigate.

4. Enter the desired metadata D and press Enter (Windows) or Return (Mac OS). Premiere Pro stores the metadata, and if that category is selected as a column in the Project panel, the metadata appears there D.

TIP One of the key benefits of entering metadata is the ability to quickly find clips based upon the descriptors entered. The Find box works well for this E.

TIP The Metadata panel shows all metadata fields, and the Project panel shows only the fields you selected for viewing there. If you've entered data in the Metadata panel and it's not appearing in the Project panel, it's likely because you don't have that field selected. See the "Working in List View" section earlier in this chapter to learn how to select columns.

TIP The process of manually inserting metadata into multiple clips is called metalogging. If you're sitting down for a massive metalogging session, try the Metalogging workspace, accessible by choosing Window > Workspace > Metalogging.

Finding faces in your clips

In Premiere Pro, there is metadata that you enter, as you just learned, and there is metadata that the application can derive by analyzing your source clips. Specifically, Premiere Pro can analyze content for faces and convert clearly spoken speech to text.

In these two tasks you'll learn how to analyze footage to find faces, and then how to find clips with faces.

To detect faces in clips:

1. In the Project panel, choose the clips to analyze **F**.

2 Right-click, and choose Analyze Content **F**. The Analyze Content dialog opens.

3. Select the Face Detection check box, and choose the desired Quality setting **G**.

4. Click OK. Adobe Media Encoder loads **H** and automatically starts analyzing the clips in the background so you can continue editing. When it's done analyzing the clips, Adobe Media Encoder will play a completion sound.

F Choose the clips to analyze, right-click, and choose Analyze Content.

G Enable Face Detection and choose a Quality setting.

H Adobe Media Encoder analyzing the clips.

To find clips with faces:

1. After your clips have been analyzed, click the magnifying glass icon in the Find box and choose Find Faces from the menu **I**. Premiere Pro displays all clips with faces **J**.

2. Click the Close Button **J** to close the Find Faces filter and restore all content.

I Click the magnifying glass drop-down and choose Find Faces.

J These are all the clips with faces. Click the Close button to restore all content.

Working with Speech Analysis

The workflow for speech analysis is very similar to that used for finding faces: Select the target file, right-click, and choose Analyze Content to open the Analyze Content dialog **K**.

Choose your language and quality settings, and if you have a reference script, attach it as either a text file (.txt) or a script from Adobe Story in ASTX format. As you would suspect, a script makes the transcription much more accurate.

Press OK, and Adobe Media Encoder analyzes the audio. When the analysis is complete, the text appears in the Speech Analysis section of the Metadata panel.

K Converting speech to text.

Working with Sequences

Sequences are where it all happens in Premiere Pro. It's where the real editing goes on, and where the video production actually occurs. Sequences are a big deal.

Some things to know about sequences: First, you can have multiple sequences in any Premiere Pro project. You can insert a sequence into a sequence to create a nested sequence. You can copy, paste, delete, rename, and search for a sequence, just like you can any other piece of content.

The thing you can't do with a sequence is change its most fundamental parameters. So when you create a sequence, you better get it right the first time. Actually, I'm being a bit dramatic; if you start editing on a sequence and later discover that you used the wrong settings, you can always copy and paste your edited clips onto the correct sequence. Either way, it's most efficient if you choose the right settings from the start.

Though there are hundreds of permutations, there are three basic scenarios, each of which calls for a different solution.

- **You want a sequence preset that matches the bulk of your source video footage.** This is the most common case: You shoot in AVCHD or DSLR, so you want an AVCHD or DSLR preset. The easiest way to accomplish this is to drag a clip in the desired format onto the New Item button, as described in the task "To create a sequence that matches your source footage."

- **You want a sequence preset that matches your target output, which is a broadcast standard.** When I produce for DVD output, I choose a 16:9 DV sequence preset even though I'm shooting in HD, because it produces better quality than working with an HD preset (see bit.ly/PP_preset). Similarly, if you're producing for 720p broadcast output, you should choose a 720p standard output even if you're shooting in 1080p. Sure, you could also use a 1080p preset and output at 720p, but you have more editing flexibility when your preset is smaller than your source footage. In these instances, it's best to choose an existing preset, as described in "To choose a sequence preset."

- **You want a sequence that matches an arbitrary project size.** When I produce 640x360 videos for web production, I create a 640x360 preset, even if I'm shooting in HD. That way, I know that the titles will fit, the logo will be in exactly the right place, and so on. Similarly, when producing a 1024x576 screencam, I first create a custom preset, following the procedure detailed in "To create a custom sequence preset."

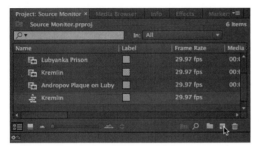

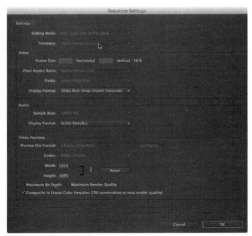

A Drag the clip onto the New Item button.

B Premiere Pro creates a sequence with the same name and matching settings.

C Opening the Sequence Settings dialog.

D The Sequence Settings dialog.

To create a sequence that matches your source footage:

Drag a clip with the format you wish to match onto the New Item button **A**. Premiere Pro creates a sequence that matches the settings of that clip and has the same name **B**; the sequence opens in the Timeline.

TIP To rename the sequence, select it, press the Tab or Enter/Return key, type the desired text, and press Enter (Windows) or Return (Mac OS).

To check your sequence settings:

1. Right-click the sequence, and choose Sequence Settings **C**. The Sequence Settings dialog opens **D**.

   Note that all the intrinsic settings in the Audio and Video areas are grayed out and uneditable. Although you can change how the format is displayed in the sequence, you can't change these intrinsic settings.

2. Click OK to close the dialog.

TIP Selecting the Maximum Bit Depth and Maximum Render Quality check boxes does improve output quality in some instances (see http://bit.ly/maxrenderquality). However, enabling these functions before editing can slow performance, and it's unlikely that you'll see any difference. For this reason, I recommend editing with these check boxes unselected and then selecting them before rendering.

TIP Note that it's not important for the editing mode to exactly match your source footage. For example, the footage I used to create this preset was AVCHD, not AVC-Intra. What's critical is that file characteristics like timebase, frame size, pixel aspect ratio, field order, and audio sample rate match.

Choosing a sequence preset

If you're attempting to create a preset that matches your source footage, I recommend that you follow the procedure outlined in the task "To create a sequence that matches your source footage." If you're choosing a sequence preset to match a specific format, you'll need to know multiple characteristics of that format, including format type, resolution, frame rate, broadcast standard, aspect ratio, whether the format is progressive or interlaced, and perhaps some others.

One way to gather this information is to have your camera and manual handy to check the settings that you used. You can also get some of this information in the Project panel by choosing the clip with the Preview Area open. See the "To open and close the Preview Area" task earlier in this chapter for more detail.

Fortunately, the preset selection interface simplifies the selection process, though the process varies from format to format.

To choose a sequence preset:

1. To create the new sequence, do one of the following:

   ▸ Click the New Item button and choose Sequence 🅴.

   ▸ Choose File > New > Sequence.

   ▸ Press Control+N (Windows) or Command+N (Mac OS).

   The New Sequence dialog opens 🅵.

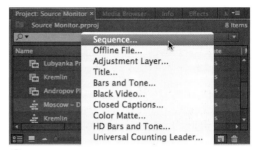

🅴 Click the New Item button, and choose Sequence.

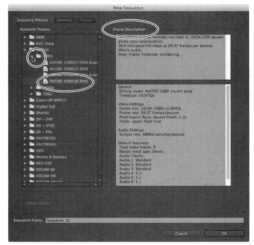

🅵 Click a preset to see the technical description.

G Type the desired name and click OK.

H The new sequence.

I Houston, we have a problem.

J Letterboxes on your source video and red lines beneath the time ruler in the Timeline also indicate a mismatch between your source footage and the sequence preset.

2. Click the triangle next to each preset category to reveal the presets and sub-categories **F**.

3. Click any preset to display its details in the Preset Description field. Repeat as necessary until you choose the correct preset **F**.

4. At the bottom of the New Sequence Dialog, type a name for the sequence **G**.

5. Click OK **G** to close the New Sequence dialog and create the sequence **H**.

TIP If you created the sequence so that it matches your source footage, try dragging one of your source clips onto the sequence. If you see the Clip Mismatch Warning dialog **I**, you know there's a mismatch. Click the Keep Existing Settings button if you didn't intend for the sequence to match your footage; click the Change Sequence Settings button if you wanted a match.

TIP If your source video shows letterboxes or if there's a red line beneath the time ruler in the Timeline **J**, you also have a mismatch between your source footage and the sequence preset. That's OK if you planned for the mismatch, but it's a problem if you didn't.

Creating custom sequence presets

When I create custom sequence presets, it's almost always for use in a totally non-broadcast setting, like screencams or streaming media. This usage dictates many of the decisions explained in the next task. If you're creating a custom sequence preset for a similar purpose, you'll find the procedure helpful.

On the other hand, if your goal is to create a format that's just like an existing preset except different in one key way—say, the number or type of video or audio tracks—you're better off starting with the existing preset, making the critical change, and then saving the new preset. You can benefit from the high-level workflow presented in this task, but you should ignore most of the suggested settings changes.

To create a custom sequence preset:

1. To create the new sequence, do one of the following:
   - ▶ Click the New Item button and choose Sequence ⓔ.
   - ▶ Choose File > New > Sequence, or press CtrlControl+N (Windows) or Command+N (Mac OS).

   The New Sequence dialog opens ⓚ.

2. Click the Settings tab ⓚ.

3. Choose Custom from the Editing Mode drop-down ⓛ. This gives you complete flexibility to change any setting.

4. Choose the desired frames per second from the Timebase drop-down ⓜ.

ⓚ Click the Settings tab to access the settings.

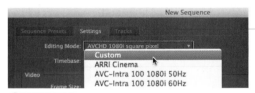

ⓛ Choose Custom for editing mode or you won't be able to change most of the settings.

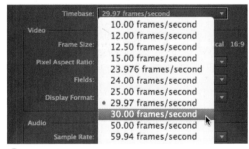

ⓜ Choose the frame rate.

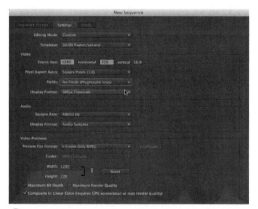

Pixel aspect ratio should almost always be square for non-broadcast projects.

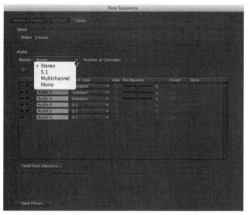

Conform your settings to those shown here.

Customize audio settings as necessary.

5. Enter the horizontal and vertical values in the Frame Size fields N.

6. From the Pixel Aspect Ratio drop-down, choose the desired pixel aspect ratio— usually Square Pixels (1.0) for non-broadcast projects N.

7. From the Fields drop-down, choose the desired settings—usually No Fields (Progressive Scan) for non-broadcast projects O.

8. From the Display Format drop-down, choose the desired format (30 fps Time-code is the recommended default) O.

9. From the Audio Sample Rate drop-down, choose the desired sample rate—usually either 48000 Hz or 44100 Hz O.

10. From the Audio Display Format drop-down, choose the desired format (usu-ally Audio Samples) O.

Leave all other settings as shown O.

11. Click the Tracks tab P to view the audio-related settings. Choose the number of video tracks to insert in the new sequence, and click the Master and Track Type drop-downs to view the available settings P and make any modifications.

continues on next page

12. To save the preset for later reuse, click the Save Preset button **P**. The Save Settings dialog opens **Q**.

13. Type the name and description, and click OK to close the dialog and save the settings **Q**.

14. At the bottom of the New Sequence dialog, type a name for the sequence **R**.

15. Click OK **R** to close the New Sequence dialog and create the sequence **S**.

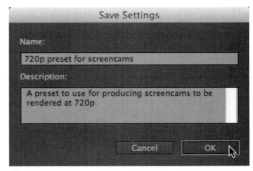

Q Saving the preset for later reuse. It will appear below all the canned presets in the Sequence Presets dialog.

R Naming the sequence preset you're creating.

S The new custom sequence preset.

A Make sure that you're in Icon view.

B Click the Sort Icons button.

C Choose User Order. Otherwise, you won't be able to sort the clips.

D Drag the clips into the desired order.

Storyboard Editing in the Project Panel

Now that we know all about the Project panel and creating sequences, let's finish up with a fun and useful exercise on storyboard editing.

Here's the back story: You've sifted through your clips in the Project panel and inserted In and Out points where appropriate. Now you want to arrange the clips in the proper order and create a sequence so you can start polishing them into a finished video. Here's the procedure.

To edit in storyboard style in the Project panel:

1. If you're not already in Icon view, click the Icon View button A.

2. To the right of the Icon View button, click the Sort Icons button B and choose User Order C. If any other sort order is selected, you won't be able to drag the clips around.

3. Drag the clips into the desired order. For example, I want the clip Andropov Plaque on Lubyanka Prison to appear before the prison clip D.

continues on next page

4. Once the clips are in the desired order, select all the clips to include in the sequence. Sort order matters here, so be sure to select the clips in the order in which you want them to appear in the sequence.

5. Drag the group of clips onto the New Item button . Premiere Pro creates a new sequence with all the clips in the selected order 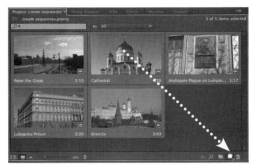 and names the sequence the name of the first selected clip.

TIP You'll learn a similar technique, using the **Automate to Sequence** feature, in Chapter 5. Automate to Sequence can send multiple clips to a sequence and insert video and audio transitions between them, but you must have an existing sequence to send the clips to; you can't use Automate to Sequence to create a sequence as we did here.

E Select the ordered clips, and drag them onto the New Items button.

F The new sequence, ready for final editing.

Working with the Timeline

Although you can perform some editing functions in the Project panel and Source Monitor, you'll do the vast majority of your editing—and spend the vast majority of your editing time—in the Timeline. Briefly, the Timeline is made up of multiple audio and video tracks onto which you insert content.

The Timeline and the Program Monitor are integrally linked. The Timeline shows the temporal progression of your project, and the Program Monitor shows what's happening at the current frame, or playhead. If you watch the timecodes on the Timeline and Program Monitor as you drag the playhead around in either panel, you'll notice that they are always in lockstep.

Timelines and sequences are also integrally linked, since a sequence is essentially a representation of content within the Timeline. Double-click a sequence in the Project panel, and it opens in the Timeline.

In this chapter, you'll learn how to configure and navigate the Timeline and how to configure the Program Monitor. You'll also learn basic ways to get content from the Project panel to the Timeline.

In This Chapter

Customizing the Timeline

Let's spend some time customizing the Timeline and learning its features Ⓐ. We'll be working with the sequence we created at the end of the last chapter, renamed Moscow Tour.

We'll discuss many of the individual features of the Timeline over the course of this and subsequent chapters, but let's briefly discuss its key features Ⓐ.

- Snap (S). Controls whether items in the Timeline snap to each other when moved. Enabled by default.

- Add Marker (M). Click to add a marker to the Timeline.

- Playhead. Marks the current frame of the video shown in the Program Monitor.

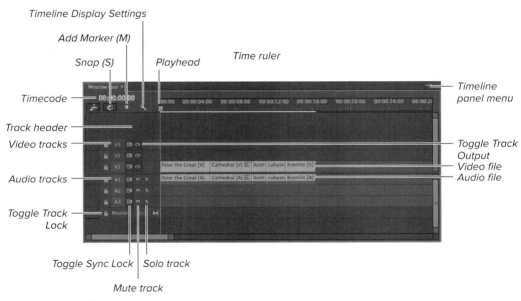

Ⓐ The Premiere Pro Timeline panel.

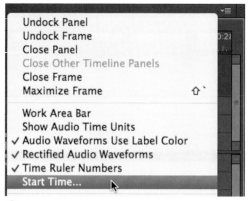

B Click here to choose a new starting timecode for your sequence.

- Timecode. Displays the location of the playhead.

- Timeline Display Settings. Opens the Settings menu.

- Time ruler. The time display within the Timeline. Runs from left to right, usually starting at zero.

- Track header. The area to the left of the Timeline track, where many track configuration adjustments are made.

- Toggle Track Output. Turns the track on and off. When a track is off, its content is no longer displayed in the Program Monitor.

- Toggle Track Lock. This button toggles locking on and off. Locking a track makes the content uneditable.

- Toggle Sync Lock. This button toggles Sync Lock on and off. Sync Lock keeps tracks in sync when certain edits are performed.

- Mute track. Mutes that track's audio during playback.

- Solo track. Plays only that track's audio during playback.

- Timeline panel menu. Contains multiple configuration options for the Timeline.

TIP By default, Premiere Pro sequences start at the timecode 00:00:00:00. To change this, choose Start Time from the Timeline panel menu **B** and, in the dialog that appears, select a different starting timecode.

TIP You can choose the colors for all content on the Timeline in the Label Defaults Preferences dialog, accessed by choosing Edit > Preferences > Label Defaults (Windows) or Premiere Pro > Preferences > Label Defaults (Mac OS).

Customizing track height

At various times during the typical project workflow, you'll want to change the appearance of your audio and video tracks. By default, the tracks are small and devoid of any indication of the content they contain. I like my audio and video files to reflect their contents, since it helps me edit faster, particularly during the early phases of production. Let's explore some options for displaying more information on the video tracks.

To expand or minimize all tracks:

1. To expand all tracks, click the Timeline Display Settings button to open the Settings menu, and choose Expand All Tracks **C**.

   Premiere Pro expands all tracks **D**. Already we can see a lot more information.

2. To minimize all tracks, click the Timeline Display Settings button **C** to open the Settings menu, and choose Minimize All Tracks **C**.

   Premiere Pro minimizes all tracks.

> **TIP** As long as we have the Settings menu open, let's look at some other configuration options available there. In particular, note the ability to show and hide the names of audio and video files in the Timeline, as well as show and hide audio and video keyframes, which you'll learn about in Chapter 8.

To expand or minimize all video or audio tracks:

1. On the right edge of the Timeline, grab one of the edges of the vertical zoom bar for either the audio or video tracks **E**.

2. Drag inward to expand track size, outward to minimize track size **F**.

C Using the Settings menu to expand or minimize all tracks.

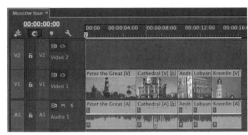

D Expanding all tracks to see more information.

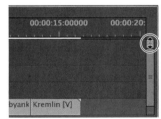

E Grab one of the edges of the vertical zoom bar.

F Drag inward to expand the tracks; drag outward to minimize the tracks.

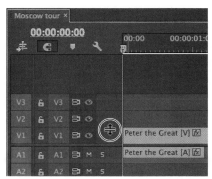

G Hover your mouse at the top of the track until the height adjustment pointer appears.

H Drag up.

I Click the track's track header area, and use your scroll wheel to adjust its size

To adjust the height of individual tracks:

Do one of the following:

- In the track header area of the Timeline, position the pointer at the top of the track that you want to expand, until the height adjustment pointer appears **G**. Drag upward to expand the track **H** and downward to minimize the track.

- Click the track header area of the track that you want to adjust **I**. Push the scroll wheel on your mouse away from you to increase video track size, and toward you to decrease it.

- Click to select the track in the Timeline area (not the track header area). Then press Control++ (Windows) or Command++ (Mac OS) to expand the track. Press Control+– (Windows) or Command+– (Mac OS) to minimize the track.

TIP For audio tracks, grab the bottom of the track and drag it down to expand, or drag it up to minimize. The keyboard shortcuts are Alt++ (Windows) and Option++ (Mac OS) to expand the selected audio track, and Alt+– (Windows) and Option+– (Mac OS) to minimize the selected audio track.

Customizing video tracks

Video thumbnails are representations of the clip content **E**. You can see them because they were enabled by default, and they became visible when you expanded the track.

You can turn thumbnails on and off even when the video track is expanded, and you can control the appearance of the thumbnails using the procedures described in the following tasks.

To enable and disable video thumbnails:

1. To enable thumbnails, click the Timeline Display Settings button to open the Settings menu, and choose Show Video Thumbnails ⓙ. When the menu item shows a check mark, the thumbnails are enabled.

2. To disable thumbnails, click the Timeline Display Settings button to open the Settings menu, and choose Show Video Thumbnails ⓙ. When the menu item does not show a check mark, the thumbnails are disabled.

To control thumbnail appearance:

Click the panel menu in the upper-right corner of the Timeline ⓚ. Select one of the following:

- Video Head and Tail Thumbnails. Shows thumbnails of the first frame and the last frame, with blank space in between ⓛ.

- Video Head Thumbnails. Shows a thumbnail of the initial frame and then blank space through the end of the file ⓜ.

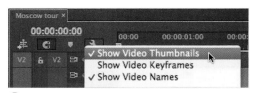

ⓙ Showing video thumbnails in the Settings menu.

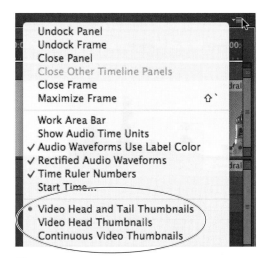

ⓚ Choose one of these three options for thumbnail display.

ⓛ Head and tail thumbnails.

ⓜ Head thumbnail.

Continuous video thumbnails.

Track name

Renaming the track.

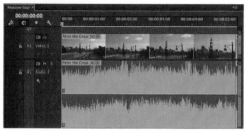

Premiere Pro's new, rectified waveform.

- Continuous Video Thumbnails. Shows thumbnails throughout the clip **N**.

TIP Once a track is expanded, the name of the track appears in the track header. You can customize this by right-clicking the track name and choosing Rename **O**.

Customizing audio tracks

Audio waveforms reflect the volume of the audio file, so a quick glance at a waveform can tell a lot about the actual contents of the file. In Premiere Pro CS7, Adobe has changed the appearance of the waveform on the Timeline from a traditional view to a "rectified" view **P**, where positive and negative values of the waveform are combined to create a single positive value presented from the bottom of the audio track. You can return to the traditional appearance via a control available in the panel menu, as you'll learn in the following task.

To switch to the traditional waveform display:

From the panel menu in the upper-right corner of the Timeline panel, choose Rectified Audio Waveforms so that the check mark disappears 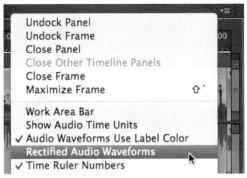 **Q**.

Premiere Pro returns to the traditional waveform view **R**.

TIP As in the Source Monitor, you can display audio timecodes in audio time units by enabling the Show Audio Time Units option in the Settings menu. Audio time units provide much greater editing precision than audio timecodes. See "Working with audio in the Source panel" in Chapter 4 for a longer discussion of audio time units.

TIP By default, audio waveforms are displayed in the color of the label. You can change the waveform color to green by deselecting Audio Waveforms Use Label Color **Q**.

TIP Note that you can disable waveforms entirely via the Timeline's Settings menu **S**.

Q Disabling rectified audio waveforms in the panel menu.

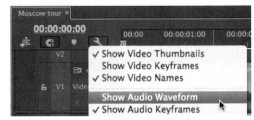

R The traditional waveform style.

S Turning off audio waveforms.

A Right-click the video track header area.

B Choose Add Track.

C Right-click the audio track header area.

Adding and Deleting Tracks

You can control the number of video tracks and the number and type of audio tracks by creating a custom preset. After you start editing, you can always add and delete tracks as needed.

To add a single video or audio track:

1. To add a single video track, right-click the video track header area **A** and choose Add Track **B**. Premiere Pro adds a video track.

2. To add a single audio track, right-click the audio track header area **C** and choose Add Track **B**. Premiere Pro adds an audio track.

> **TIP** You can also create a new track by dragging a clip from the Project panel to the blank area above the video tracks and below the audio tracks.

> **TIP** When you use this option to add an audio track, Premiere Pro adds a standard audio track, which can accept only mono or stereo audio. If you need to add a different kind of track, use the technique described in "To add multiple tracks," on the next page.

To delete a single video or audio track:

To delete a single audio or video track, right-click the track header **D** and choose Delete Track **E**.

Premiere Pro deletes the selected track.

To add multiple tracks:

1. Right-click the track header area **F** and choose Add Tracks **G**.

   Premiere Pro opens the Add Tracks dialog.

D To delete a single track, right-click it and...

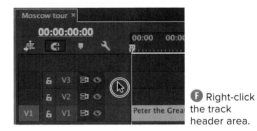

E ...choose Delete Track.

F Right-click the track header area.

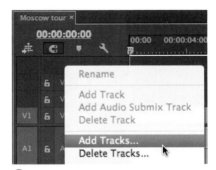

G Choose Add Tracks.

H Choose the number and placement of video tracks.

I Choose the number, placement, and track type for audio tracks.

J Choose the number, placement, and track type for submix tracks.

2. Specify the number of video tracks to add, and choose their placement **H**.

3. Specify the number, placement, and track type for audio tracks **I**.

4. Specify the number, placement, and track type for any audio submix tracks **J**.

5. Click OK to close the Add Tracks dialog and add the specified tracks **I**.

About Audio Tracks in Premiere Pro

Premiere Pro uses six different audio tracks.

- Standard: A standard track can contain both stereo and mono audio tracks and is the default for new audio tracks.

- Mono: Contains one audio channel. If you drop a stereo file into a mono track, the stereo is converted to mono.

- 5.1: Contains only 5.1 surround sound tracks, which include three front audio channels (left, center, and right); two rear channels (left and right); and one low-frequency subwoofer channel.

- Adaptive: Can contain mono or stereo tracks, and are used when you need to map the source audio to different output channels.

- Audio submix track: A synthetic track that contains no audio other than audio sent to the submix from other audio tracks.

- Master audio track: Controls the combined output of all tracks in the sequence so, for example, you can adjust overall track volume via a single slider in the Audio Mixer.

To delete multiple tracks:

1. Right-click the track header area **F** and choose Delete Tracks **K**. Premiere Pro opens the Delete Tracks dialog.

2. To delete video tracks, select the Delete Video Tracks check box and identify the tracks to delete in the associated drop-down menu **L**.

3. To delete audio tracks, select the Delete Audio Tracks check box and identify the tracks to delete in the associated drop-down menu **M**.

4. To delete audio submix tracks, select the Delete Audio Submix Tracks check box and identify the tracks to delete in the associated drop-down menu **M**.

5. Click OK to close the Delete Tracks dialog and delete the specified tracks **M**.

K Choose Delete Tracks to delete multiple tracks.

L Identify the video tracks to delete.

M Identify the audio tracks to delete.

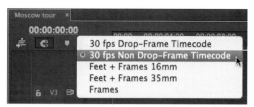

A Your choices for timecode display format (when timecode, rather than audio time units, is selected).

Choosing the Timecode Display Format

Atop the Timeline is the time ruler, which has a control **A** that lets you determine how time is displayed. For most producers, the choice comes down to the top two options in the drop-down menu **A**, Drop-Frame Timecode and Non Drop-Frame Timecode. Which should you use?

The short answer is that if you're producing a video that has to precisely match a particular time—like a program that's exactly an hour long, or a 30-second commercial—use drop-frame timecode. If you don't care that your 10-minute video actually takes .6 seconds longer, then use Non Drop-Frame Timecode or whichever timecode was used by your source format.

Here's why: Interestingly, the timecode on tape has nothing to do with time. Rather, the timecodes mark specific frames in the video, which occur at 29.97 frames per second, or every 1/29.97 of a second. Which means that 30 frames of 29.97 video actually takes 29.97/30 of a second, which is pretty close to a second, but not quite. Over time, the differences add up. For example, at 1:00:00:00 (one hour of video), the actual time that has elapsed is 60 minutes and 3.6 seconds, a difference insufficient to bother anyone who's not broadcasting on a regular schedule, but worth paying attention to if your production demands more precision.

To correct this, drop-frame timecode skips ahead two frames every minute except for every tenth minute. No frames are actually dropped, but at minute one, for example, the timecode will jump from 00;00;59;29 to 00;01;00;02. In non drop-frame time-code, the progression is from 00:00:59:29 to 00:01:00:00. So if you need your hour-long video to be exactly an hour, use drop-frame timecode. If you don't, follow the timecode of the source footage.

And yes, sharp-eyed readers, drop-frame timecode is shown with semicolons (;) separating the digital pairs, whereas non drop-frame timecode uses colons (:).

To choose a timecode display format:

1. Hover your pointer over the timecode in either the Timeline or the Program Monitor, and your pointer will change to a hand with two black arrows. Do not click .

2. Right-click, and the timecode display options will appear .

3. Choose the desired timecode display format.

   Premiere Pro changes the time ruler display.

TIP Whichever timecode display format you choose will apply to both the Timeline and the Program Monitor.

TIP If you've elected to display audio time units via the panel menu, your choices will be Audio Samples and Milliseconds **C**.

B Hover your pointer over the timecode. Do not click.

C Your options when you are using audio time units.

About the Tools Panel

Now that we're about to actually do some things in the Timeline, I should introduce you to the Tools panel **D**. It appears to be one of the few panels you can't actually close, which is OK because it's so useful and doesn't take up much space. If you lose track of its location, choose Window > Tools to highlight the panel.

Some of the tools are simple and obvi-ous, like the Selection tool and Zoom tool, which we'll discuss in this chapter. You'll learn about most of the other tools in later chapters.

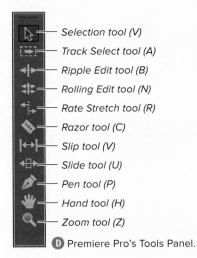

Selection tool (V)
Track Select tool (A)
Ripple Edit tool (B)
Rolling Edit tool (N)
Rate Stretch tool (R)
Razor tool (C)
Slip tool (V)
Slide tool (U)
Pen tool (P)
Hand tool (H)
Zoom tool (Z)

D Premiere Pro's Tools Panel.

Drag in to
zoom in
(see more detail)

Drag out to
zoom out
(see less detail)

A Zooming in with the zoom bar.

B Choosing the Zoom tool (press Z).

C Click the region that you want to zoom in on.

D Alt-click (Windows) or Option-click (Mac OS) to zoom out.

E Choosing the Selection tool (press V).

Navigating in the Timeline

When you create a 90-minute video in a Timeline that measures about 4 inches by 8 inches on your monitor (smaller with notebooks), you need to be facile at zooming in and out, moving around, and arranging (and rearranging) Timeline components.

As with most panels in Premiere Pro, you can maximize the Timeline within the application by pressing the accent key (`) on the keyboard (to the left of the 1 key and directly above the Tab key). Let's cover some of the most common navigational tools and techniques specific to the Timeline.

To zoom in and out on the Timeline:

Do one or more of the following:

- Grab one edge of zoom bar at the bottom of the Timeline or Program Monitor **A**. The pointer turns into a pointer with two arrows. Drag the edge toward the middle to zoom in on the Timeline (and show more detail); drag out from the middle to zoom out and show less detail.

- Click the Zoom tool (Z) in the Tools panel **B**. Navigate to the spot on the Timeline that you'd like to zoom in on, and click as many times as necessary to achieve the desired level of zoom **C**. To zoom back out, Alt-click (Windows) or Option-click (Mac OS) **D**. When you're done, click the Selection tool in the Tools panel (or press V) **E**.

continues on next page

- Click the Zoom tool (Z) in the Tools panel **B**. Drag a marquee around the area of the Timeline you'd like to zoom in on **F**. When you're done, click the Selection tool in the Tools panel (or press V) **E**.

- When you're zoomed in on the Timeline and want to quickly zoom out and see the entire project, press the backslash (\) key; press it again to return to your initial zoom level.

TIP The backslash key is one of the most useful keyboard shortcuts in the entire program, and (I think) the first one I ever learned.

TIP The easiest way to zoom in on a specific region is to drag the playhead to that region and drag the zoom bar inward **A** to the desired zoom level. I find that the Zoom tool jumps around too much when zooming in.

Adjusting audio and video track space

At various points in a project, you may want to work on video and ignore audio, or vice versa. If you have enough audio or video tracks, some will move out of view in some Timeline configurations. Let's cover some adjustments and navigational tools designed to assist editing in these circumstances.

To reallocate space between video and audio tracks:

1. In the track header area of the Timeline, position the pointer over the dividing line between the video and audio tracks until the height adjustment pointer **G** appears.

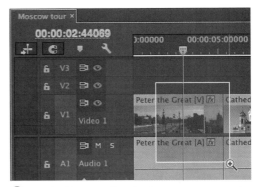

F Use the Zoom tool to drag a marquee around the area you want to zoom in on.

G Hover your pointer over the line between the video and audio tracks. The adjustment pointer appears.

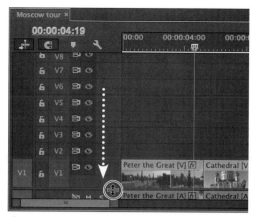

H Drag downward to maximize video area.

I Drag upward to maximize audio area.

J Grab the vertical zoom bar in the textured grab area. No special pointer will appear.

K Drag upward or downward to reveal more tracks.

2. Drag downward to hide audio tracks and maximize space for video editing **H**.

3. Drag upward to hide the video tracks and maximize space for audio editing **I**.

To show hidden audio or video tracks:

1. Select the textured grab area of the vertical zoom bar to the right of the video or audio tracks **J**. No special pointer will appear (note on the left that only video tracks V1–V4 are showing).

2. Drag upward or downward as required **K**. (Note that video tracks V7–V9 are now visible.)

TIP You can also use the scroll wheel on your mouse to scroll up and down in the audio and video area. Click in the Timeline itself **L** and scroll. Don't click in the track header, which will adjust the height of the selected track when you scroll.

L Click in the Timeline area, and you can use your mouse's scroll wheel to move through the tracks.

Moving around in Premiere Pro

We're almost done with these navigational tasks, but there's one more concept to cover: the difference between the viewing window and the location of the playhead. The viewing window is the region in the Timeline that's open for viewing. In previous tasks, you've learned to expand and contract the viewing window and to show and hide the video and audio tracks within it, but not how to move within the window (though I'm guessing that you figured it out for yourself).

 To move the viewing window, drag the zoom bar.

To move the viewing window:

Grab the textured area on the zoom bar beneath the Timeline and drag it left or right .

Premiere Pro adjusts the viewing window to the selected location.

To move the playhead:

Do one or more of the following:

- Drag the playhead to the desired location.

- Use the playback controls in the Program Monitor to play the video to the desired location.

- Press the Home key to move the playhead to the start of the sequence.

- Press the End key to move the playhead to the end of the sequence.

- Press the Left and Right Arrow keys to move the playhead frame by frame (or audio time unit by audio time unit) within the sequence.

- Press the Up and Down Arrow keys to move the playhead from edit point to edit point in the sequence (essentially, clip to clip).

Monitoring Audio and Video

Most productions contain multiple tracks of audio and video, and at various points during the project, you may wish to see or hear only some or just one of the video or audio tracks.

You can see an example of this in , where there's a title on V2 and three audio tracks, one containing the audio shot with the video, and the others containing narration and background music tracks. With video, you can enable and disable a track via the Toggle Track Output button in the track header.

With audio you can mute any or all tracks, or you can solo any individual track, which mutes all others.

Toggle Track Output button

Mute track

Solo track

Ⓐ Our starting point.

To disable a video track:

1. To disable a track, click the Toggle Track Output button in the track header (you'll see a slash over the eye icon) **B** . The track is disabled, and it disappears from the Program Monitor.

2. To restore the track, click the Toggle Track Output button again .

> **TIP** These adjustments remain until you change them back, so if you don't mean for a video track to disappear, or an audio track to stay permanently mute, remember to reverse any changes here.

To mute or solo an audio track:

1. To mute one or more audio tracks, click the M in the track header of the desired tracks **C**. Premiere Pro mutes the selected tracks.

2. To solo any single track, click the S in the track header of that track **D**. Premiere Pro mutes the other tracks.

B V2 is disabled, and the title disappears from the Program Monitor.

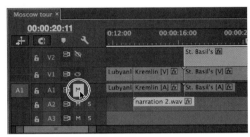

C Click M to mute one or more tracks.

D Click S to solo any audio track. Note that the other two tracks are muted.

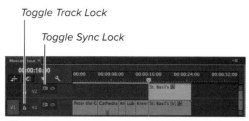

Toggle Track Lock

Toggle Sync Lock

A Our starting point. Note that the St. Basil's title and clip are aligned 16 seconds into the sequence.

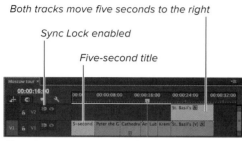

Both tracks move five seconds to the right

Sync Lock enabled

Five-second title

B With Sync Lock enabled, the St. Basil's clip and title shifted five seconds to the right.

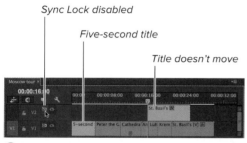

Sync Lock disabled

Five-second title

Title doesn't move

C With Sync Lock disabled, the St. Basil's clip shifts five seconds to the right, but the title doesn't move.

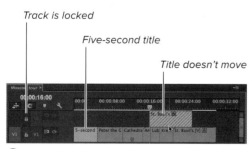

Track is locked

Five-second title

Title doesn't move

D The locked track stays put.

Sync Lock and Track Lock

Now that we have items on two tracks in the Timeline, we should talk about Sync Lock and Track Lock. Sync Lock is enabled by default on all tracks and ensures that all tracks are affected equally by certain adjustments made to any track.

For example, note that the St. Basil's title is located directly above the St. Basil's clip, exactly 16 seconds into the video **A**. If I inserted a five-second intro title on V1, I would still want the St. Basil's title to be located above the corresponding clip, and with Sync Lock enabled for both tracks, Premiere Pro would move both clips five seconds to the right **B**. Perfect; just what we wanted.

Now suppose the title had nothing to do with the clip but just needed to appear 16 seconds into the video. With Sync Lock enabled in both tracks, adding a five-second title to track V1 would move V2 five seconds as well, which isn't what we want in this case. So, you would disable Sync Lock on V2 **C** and add the title to V1, and the title wouldn't move.

Any time you don't want the content on some tracks adjusted for edits made in other tracks, disable Sync Lock for the tracks that you don't want affected.

Track Lock is totally different, and simply locks the track from either direct editing or from adjustments made to other synced tracks **D**.

To enable and disable Sync Lock:

1. Sync Lock is enabled by default. To disable Sync Lock, click the Toggle Sync Lock button Ⓐ. When you see a line over the Sync Lock icon, Sync Lock is disabled ▧.

2. To enable Sync Lock, click the Toggle Sync Lock button Ⓐ. When the line disappears, Sync Lock is enabled ▤.

TIP To insert a clip without shifting clips in other tracks, press Control+Alt (Windows) or Command+Option (Mac OS) while dragging the clip into the track.

To enable and disable Track Lock:

1. To lock a track, click the Toggle Track Lock button Ⓐ; the lock icon closes, and Premiere Pro displays a diagonal line pattern on the track Ⓓ.

2. To unlock a track, click the Toggle Track Lock button; the lock icon opens Ⓐ and the diagonal line pattern disappears.

How Premiere Pro Works with Tracks

Another topic we should discuss now that we have content on multiple tracks  is how Premiere Pro works with tracks, which differs between audio and video.

Let's start with video. There are three video tracks with content in Ⓔ, V1 has the street scenes from Moscow, V2 has my scintillating narration about the trip, and V3 has the St. Basil's title.

Premiere Pro combines these tracks from the top down. Whatever is on a higher track obscures the content on the lower track. So if the street scenes from Moscow were on V3 instead of V1, you wouldn't see the title or the narration.

Content on higher tracks obscures content on lower tracks unless the higher tracks are either smaller or transparent. I made the narrative on V2 smaller (using the Motion controls you'll learn about in Chapter 8) by creating what's commonly referred to as a picture-in-picture. If I had left the narration video at its original resolution, which was the same as the Moscow street scenes, it would totally obscure the lower track.

You can see through the background frame of the title because I made it transparent, which you'll learn about in Chapter 13. The text isn't transparent, so you can't see through it. Besides titles, the most common application of combining clips with transparency is com-positing, or greenscreen, effects, which you'll learn about in Chapter 9.

Audio is completely different. In the figure, there are three audio tracks: background audio captured with the street scenes (V1), the audio from my narration (V2), and the background music (V3).

Premiere Pro affords these tracks equal weight in the mix, regardless of track positioning. You adjust the audio mix—say, to make the narration louder and the ambient audio lower—by boosting or reducing volume on one or more individual tracks. You adjust overall volume by adjusting the volume of the master audio track. You'll learn to do all this and more in Chapter 14.

Ⓔ A simple Timeline for demonstration purposes.

Getting Clips to the Timeline

The technique you use to get clips to the Timeline will vary according to the type of projects that you produce, how long you've been editing, and how frequently you edit. Premiere Pro works well for virtually all users, from casual beginners to pros who edit all day every day.

For example, new editors may set In and Out points in the Source Monitor (or not), drag the clips to the Timeline one by one, and make final trims on the Timeline—all with the mouse. At the other end of the spectrum, an editor integrating hundred of source clips into a complicated independent film production may want to perform all editing activities via keyboards short-cuts, which is quicker and the traditional workflow for film editors.

Getting your first clip to the Timeline via your mouse is the simplest of all edits, so let's start there.

To drag a clip to an empty Timeline:

Drag the clip from the Source Monitor to the desired location and track on the Timeline . Note that Premiere Pro shows the timecode of the selected location at the bottom left of the Program Monitor. Premiere Pro inserts both the audio and video components of the source file into the selected location .

TIP Typically, you'd drag your first clip to the beginning of the Timeline on V1, but I wanted to demonstrate that you can drag the clip to any location, any track.

A Drag the clip from the Source Monitor to the desired location and track.

B Premiere Pro inserts it there.

C Or, you can drag just the video to a video track.

D Or just the audio to an audio track.

E Here's what it looks like to have multiple open sequences.

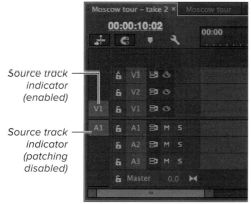

F These source track indicators identify the tracks into which Premiere Pro will insert the audio and video from the Source Monitor.

Source track indicator (enabled)

Source track indicator (patching disabled)

TIP To drag just the video portion of a clip from the Source Monitor to a video track, drag the Drag Video Only ⊞ button from the top of the Source Monitor's transport controls **C** to the selected location. To drag just the audio portion, drag the Drag Audio Only button ⊞ **D** to the desired location.

TIP Note the multiple sequences at the top of the Timeline panel **E**. To switch from one to the other, just click the tab. To close any sequence, click the Close button on the right of the tab. Or, you can arrange the sequences by dragging the tabs to the desired locations.

Targeting tracks

When you drag a clip to the Timeline, you're telling Premiere Pro where to insert it. How do you tell Premiere Pro which track to use when you're adding clips by using the buttons beneath the Source Monitor or their respective keyboard short-cuts? And how do you specify the location on that track? Let's take these issues one at a time.

To the left of the Timeline are two buttons called source track indicators **F**. Note that these appear only when a clip is loaded in the Source Monitor.

These locators identify the tracks into which the audio and video will be inserted. The default locations for the indicators are V1 and A1, unless the content in the Source Monitor isn't compatible with these tracks. For example, if the audio in the selected file is 5.1 surround sound, the source track indicator will shift to a 5.1 surround sound audio track. Audio files will show only an audio track indicator, much as video files will show only a video track indicator.

Note that the source track indicators can either be enabled or disabled. When you disable the audio and enable the video **F**, video is inserted into the selected video track, but no audio is inserted into the selected track. Vice versa when audio is enabled and video isn't.

What about the temporal location on the selected track? You select that by moving the playhead to the desired location.

To target a track:

To target an audio or video track, click the source track indicator **G** and drag it to the desired track **H**.

G Click the source track indicator to select it.

To disable or enable the source track indicator:

1. To disable the source track indicator (enabled is the default state), click it **G**. When the button is no longer high-lighted, it is disabled **F**.

2. To enable the source track indicator, click it. When the button is highlighted, it's enabled **F**.

H Then drag it to the desired track.

To specify the timecode location for clips inserted via button controls or keyboard shortcuts:

Do one of the following:

- Drag the Timeline playhead to the desired location **I**.

- Use playback controls (or keyboard shortcuts) to navigate the playhead to the desired location.

- Click the timecode in either the Time-line or the Program Monitor to make it active, type the desired timecode (with no punctuation), and press Enter (Win-dows) or Return (Mac OS). For example, to move the playhead to 00:00:10:02, you would type 1002.

I Drag the playhead to the desired clip location.

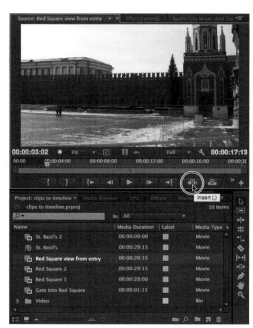

J Click either Insert or Overwrite to insert a clip when the Timeline is empty.

To insert a clip using button controls:

1. Drag the source track indicators to the desired track.

2. Navigate the playhead to the desired location.

3. In the Source Monitor's Tools panel, click either the Insert button or the Overwrite button .

   Premiere Pro inserts the clip in the selected location.

TIP In the next task we'll look at the difference between the Insert and Overwrite functions, but when inserting a clip into an empty Timeline, it makes no difference which you use.

TIP Premiere Pro also offers a hybrid drag-and-drop option: Choose the location for the clip, drag the clip from the Source Monitor, and drop it into the Program Monitor **K**.

K A third option for adding clips to the Timeline.

Insert and Overwrite Edits

Let's look at the difference between insert and overwrite edits from the perspective of a common problem. As you can see in **A**, the "Moscow tour – take 2" sequence starts with the Day 1 title, and then has multiple clips from Red Square. After inserting these clips I realized that I had forgotten to start with a shot of Red Square's entrance gate. I want to insert that clip and push all the subsequent clips on V1 back by the length of the inserted clip. This is a classic insert edit, where the inserted footage pushes all footage located after the insertion point to the right for the duration of the inserted footage.

Just to complicate things, I want the Red Square title on V2 to stay in place—a perfect opportunity to use the Sync Lock feature.

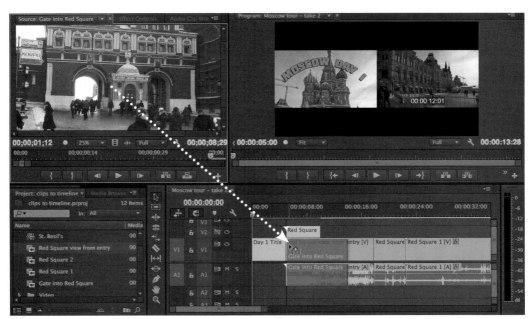

A I need to add the clip in the Source Monitor to V1 after the Day 1 title. I want to push all clips on V1 back, but I don't want to move the Red Square title on V2.

B Disabling Sync Lock for tracks that I don't want to adjust.

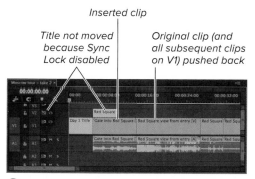

C Press Control (Windows) or Command (Mac OS) to convert the overwrite pointer to the insert pointer.

Inserted clip

Title not moved because Sync Lock disabled

Original clip (and all subsequent clips on V1) pushed back

D Mission accomplished: clip inserted, all clips on V1 pushed back, title on V2 stays in place.

To perform an insert edit by dragging:

1. If there are any clips that you don't want to move with the inserted clip, disable Sync Lock [icon] for those tracks **B** (see the tips for a keyboard shortcut for this).

2. Drag the clip from the Source Monitor to the target location and track in the Timeline **A**. Notice that once you drag the clip to the tracks, the pointer turns to the overwrite pointer [icon] and a vertical line appears at the insert point **A**.

   When you drag the clip to a track with content, this content appears in the Program Monitor. The last frame before the inserted file is shown on the left, and the first frame after the inserted file is shown on the right.

3. Press the Control (Windows) or Command (Mac OS) key **C**. The overwrite pointer changes to the insert pointer [icon] and the vertical line shows arrows pointing to the right.

4. Release your pointer. Premiere Pro inserts the clip, pushing back all subsequent clips on that track, and any other track on which Sync Lock was not disabled **D**.

> **TIP** Press the Shift key while you're dragging the content into the Timeline to have the playhead snap at edit points on the Timeline.

> **TIP** If you press Control+Alt (Windows) or Command+Option (Mac OS) when you drag the clip into the Timeline, the pointer changes to the insert target tracks pointer [icon] and Premiere Pro performs the insert edit solely on the target track, obviating the need to disable Sync Lock for tracks that you do not want to adjust for the insert edit.

To perform an insert edit via button controls or keyboard shortcuts:

1. Drag the source track indicators to the desired track **E**.

2. Navigate the playhead to the desired location. Use the Up and Down Arrow keys to move the playhead to the precise intersection between the two clips.

3. In the Source Monitor's Tools panel, click the Insert button ![insert button] , or press , (the comma key).

   Premiere Pro inserts the clip at the selected location.

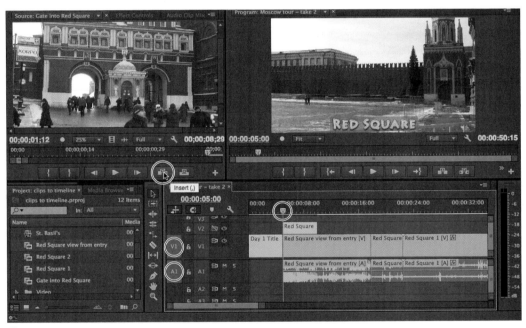

E Setting up for the insert edit: tracks targeted, playhead in the desired position, ready to click the Insert button.

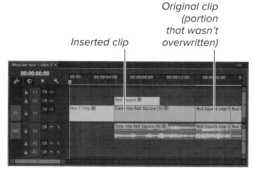

F Drag the clip to the target edit point.

Inserted clip

Original clip
(portion
that wasn't
overwritten)

G Here's the result.

Overwrite edits

In contrast to insert edits, overwrite edits push no content back on the track on which they replace footage. We can use the same basic setup as the insert edit task, with a different goal: to replace footage on V1 rather than push it back. Note that because an overwrite edit doesn't push any tracks back, there's no need to worry about Sync Lock.

To perform an overwrite edit by dragging:

1. Drag the clip from the Source Monitor to the target location and track in the Timeline F. Notice that once you drag the clip to the tracks, the pointer turns to the overwrite pointer and a vertical line appears at the insertion point.

   When you drag the clip to a track with content, this content appears in the Program Monitor. The last frame before the inserted file is shown on the left, and the first frame after the inserted file is shown on the right.

2. Release your pointer.

   Premiere Pro overwrites content on the target track up to the duration of the clip in the Source Monitor G. No other tracks are affected.

To perform an overwrite edit via button controls or keyboard shortcuts:

1. Drag the source track indicators to the desired track **H**.

2. Navigate the playhead to the desired location. Use the Up and Down Arrow keys to move the playhead to the precise intersection between the two clips.

3. In the Source Monitor's Tools panel, press the Overwrite button ![overwrite button], or press . (the period key).

   Premiere Pro inserts the clip at the selected location, overwriting the existing content.

TIP If you don't want to overwrite the audio or video component, disable the source track indicator for that track. For example, if you were inserting a clip of B-roll (essentially, background video) over a video interview, you might want to overwrite the interview video but not the audio. To accomplish this, disable the audio source track selector before pressing the . (period) key.

H Setting up for the overwrite edit: tracks targeted, playhead in the desired position, ready to press the Overwrite button.

Overwrite Edits in Practice

When I first started editing (pre-Premiere Pro), many editing tools offered only one Timeline track for video. With these tools, if you wanted to replace existing footage on the Timeline, you had to use an overwrite edit or the equivalent.

Today, Premiere Pro has 99 tracks, and many projects never exceed four or five tracks. Rather than perform an overwrite edit in these instances, I typically insert the clip on a track above the clip that I want to overwrite 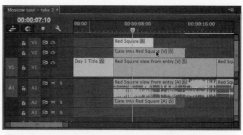.

This produces the same result, but it has several positives, at least for the types of projects that I produce. First, it makes the edit point very visible in case I need to find it again. Second, having the clips on separate tracks makes it easier to adjust the place- ment and content of the inserted clip. Third, it leaves the original clip in place in case I later change my mind, though it's typically easy enough to retrieve the overwritten portion.

The negatives are that if you meant to replace the audio on the overwritten track, you'll have to do so manually. It also can be complicated to insert transitions when the edges of the two clips are adjacent to another clip, as the clips in V1 and V2 are adjacent to the Day 1 Title clip. Specifically, with some dissolve transitions, the clip on V1 will appear during the transition. If this becomes a problem, you can drag the top clip directly down into the bottom clip, with the overwrite pointer letting you know that you're about to overwrite the bottom clip. Note that the yellow timecode box lets you know if you're shifting the location to the left or right. At 00:00:00:00, the edit is perfectly in place.

This edit produces the same effect as the overwrite edit but has several benefits.

You can perform an overwrite edit on the Timeline by dragging one track onto another.

Three- and Four-Point Edits

Most novice editors hear the terms three-point edit and four-point edit and assume that they refer to advanced editing functions that occur only in high-end productions. The fact of the matter is that every edit we've discussed so far has been a three-point edit (you're *that* good, and you didn't even know it).

The file in the Source Monitor has two points: the In point and the Out point, or the beginning and end if you didn't mark the In and Out points. The playhead in the Timeline is the third point. Press the Insert or Overwrite button, and voilà: a three-point edit. Simple enough.

But all these edits involved *starting* clip playback at a specific location. What if you want the clip to *end* at a specific location? Or what if you have a specific gap that you need to precisely fill?

The problem we'll use to explore these concepts is shown in Ⓐ. I've got ten seconds of narration on A1, and two clips, St. Basil's 1 and 2. St. Basil's 2 has a striking shot at the end, so I want it to align with the end of the narration. I want the selected region in St. Basil's 1 to fill in the remaining gap.

The secret to producing these types of edits is setting In and Out points in the Timeline. The procedure is very similar to setting In and Out points in the Source Monitor—which we covered in Chapter 4, if you want a quick review.

Ⓐ Our mission: Fill in the ten-second narration with the two clips in the Project panel. The playhead is at the target end point, and I'm selecting my Out point.

To force a clip to end at a certain point via a three-point edit:

1. In the Timeline or Program Monitor, navigate the playhead to the target Out point Ⓐ. Press the Up and Down Arrow keys to move to an existing edit point.

2. In the Program Monitor, click the Mark Out button ▐ } ▐ or press O.

    Premiere Pro sets the Out Point.

3. Drag the source track indicators to the desired track Ⓐ.

4. In the Source Monitor, make sure you have In and Out points set in the source clip.

5. Press the Overwrite button ▐▄▐ Ⓑ.

    Premiere Pro inserts the selected region of the source clip into the Timeline, with playback ending at the selected Out point.

Clip ends at Out point

Ⓑ St. Basil's 2 now ends at the Out point.

To fit to fill via a four-point edit:

1. In the Timeline or Program Monitor, navigate the playhead to the target Out point **C**.

2. In the Program Monitor, click the Mark Out button ▯ or press O.

   Premiere Pro sets the Out point.

3. In the Timeline or Program Monitor, navigate the playhead to the target In point **D**.

4. In the Program Monitor, click the Mark In ▯ button or press I.

   Premiere Pro sets the In point.

5. Drag the source track indicators to the desired track **C**.

C Setting the Out point in the Timeline.

Marked target area

Mark In   *Mark Out*

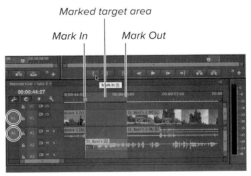

D Setting the In point and marking the target area for the clip.

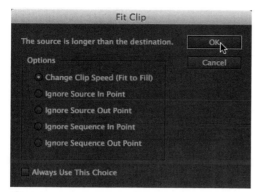

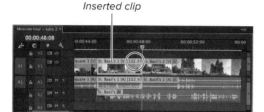

⑤ Here's where you tell Premiere Pro what to do with the time discrepancy between the source clip and the target region.

Inserted clip

⑥ Here's the result.

6. In the Source Monitor, make sure you have In and Out points set in the source clip.

7. In the Source Monitor, press the Overwrite button 🖳.

   Premiere Pro opens the Fit Clip dialog **⑤**.

8. Since the object of the exercise is to fit the clip from the Source Monitor into the target region in the Timeline, click the Change Clip Speed (Fit to Fill) option, and press OK to close the dialog **⑤**.

   Premiere Pro inserts the clip into the marked space **⑥**, making the required speed adjustments. The 102.97 in the clip means that it's playing about 3 percent faster than normal, which shouldn't cause any audio or visual problems.

TIP If you change the speed significantly, the video may look too fast or too slow and the audio may sound distorted. Preview the inserted footage immediately after making the edit to determine if you have a problem.

Playing Clips in the Program Monitor

We spent a lot of time in Chapter 4 detailing the configuration options for the Source Monitor, and virtually all work identically in the Program Monitor.

Whereas the Source Monitor displays clips opened from the Project panel or Timeline, the Program Monitor displays the output from the Timeline **A**. That's why the timecode in the Program Monitor is always the same as the one in the Timeline. What's

shown in the Program Monitor is the frame located at the playhead, and the aforementioned timecodes mark the location of the playhead.

You can move the playhead via the playback controls in the Program Monitor, via keyboard shortcuts in the Timeline, or simply by dragging the playhead in either panel. However you do it, the Program Monitor and Timeline forever stay in sync.

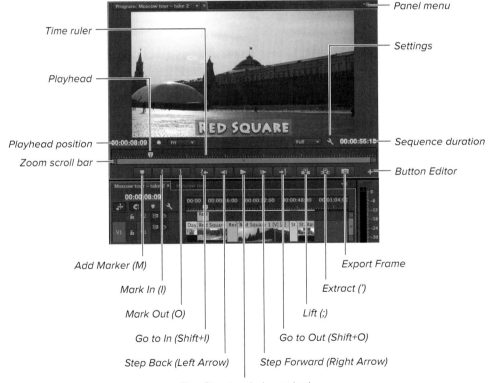

Time ruler
Playhead
Playhead position
Zoom scroll bar

Panel menu
Settings
Sequence duration
Button Editor

Add Marker (M)
Mark In (I)
Mark Out (O)
Go to In (Shift+I)
Step Back (Left Arrow)
Play-Stop toggle (spacebar)

Export Frame
Extract (')
Lift (;)
Go to Out (Shift+O)
Step Forward (Right Arrow)

A Playback and related controls in the Program Monitor.

B The Program Monitor's panel menu contains many configuration options.

C Here's where you control the zoom level of video in the Program Monitor.

D This controls playback resolution, or the quality of the real-time preview.

E The Button Editor lets you configure the buttons shown in the Program Monitor.

Configuring the Program Monitor

Many of the Program Monitor's key configuration controls are located in the panel menu **B**, including the following:

- Mode selection: Change the viewing mode from Composite Video to a range of video scopes mostly used during color and brightness correction.

- Control interlaced display: Display the first field, the second field, or both during interlaced display.

- Playback Resolution: Control video resolution during playback and while the video is paused.

- Show Transport Controls: Editors who exclusively use keyboard shortcuts can hide the transport controls entirely.

- Show Dropped Frame Indicator: A small ball in the Program Monitor that turns orange when you drop frames during playback.

- Time Ruler Numbers: Enabled by default in the Timeline, but disabled by default in the Program Monitor.

- Safe Margins: Useful when producing for broadcast.

The following controls are located in the Program Monitor:

- Select Zoom Level **C**: Controls the resolution of the video shown in the Program Monitor.

- Select Playback Resolution **D**: Controls the quality of the video during real-time playback (duplicates the Playback Resolution option available in the panel menu).

- Button Editor: Opens the Button Editor, which lets you pick and choose the buttons in the Program Monitor **E**.

About Lift and Extract

Adobe invests significant thought and energy into streamlining and simplifying the Premiere Pro interface, and to the extent that the Lift and Extract buttons made the cut as default buttons on the Program Monitor, it means that Adobe feels they are important tools.

The workflow is the same for both the Lift button and the Extract button: Set In and Out points in the Timeline **F**.

Lift deletes the selected region but leaves a gap in the Timeline **G**. Extract deletes the selected region and closes the gap **H**. Both functions copy the deleted portion of the clip to the clipboard so you can paste it somewhere else.

Some producers like using the Life and Extract functions; I prefer using Ttimeline-based tools you'll learn over the next two chapters, such aslike the Razor and Ripple Delete functions, to accomplish the identical edits.

F To use Lift or Extract, start by marking In and Out points in the Timeline.

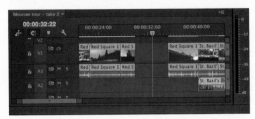

G Lift deletes the selected region but leaves a gap.

Extract closes gap *Shifts content over*

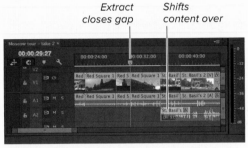

H Extract deletes the selected region and then closes the gap by shifting content over from the right.

6

Editing in the Timeline

Whenever you learn a new skill, be it touch-typing or golf, you spend hours learning the fundamentals before you move on to higher-level functions. No matter how talented you are, failing to master the basics dooms your overall game to mediocrity.

This is your editing fundamentals chapter. Although failing to master these techniques won't forever degrade the quality of your productions, it will make you far less efficient. Spend an hour or two here, and it will pay you back in spades.

You'll learn the fundamentals behind the seemingly simple task of dragging clips around on the Timeline. As you'll see, the default behaviors here are almost guaranteed to deliver an unwanted result that a few modifier keys can quickly resolve. You'll also learn other key skills, like how to maintain audio sync (except when you no longer want it) and how to work with high-resolution images.

In This Chapter

Selecting Clips on the Timeline

You select a clip on the Timeline because you want to do something to it: move it, trim it, or add an effect to it. You select multiple clips because you want to do something to all of them, usually to move them, unlink the audio from the video, or apply an effect. To deselect all selected clips and start fresh, just click any empty region in the Timeline. Selecting a single clip or multiple clips at once is temporary and lasts only until you deselect them. For more permanent associations, see the section "Grouping and Ungrouping Clips" later in this chapter.

Most source clips captured via camcorders contain audio and video. In the parlance of Premiere Pro, these are *linked* clips; wherever you drag or otherwise place the video, the audio will follow. Ninety-nine percent of the time, this is what you want, but for times where you want to edit them separately, there's a modifier key for that.

As you'll see, we're going to take a break from the clips from Russia to work with some synthetic clips created to help demonstrate some of the principles we'll tackle in this chapter. We have numbered clips of equal length on Video 1, with additional content on Video 1 and Video 2. All clips have synced audio.

To select a single clip on the Timeline:

Click the target clip **A**. Premiere Pro highlights its border.

TIP To deselect a clip or clips, click any empty region in the Timeline.

TIP Note that you can't select clips in a locked track with this or any other technique.

Selected clip

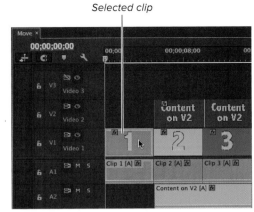

A The selected clip has a border around it.

Only video selected

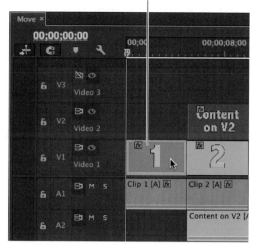

B Because I used the Alt/Option modifier, only the video track is selected.

To select just the audio or video of a single clip on the Timeline:

Alt-click (Windows) or Option-click (Mac OS) either the video or audio track to select it. Premiere Pro highlights the border of the selected media component **B**.

TIP Release the Alt (Windows) or Option (Mac OS) key before you drag the selected clip in any direction. If you keep that key pressed, Premiere Pro will copy the clip as you drag. For more information, see the task "To duplicate a clip by dragging" later in this chapter.

TIP Note that when using the Alt/Option key modifier, you are *temporarily* unlinking the audio and video for one edit. To permanently unlink audio and video, see "Linking and Unlinking Clips."

To select multiple clips on the Timeline:

Do any of the following:

- Press Shift and click multiple clips 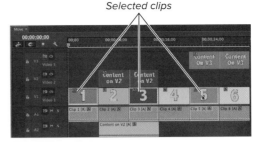 **C**.
  To deselect any clip from the group, click it again.

- Click any empty region in the Timeline and drag to select the clips **D**. Premiere Pro creates a marquee around the dragged area and includes all clips within the box. For linked clips, if the video or audio component is within the box, both components are selected.

- To select just the audio or video component of multiple clips, press the Alt (Windows) or Option (Mac OS) key while selecting multiple clips via either of the above options **E**.

  Premiere Pro highlights the borders of all selected clips or components of clips.

Selected clips

C Press the Shift key and select multiple clips.

Click in an empty region and drag to select.

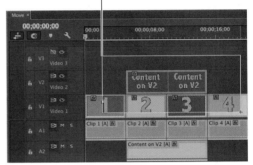

D Drag to select clips. By default, when you select the video region, Premiere Pro also selects the audio.

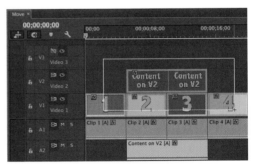

E Because I pressed the Alt/Option key as I dragged, only the video was selected.

Selection tool (V)

Track Select tool (A)

Ripple Edit tool (B)

Rolling Edit tool (N)

Rate Stretch tool (R)

Razor tool (C)

Slip tool (V)

Slide tool (U)

Pen tool (P)

Hand tool (H)

Zoom tool (Z)

F Premiere Pro's Tools panel.

To select all clips in multiple tracks:

1. In the Tools panel, click to choose the Track Select tool, or press A **F**. The pointer changes to the multitrack pointer ⬆.

2. Do one of the following:

   ▸ Press Shift to convert the pointer to the track pointer ➡. To select all clips on all tracks from one particular clip to the end of the sequence, Shift-click that clip **G**.

   ▸ To select all clips on a single track from one particular clip to the end of the sequence, click that clip **H**.

TIP Note that the default behavior of the Track Select tool has changed in Premiere Pro CS7. In previous versions, the default was the Track Select tool (single arrow) and you pressed Shift for the Multi-Track Select tool (double arrow). With CS7, Adobe has reversed that behavior.

TIP You can select just audio or just video with this selection technique by pressing Alt/Option+Shift.

Click 2 to select it and all subsequent clips on the Video 1 track.

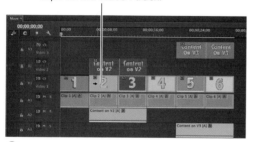

G The Multi-Track Select tool at work.

Shift-click 2 to select it and all subsequent clips on all tracks.

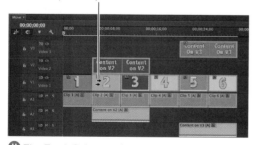

H The Track Select tool at work.

Grouping and Ungrouping Clips

Selecting multiple clips is temporary; once you deselect the clips by clicking an empty region in the Timeline, the association is dissolved. If you want a more permanent linkage, use the grouping function discussed here.

Note that grouping and ungrouping is different from linking and unlinking. You'll use unlinking to separate the audio and video components of a single clip. You'll use grouping to group multiple disparate clips.

You group clips so you can move them together, apply the same effects to them, or otherwise edit them consistently throughout the project. Note that while you can apply effects to a group of clips, you can't modify the effect without ungrouping them or selecting an individual clip within the group.

To group clips:

1. Select the target clips on the Timeline 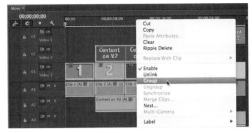.
2. Do one of the following:
   ▸ Right-click and choose Group Ⓐ.
   ▸ Choose Clip > Group.
   ▸ Press Control+G (Windows) or Command+G (Mac OS).

   Premiere Pro groups the clips. There's no special grouping designation, but when you select one clip in the group, Premiere Pro highlights the borders of all clips in the group.

Ⓐ Select the target clips, then right-click and choose Group.

> **TIP** To add more clips to a group, Alt-click (Windows) or Option-click (Mac OS) the additional clips, then select one of the options listed in step 2 to re-create the group. Note that you'll have to choose audio and video components of a linked clip separately to include them in a group.

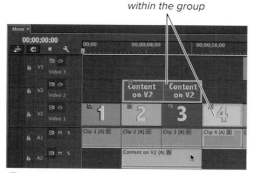

B Right-click any clip in the group, and choose Ungroup.

Selected clips
within the group

C Selecting multiple clips within a group.

To ungroup clips:

1. Select any clip in the group.

2. Do one of the following:

   ▸ Right-click and choose Ungroup **B**.

   ▸ Choose Clip > Ungroup.

   ▸ Press Shift+Control+G (Windows) or Shift+Command+G (Mac OS).

   Premiere Pro ungroups the clips.

To select one or more clips within a group:

With none of the clips in the group selected, do one of the following:

- Alt-click (Windows) or Option-click (Mac OS) the target clip. This selects solely the clip and not the group, so you can perform edits like customizing applied effects or motion controls.

- To select multiple clips within the group, Shift-Alt-click (Windows) or Shift-Option-click (Mac OS) the target clips **C**.

TIP You can use either of these techniques to remove clips from the group. Just select the clips, right-click, and choose Ungroup, and the selected clips are removed from the group.

Working with Snapping

The next major section involves dragging clips around the Timeline. To accomplish this quickly and with precision, you need to know what snapping is, how it works, and how to enable and disable it.

When snapping is enabled (A) and you drag a clip horizontally along a track, both edges of the clip automatically snap to, or align with, other content on the currently selected and other tracks. That way, if you'd like to align the edge of a title to the start of the clip, it's very easy: Just drag the title until the front edge snaps to the start of the clip, and then release. You can see this in (B), where I'm dragging the St. Basil's title to match the start of the St. Basil's clip on V1. Snapping has both a feel component—when the content snaps to the edges—and a visual component, which is the black vertical line with the two white indicators that indicate that the clip edges align (B).

When you're trying to align two clips—or to align a clip with a Timeline marker or the pointer—snapping is very useful. In contrast, if you're trying to align the title to a point five frames into the clip, snapping is a pain, because unless you're zoomed in to the Timeline, Premiere Pro will snap the edge of the title to the edge of the clip. You can enable or disable snapping—even in mid-drag—by pressing S.

To enable and disable snapping:

Click the Snap button  on the upper left of the Timeline, or press the S key.

> **TIP** When the Snap button appears depressed, snapping is enabled.

(A) Here's where you enable and disable Snap.

Alignment indicators

(B) Snapping makes it easy to align the start of the St. Basil's title with the start of the St. Basil's clip.

Dragging Clips in the Timeline

When you see a title like "Dragging Clips in the Timeline," you may think to yourself, "I know how to do that" and skim ahead. But, to steal a line from Springsteen (which, having grown up in New Jersey, I have to do at least once a book), this is one of those "I found the key to the universe in the engine of an old parked car" kind of moments. There's a lot more here than the title suggests, so read on.

When you have only one clip on the Timeline, you can move it anywhere on any track just by dragging. Once you have multiple clips on multiple tracks, things get much more complicated. There are three things you need to think about when you drag a clip from one location to another:

- What happens where the clip used to be?
- What happens to clips on the track where you drop the clip?
- What happens to clips on other tracks?

When addressing what happens to where the clip used to be, there are two options, both named after edit buttons on the Program Monitor. The first option is to leave a gap, which is referred to as a lift edit. The other option is to close the gap by shifting all subsequent content on the track to the left, which is called an extract edit. By default, the extract edit shifts content not only on the track that the edit occurs on, but also on all synced tracks.

There are also two options for what happens where you drop the clip. With an overwrite edit, the dropped content overwrites the content that exists at that location. With the insert edit, Premiere Pro pushes back all content on that track to accommodate the dropped clip. As with the extract edit, the insert edit by default affects both the track where the edit occurs and all synced tracks.

A represents the starting point for the next series of screenshots. Note several changes from the screenshots in the previous section. First, I pushed the "Content on V3" clip to the edge of Clip 6 (from Clip 5). Second, I added markers to the Timeline at the locations of the "Content on V2" and "Content on V3" clips, which will make the adjustments to these tracks easier to see.

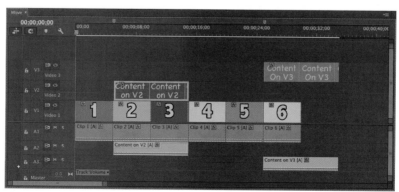

A The starting point for the following set of tasks.

In all tasks, the basic edit is to drag Clip 5 to the location currently inhabited by Clip 2. Since we'll be treating audio identically in all these edits, I'll exclude the audio from the next series of screens to save space and show more detail.

Let's see what happens when I drag Clip 5 to the start of Clip 2 and release **B**—essentially, the default drag-and-drop edit. To use our newly learned terminology, Premiere Pro performs a lift/overwrite edit, leaving a gap where Clip 5 was and overwriting Clip 2 with Clip 5.

All editors are different, and this approach may suit your purposes sometimes, but this is very seldom what I actually want to accomplish. I would guess that Adobe chose this as the default drag-and-drop edit because it affects only the Video 1 track. If the default edit involved an extract edit, an insert edit, or both (the horror!), a simple drag-and-drop operation could shift content on all tracks and totally discombobulate a newbie's carefully constructed Timeline.

First, if you're performing either an extract or insert edit and you have content on multiple tracks, you have to consider what you want to happen to that content after you perform these edits. If you want the content to adjust with the edits, make sure that Sync Lock is enabled. Otherwise, disable

Sync Lock. (I discuss Sync Lock and Track Lock in Chapter 5.)

Second, to toggle between a lift edit (the default) and an extract edit, you have to press the Control (Windows) or Command (Mac OS) key before you click the clip you'll be dragging.

Third, once you start to drag the clip, you must change modifier keys to choose between an insert edit and an overwrite edit. If you release (or never pressed) the Control/Command key, you have the default overwrite edit. If you press (or keep pressing) the Control/Command key, you choose the insert edit. As you'll see in these tasks, Premiere Pro changes the icon to reflect the type of edit it's about to perform.

Finally, to reward those readers who made it this far, if you press Control+Alt (Windows) or Command+Option (Mac OS) after you start dragging your clip, you perform a rearrange edit, which is an extract/insert edit that doesn't affect any other tracks in the Timeline. This is the result I want most of the time when I'm dragging clips on the Timeline, and this is the perfect way to accomplish it. If you're tempted to skip to another section, at least read the task about the rearrange edit—a subtle but highly convenient feature.

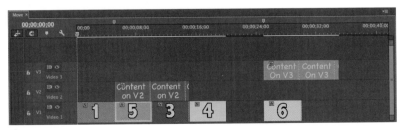

B The default lift/overwrite edit.

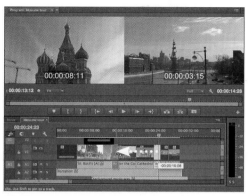

 You can drop clips between other clips, guided by feedback from the two-up view in the Program Monitor.

Just a couple of more notes before we get to the tasks:

As mentioned, all of the tasks will involve dropping Clip 5 at the intersection between Clip 1 and Clip 2. You can drop the clip at any point in the Timeline **C**, not just at an existing intersection. In **C**, I'm dragging the third-from-last clip on the Timeline to the left, between the St. Basil's clip and the Peter the Great clip.

When you drag content in the Timeline, the Program Monitor changes to a two-up view. On the left side is the frame immediately before the drop point; the timecode is that of the original clip. On the right is the frame immediately after the drop point; the timecode is from that clip.

To perform a lift/overwrite edit:

1. Click the target clip. The pointer doesn't change because you haven't pressed the Control/Command key.

2. Start dragging the clip to the target location. The pointer changes to the overwrite pointer .

3. Release the pointer at the target location. Premiere Pro leaves a gap at the original location of Clip 5 and overwrites Clip 2 with Clip 5 **B**. No other content on any track moves.

To perform an extract/overwrite edit:

1. Hold down the Control/Command key and hover the pointer over the target clip. The pointer changes to the extract pointer .

2. Start dragging the clip. The pointer changes to the insert pointer .

continues on next page

3. Release the Control/Command key. The pointer changes to the overwrite pointer .

4. Release the pointer at the target location **D**. Clip 6 shifts to the left to close the gap, as does the "Content on V3" clip. If that's not what you intended, disable Sync Lock for this track before making the edit.

To perform a lift/insert edit:

1. Click the target clip. The pointer doesn't change because you haven't pressed the Control/Command key.

2. Start dragging the clip to the target location. The pointer changes to the overwrite pointer .

3. Press the Control/Command key. The pointer turns into the insert pointer .

4. Release the pointer at the target location **E**. Premiere Pro leaves a gap at the original location of Clip 5 (the lift edit) and pushes back the content on V1 to accommodate Clip 5 (the insert). Since I didn't disable Sync Lock on V1 and V2, the content on both tracks shifted to the right. If that's not what you intend, disable Sync Lock for these tracks before making the edit.

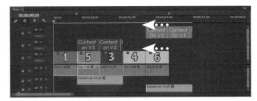

D The extract/overwrite edit. Clip 6 shifted left to close the gap, and the "Content on V3" clip shifted as well, because Sync Lock was enabled.

E The lift/insert edit. Note the gap where Clip 5 started, and that all content in all tracks was pushed back to accommodate Clip 5.

F The extract/insert edit.

G The rearrange edit—the perfect editing technique for later-stage projects when you have content on multiple tracks.

To perform an extract/insert edit:

1. Hold down the Control/Command key and hover the pointer over the target clip. The pointer changes to the extract pointer ![extract pointer].

2. Start dragging the clip. The pointer changes to the insert pointer ![insert pointer].

3. Release the pointer at the target location **F**. Premiere Pro extracts Clip 5, closing the gap, and inserts Clip 5 after Clip 1, pushing all other clips back. The "Content on V2" clip is pushed back by the duration of the insert edit. The "Content on V3" clip remains in place, because the shift from the extract edit (-5:00) is offset by the shift from the insert edit (+5:00).

To perform a rearrange edit:

1. Start dragging the target clip.

2. Press Control+Alt (Windows) or Option+Command (Mac OS). The pointer turns into the recycle pointer ![recycle pointer].

3. Drag the clip to the target location and release the pointer. Premiere Pro performs an extract/insert edit that affects only the Video 1 track **G**.

Moving Clips via Keyboard Controls and the Keypad

Sometimes you'll want to move a clip a frame or two to the left or right. A good example is the edit discussed in the previous section, where you want a title to align five frames from the start of a clip. Another example is when you're trying to sync clips in a multicam sequence. In both cases you need to move the clip with precision.

There are two approaches: by using keyboard controls and via the numeric keypad on an extended keyboard. (The latter technique requires an extended keyboard.)

Be careful when you use either to shift clips on tracks where there are adjacent clips, because the default behavior is to overwrite those clips.

I'll demonstrate both techniques using the St. Basil's title, which I want to appear 30 frames from the start of the St. Basil's clip.

To move clips via keyboard controls:

1. Select the clip or clips to move .

2. To move the clip one frame, press Alt+Right/Left Arrow (Windows) or Option+Right/Left Arrow (Mac OS). Use the Left Arrow key to move to the left, the Right Arrow key to move right.

3. To move the clip five frames at a time, press Alt+Shift+Right/Left Arrow (Windows) or Option+Shift+Right/Left Arrow (Mac OS) 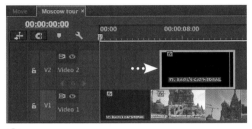. Use the Left Arrow key to move to the left, the Right Arrow key to move right.

Ⓐ Our goal: Move the St. Basil's title 30 frames to the right.

Ⓑ Mission accomplished.

C Press the + key on your extended keyboard.

D Enter the number of frames you want the video to shift; use the – key to move clips to the left.

E Mission accomplished.

To move clips via the numeric keypad:

1. Select the clip or clips to move **A**.

2. Press the + key on the extended keyboard. Premiere Pro blanks out the Timecode box on the upper left of the Timeline **C**.

3. Enter the number of frames you'd like to shift the clip to the right. To shift the clip to the left, press the – key and enter the number of frames **D**.

4. Press Enter (Windows) or Return (Mac OS). Premiere Pro shifts the clip the specified duration **E**.

Moving Clips from Track to Track

Often during editing, you'll have to move content vertically from one track to another, changing the track but not the timing of the content within the project. Premiere Pro simplifies this task by providing feedback to ensure that you don't move the clip forward or backward in the Timeline when making this adjustment. As long as you're moving the audio or video component vertically to another track, and not horizontally within the same track, you don't have to unlink the content first or use the Alt (Windows) or Option (Mac OS) modifier to select one track or the other.

Note that you can drop the content only on a compatible track; for example, you can't drop a 5.1 surround sound audio track on a standard audio track. The solution is to drop the content beneath the lowest existing track (or above the current highest track for video), and Premiere Pro will automatically create a compatible track. As you'll see, this same solution works if you'd like to create a new track for the selected content.

To move content from one track to another at the same location:

1. Click the target clip.

2. Drag the clip up or down to the target track **A**. Premiere Pro displays the over-write pointer ![icon]. Note the timecode box, which tells you when you're moving the clip vertically (no timecode change) or horizontally and shifting position in the project. If there are compatible tracks, Premiere Pro will temporarily park the content in each compatible track as you move toward your destination; release the pointer to drop the content in any compatible track.

Original track location

A Since there are compatible video tracks, Premiere Pro parks the clip in each one as you drag by it.

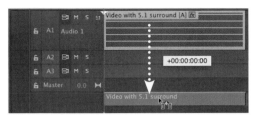

There are no other 5.1 surround tracks, so Premiere Pro immediately parks the audio file below the Master...

The new 5.1 surround sound track

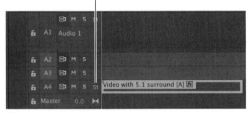

C ...and creates a new 5.1 surround sound track.

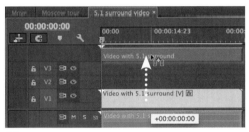

D Dragging this video clip above the last existing track...

The new track

E ...to create a new video track.

If there are no compatible tracks (as with this 5.1 surround track), Premiere Pro will immediately park your content below the last existing track **B** (or above the current highest track for video) and create a new track **C**.

To move content to a new track at the same location:

1. Click the target clip.

2. Drag upward past the last existing video track **D**, or downward past the last existing audio track.

3. Release your pointer. Premiere Pro automatically creates a track compatible with the selected content **E**.

Working with Track Targeting

Most of the edits discussed so far have been applied to a single clip, even though their effect might ripple through multiple tracks. Now we'll look at several edits, or edit functions, that can be applied directly across multiple tracks.

A good example is the lift edit, which you learned about in Chapter 5. The basic procedure is to mark In and Out points in the Timeline and then click the Lift button beneath the Program Monitor **A**. This lifts the video in the marked region from all tracks **B**, and because it's a lift (as opposed to an extract), it leaves a gap. Let's suppose you wanted to exclude a track from this edit. To accomplish this, you would toggle track targeting off for that track using the "Toggle track targeting" button **C**. When targeting is enabled, the track is light gray; when targeting is disabled, the track is dark gray. Let's see what happens when I disable Track 2.

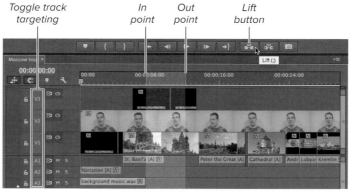

Toggle track targeting   *In point*   *Out point*   *Lift button*

A Setting up for the lift edit. I have marked the In and Out points and am ready to click the Lift button.

B Here's the result: The video is lifted from all three tracks.

C Disabling track targeting for V2. When track targeting is enabled, the background is lighter.

D Now the lift edit excludes V2.

If I repeat the edit now, video on Track 2 is not affected **D**. It's similar to locking the track, but you can perform all direct edits on content on that track; it's only Timeline-wide edits that are excluded.

To enable and disable track targeting:

On the target track, click the "Toggle track targeting" button to enable or disable track targeting **C**. When the track is light gray, targeting is enabled; when dark gray, it's disabled.

Cut, Copy, Paste, and Paste Insert

Most readers know these terms, but let's quickly review.

- Cut. This edit deletes the selected clip, leaving a gap, and copies it to the clipboard. It's pretty much the same as a lift edit.

- Copy. This edit copies the selected clip to the keyboard and doesn't otherwise affect the selected clip.

- Paste. This edit pastes the clip in the clipboard to the selected track at the playhead location, performing an overwrite edit that replaces existing footage.

- Paste Insert. This edit pastes the clip in the clipboard to the selected track at the playhead location, performing an insert edit that pushes all existing footage to the right on the target track and all synced tracks.

When you're pasting your clips, use the track-targeting technique described in the previous section. Premiere Pro pastes the clip on the lowest track with track targeting enabled. If that's not what you want, you need to disable track targeting for all tracks lower than your target. If track targeting is disabled for all tracks, Premiere Pro pastes the content on the lowest possible track.

In addition, when you're using the Paste Insert option, you have to remember that the insert edit will shift content on the target track and all synced tracks. If this isn't what you want, you need to disable Sync Lock on those tracks.

As an alternative to copying and pasting your clips, you can also drag another version of that clip from the Project panel. Each clip that you source in this fashion is completely independent, so edits made to one don't affect another. Copying and pasting is the better approach when you've made changes to the clip in the Timeline that you'd want in the new instance, such as color or brightness correction. Redeploy a new clip from the Project panel if you need to start fresh and don't need these adjustments. Just to make the demonstration fun, I'm going to copy two clips from tracks V1 and V2 and paste them into V3.

You can also duplicate a clip by dragging, which I'll demonstrate later in this section.

Selected clips

A Nothing exotic here, just right-click the clips and choose Copy.

B Moving the playhead to the target position.

C Disabling track targeting on V1 and V2.

To copy and paste a clip or clips:

1. Click the target clip or clips. Or, Alt-click (Windows) or Option-click (Mac OS) to select either video or audio in a clip or clips. (I'm selecting the "Content on V2" clip and Clip 5 **A**.)

2. Do one of the following:

   ▸ To delete the clip, copy it to the clipboard, and leave a gap in the Timeline, right-click and choose Cut. Or press Control+X (Windows) or Command+X (Mac OS).

   ▸ To copy the clip to the clipboard, right-click and choose Copy. Or press Control+C (Windows) or Command+C (Mac OS) **A**.

3. Navigate the Timeline playhead to the selected paste location **B**.

4. Toggle track targeting off on all tracks lower than your target. Since my target here is V3, I'm disabling V1 and V2 **C**. Note that track targeting is disabled for all audio tracks.

5. If performing a Paste Insert, disable Sync Lock on all tracks that you don't want to be affected by the edit.

continues on next page

6. Do one of the following:

- Choose Edit > Paste , or press Control+V (Windows) or Command+V (Mac OS). Premiere Pro pastes the selected clip or clips to the selected tracks at the playhead location, performing an overwrite edit that writes over any existing content.

- Choose Edit > Paste Insert, or press Control+Shift+V (Windows) or Command+Shift+V (Mac OS). Premiere Pro pastes the selected clip or clips to the selected tracks at the playhead location, performing an insert edit that pushes back all content on the selected and synced tracks.

In this case, since there was no content subsequent to the playhead in the Timeline, it didn't matter whether I chose Paste or Paste Insert 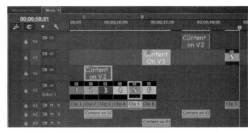. Note that Premiere Pro inserted Clip 5 on V3, and created V4 to maintain the spatial relationship between the "Content on V2" clip and Clip 5. Note also that Premiere Pro pasted the audio from the two copied clips on A1 and A2 because track targeting was disabled for all audio tracks.

To duplicate a clip by dragging:

1. Select the target clip 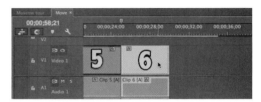.

2. Alt-drag (Windows) or Option-drag (Mac OS) the clip to a new location on the Timeline .

Premiere Pro duplicates the selected clip .

D Maintaining the visual narrative by showing you which paste option I used.

E The result: Premiere Pro placed the video clips on the targeted frames and created a new track for the "Content on V2" clip. Audio went to A1 and A2 because track targeting was disabled for all audio clips.

F Copying Clip 6, video and audio.

G Alt/Option-drag.

H There we are: the new copy.

TIP Alt-click (Windows) or Option-click (Mac OS) a clip to select the video or audio component of a linked clip. Keep Alt/Option depressed when you move the clip, and Premiere Pro will duplicate the selected component.

TIP Note the overwrite pointer 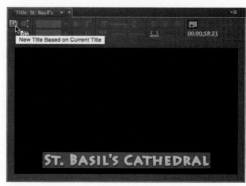 shown in **G**. This tells you that if you drag the clip over an adjacent clip, Premiere Pro will overwrite it.

TIP You can duplicate both clips and sequences in the Project panel by selecting the clip or sequence, right-clicking, and choosing Duplicate. Once duplicated, the two articles are completely separate and edits done to one don't affect the other, excepting titles, as discussed in the sidebar "Duplicating Titles."

Duplicating Titles

I want to warn you that neither procedure described in this section works with titles. With all other clips, when you create a copy, you can edit either copy independently of the other.

In contrast, when you copy a title outside the Project panel, you just create another use of that same title. For example, suppose I copied the St. Basil's title we've seen several times, and renamed the copy The Kremlin. If I changed the text in the title from St. Basil's to The Kremlin, the text in both titles would change—it's the same title, deployed twice.

Here's the procedure for creating a new title you can edit without overwriting the old. First, load the title into the Titler utility. Then click the New Title Based on Current Title button **I** to create a new title that you can name and then edit without overwriting the original. We'll discuss this in detail in Chapter 14, but it's worth noting now while you're learning about copying.

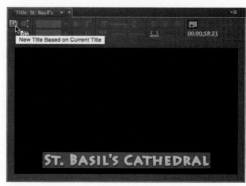

I The preferred technique for duplicating titles.

Deleting Clips on the Timeline

There are two general techniques used to delete clips on the Timeline: delete and ripple delete. Deleting a clip is similar to the lift edit: The clip is gone, but the gap remains. This may be useful when you want to replace one clip with another, but see the "Replacing a Clip on the Timeline" section later in this chapter if that's your goal.

The ripple delete function deletes the clip and closes the gap, but it also closes the gap on all tracks that remain synced. If you don't want a track to be affected, disable Sync Lock on that track.

In both tasks, I will select Clip 1 and Clip 2.

To delete one or more clips on the Timeline:

1. Select the clips to delete 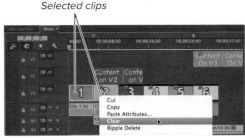.

2. Do one of the following:

   ▸ Press Backspace (Windows) or Delete (Mac OS).

   ▸ Right-click and choose Clear Ⓐ.

   Premiere Pro deletes the clip and leaves the gap Ⓑ.

Selected clips

Ⓐ Choose the clips to delete, right-click, and choose Clear.

The gap

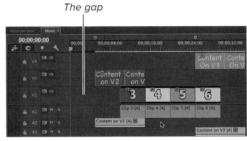

Ⓑ Gone, with only the gap remaining (think lift edit).

Selected clips

C Choose clips to delete, right-click, and choose Ripple Delete.

D Gone, and all content on all tracks rippled to the left (think extract edit).

To ripple delete one or more clips in the Timeline:

1. Deselect Sync Lock to disable the ripple adjustment for any tracks that you don't want to adjust (if necessary).

2. Select the clips to delete **C**.

3. Do one of the following:

   ▸ Press Shift+Backspace (Windows) or Shift+Delete (Mac OS).

   ▸ Right-click and choose Ripple Delete **C**.

   Premiere Pro closes the gap, shifting all content on all synced tracks to the left **D**.

TIP Use the Alt (Windows) or Option (Mac OS) modifier to select and delete only the audio or video component of a linked clip.

TIP Again, the ripple delete affects all tracks on the Timelime. If that isn't the desired result, disable Sync Lock on tracks that you don't want affected.

Finding and Deleting Gaps in the Timeline

If you move clips around in a project, you may leave gaps between some clips, even with snapping enabled 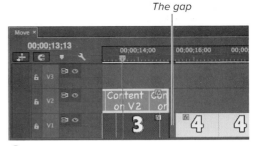. For this reason, it's good practice to search for gaps as one of the later stages of any project.

Fortunately, Premiere Pro makes the gaps easy to find and delete.

To find gaps in the Timeline:

Do one of following:

- To find gaps *after* the playhead in the sequence, choose Sequence > Go to Gap > Next in Sequence (or press Shift + ;) **B**.

- To find gaps *before* the playhead in the sequence, choose Sequence > Go to Gap > Previous in Sequence (or press Control+Shift+; [Windows] or Shift+; [Mac OS]).

- To find the next gap on the selected *track*, choose Sequence > Go to Gap > Next in Track.

- To find the previous gap on the selected *track*, choose Sequence > Go to Gap > Previous in Track.

    If there are more gaps, Premiere Pro moves the playhead to the next gap **C**.

    Next, you'll learn how to delete the gap.

The gap

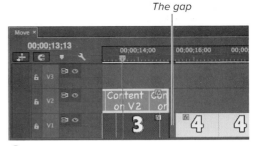

A Searching for gaps between clips.

B Choose the desired search pattern.

Playhead shifts to gap

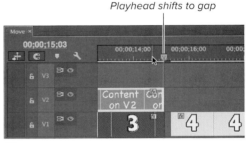

C The playhead moves to the next gap.

D Right-click the gap and choose Ripple Delete.

E Content shifts to the left to close the gap.

To ripple delete a gap in the Timeline:

1. Deselect Sync Lock to disable the ripple adjustment for any tracks that you don't want to adjust (if necessary).

2. Select the gap to delete **D**.

3. Right-click and choose Ripple Delete **D**.

   Premiere Pro closes the gap, shifting all content on all synced tracks to the left **E**. I'm showing only video tracks, but the result is the same for audio tracks.

When Ripple Delete Goes Gray

Sometimes when you desperately need to use the Ripple Delete command to close a gap in your project, the control goes gray. This is because Ripple Delete isn't available if it will move any other content in any other track out of sync.

For example, in **F** I'm trying to ripple delete the audio component of the first Red Square clip. As you can see, Ripple Delete is disabled.

Even if you turn off Sync Lock, Premiere Pro will stubbornly refuse to make the Ripple Delete command available. The only solution is to lock all other active tracks, which should make Ripple Delete available **G**. Once applied, however, you see that the audio sync between the video on V1 and the audio on A1 has been lost **H**.

I override the grayed-out Ripple Delete command in this fashion a lot when editing screencams, where the sync between the audio and the video isn't so critical. Be very careful when applying this technique to talking-head clips, because the loss of sync could be problematic.

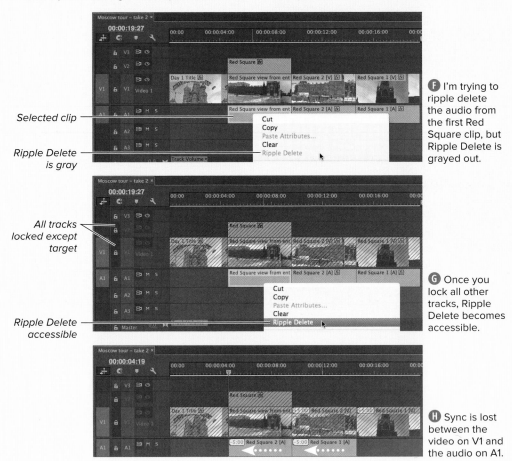

Selected clip

Ripple Delete is gray

F I'm trying to ripple delete the audio from the first Red Square clip, but Ripple Delete is grayed out.

All tracks locked except target

Ripple Delete accessible

G Once you lock all other tracks, Ripple Delete becomes accessible.

H Sync is lost between the video on V1 and the audio on A1.

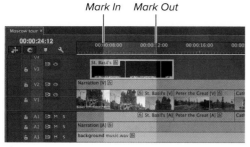

Mark In   Mark Out

A Mark the In and Out points to start the lift or extract edit.

Performing Lift and Extract Edits

We've beaten around these particular bushes a few times, but let's detail the concepts and procedures for those few readers who aren't reading this book from front to back (har, har).

A lift edit lifts the selected content and leaves a gap in the Timeline where the content existed. An extract edit lifts the selected content and closes the gap, shifting content located to the right of the gap on any synced tracks.

To be clear, even if you disable track targeting on a track so that the extract or lift edit doesn't directly affect that track, the ripple effect from the extract edit still will. For this reason, to avoid impact on other tracks when performing an extract edit, you may have to disable track targeting and Sync lock. Or just lock the tracks, of course.

Here's the procedure.

To perform a lift or extract edit:

1. Set In and Out points in the Timeline or Program Monitor **A**.

2. Disable track targeting for all tracks that you don't want affected by the edit (not applicable in this case).

3. Click Sync Lock for all tracks that you don't want affected by the edit (again, not applicable).

continues on next page

4. Do one of the following:

▸ To lift the selected content and leave a gap in the Timeline, click the Lift button ![lift button] in the Program Monitor or press ; (semicolon). Premiere Pro performs the lift edit **B**.

▸ To extract the selected content and ripple all changes to close the gap, click the Extract button ![extract button] in the Program Monitor or press ' (apostrophe). Premiere Pro performs the extract edit **C**.

5. If desired, paste or paste insert the content at another location on the same or a different sequence.

TIP Once Premiere Pro performs the lift or extract edit, it clears the selected In and Out points. If you change your mind and don't want to perform the edit, you can do the same by right-clicking the Timeline time ruler and choosing Clear In, Clear Out, or Clear In and Out **D**.

TIP The extract edit, in particular, is useful when you want to delete a multitrack chunk of content from a sequence or move a multitrack chunk from one place to another.

TIP Note that once you mark In and Out points, the Copy command copies the selected region to the clipboard if no other clips are selected at the time. This is a great way to grab content from one part of a project to use in another where you don't want to delete the content in its existing location. For example, this works well when grabbing short snippets of content from the body of a video to use in the intro, or in a condensed version of the longer video.

Gap

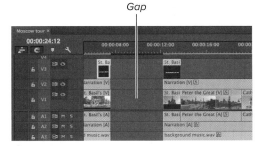

B The lift edit leaves a gap where the selected content once was.

Gap closed

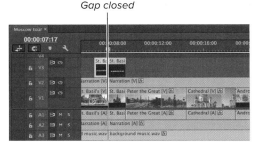

C The extract edit closes the gap where the content was.

D If you change your mind, here's how you clear the In and Out points.

A Your three options in a replace edit.

Insufficient media in
replacement clip

B The zebra pattern indicates that the
replacement clip had insufficient media.

Replacing a Clip
on the Timeline

This is one of Premiere Pro's coolest and
most useful functions. Though it's not an
edit that you'll use a lot, when you do, it
will save you serious time and aggravation.
Here's the setup. You've used a clip in the
Timeline, and now you need to replace
it with another clip. You could delete the
first clip and then insert the second, but if
you've applied effects to the first clip, they
wouldn't carry over.

The replace edit is easiest if you're switching one piece of content for another of
similar duration, like one 5-second image
for another. When you're using real-world
clips of different lengths, the procedure is
more complex. Here's an overview.

You can replace the clip in the Timeline
with a clip from the bin **A** (which we've
been calling the Project panel) or from the
Source Monitor. If the clip in the bin has
marked In and Out points, Premiere Pro
will insert the clip starting with the In point;
if not, it will start with the first frame.

If there isn't sufficient content in the new
clip (a 5-second clip replacing a 10-sec-
ond clip), a zebra pattern in the Timeline
will indicate this **B**. If there's more than
enough content (a 20-second clip replacing a 10-second clip), Premiere Pro will
replace the old clip with the new clip, but
only up to the original border of the old
clip. It won't push back or overwrite any
adjacent content.

If you replace the clip in the Timeline with a
clip from the Source Monitor, you have two
choices. Replace With Clip > From Source
Monitor works exactly like replacing a clip
from the bin. The second option, Replace
With Clip > From Source Monitor, Match

Frame 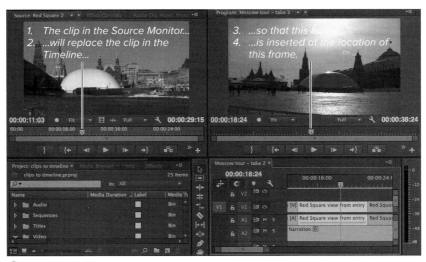 inserts the clip so that the frame showing in the Source Monitor replaces the frame showing in the Program Monitor. This is useful when your narration addresses a specific item (like Lenin's Tomb in the example) and you want that item to appear in the replacement clip exactly where it appeared in the original clip.

With Match Frame edits, Premiere Pro adjusts the In and Out points automatically from that starting point, and if there's insufficient content at either the start or end of the clip, it will display the zebra pattern. I'll demonstrate the Match Frame technique in the task.

In all cases, any effects or other adjustments made to the initial clip in the Timeline will be applied to the replacement clip. This includes motion adjustments (for picture-in-picture), speed adjustments, and any effects.

To replace a clip in the Timeline using the Replace With Clip function:

1. Prepare the clip that you'll be inserting into the Timeline (if necessary) by marking In and Out points and (for Match Frame edits) positioning the playhead at the desired frame. Here, I'm positioning the ballooned structure (Lenin's Tomb) in the Source Monitor, to replace the same view in the clip in the sequence shown in the Program Monitor **C**.

2. For a Match Frame edit, position the playhead in the Timeline at the desired frame. I've got the playhead at Lenin's Tomb shot from a different angle, and the glare from the sun makes it a poor shot **C**.

1. The clip in the Source Monitor...
2. ...will replace the clip in the Timeline...

3. ...so that this frame...
4. ...is inserted at the location of this frame.

C Setting up the Match Frame replacement edit.

3. Right-click the clip on the Timeline and choose Replace With Clip and the desired option. I'm choosing From Source Monitor, Match Frame **A**. Premiere Pro inserts the clip from the Source Monitor, matching the playhead location in the Source Monitor to the playhead location in the Timeline and Program Monitor **D**.

TIP You can perform this edit via keyboard shortcuts. To use the In point of a new clip in the Project panel or Source Monitor, press the Alt (Windows) or Option (Mac OS) key while dragging the new clip onto the old in the Timeline.

TIP A similar technique is to replace footage in the Project panel with other clips on your hard drive, which is useful when you want to replace a clip used in multiple places in the project with another. To do this, select the clip in the Project panel, right-click, and choose Replace Footage. Navigate to and select the new clip, and Premiere Pro will replace the old clip with the new wherever it's deployed in the project.

D The Red Square 2 clip replaced the "Red Square view from entry" clip with the selected frame in Red Square 2, matching the location of the selected frame in "Red Square view from entry."

Splitting Clips

Splitting clips is a fundamental editing action you'll perform many, many times over the course of most projects. When you split a clip, you create two discrete clips, and each has full access to all frames in the source clip, though they obviously use different In and Out points.

By default, as with most edits, when you split a linked clip containing both audio and video, you split both tracks, though the Alt /Option modifier key can limit this when splitting with the Razor tool.

In addition to splitting a single clip, you'll learn two ways to split multiple clips. The first, using the Razor tool, cuts all tracks except locked tracks, including those where track targeting is disabled. The second method, which is implemented via menu commands or keyboard short-cuts, doesn't split locked tracks, but it can split tracks with track targeting disabled, depending on the option you choose. To help make this point, the track targeting in all tasks is *enabled* for V1/A1 and V2/A2, and *disabled* for V3/A3.

Note that in Premiere Pro CS7, there is a new Through Edit indicator to let editors know when adjacent clips are split clips that haven't been trimmed in any way. This is useful if you are adding transitions between clips on a track but don't want to add a transition to a through edit.

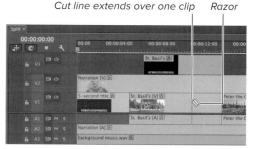

Ⓐ Clicking the Razor tool (C is an essential keyboard shortcut to learn).

Cut line extends over one clip   *Razor*

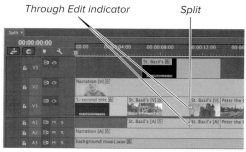

Ⓑ Before the split. Notice that the cut line extends only over V1 and A1.

Through Edit indicator   *Split*

Ⓒ After the split. Notice that only V1 and A1 were split.

To split a clip with the Razor tool:

1. In the Tools panel, click the Razor tool Ⓐ, or press C. The pointer converts to the razor pointer 🔷.

2. If desired, press the Alt (Windows) or Option (Mac OS) key to split either the audio or video component of a linked clip.

3. Hover the pointer over the target clip on the Timeline. Note that the vertical line appears only over a single clip Ⓑ.

4. Click the clip at the desired split location. Premiere Pro splits the clip Ⓒ. Note the Through Edit indicators at the split between V1 and A1. These were the only two clips that Premiere Pro split.

TIP Remember to click V to restore the selection pointer when you're done splitting; otherwise, you'll inadvertently split the next piece of content that you click.

To split multiple clips with the Razor tool:

1. In the Tools panel, click the Razor tool, or press C. The pointer converts to the razor pointer 🔹.

2. Press the Shift key. The razor pointer converts to the multirazor pointer 🔹.

3. Hover the pointer over the target clip on the Timeline. Note that the vertical line appears over all clips in all tracks **D**.

4. Click any clip at the desired split location. Premiere Pro splits all clips in all tracks at that location, including tracks with targeting disabled but not including locked tracks **E**.

TIP If you're going to use this technique, lock any tracks that you don't want split.

Track targeting disabled   *Vertical line over all tracks*   *Multirazor pointer*

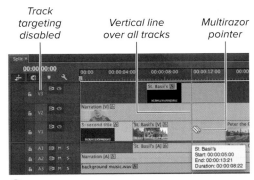

D Just before the multirazor split.

Even the track with targeting disabled   *All tracks split*

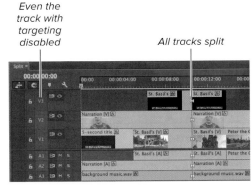

E After the multirazor split.

F Note the two options. Add Edit excludes tracks on which targeting has been disabled; Add Edit to All Tracks doesn't.

Track not split

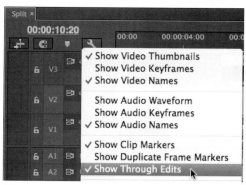

G The track with targeting disabled wasn't split.

H You enable and disable the Through Edit indicator in the Timeline's Settings menu, accessed by clicking the wrench icon.

To split clips using menu commands:

1. Navigate the playhead to the desired split location.

2. Do one of the following:
   - ▸ Choose Sequence > Add Edit (Control/Command+K) **F**. Premiere Pro splits all clips on all tracks except for locked tracks or tracks with targeting disabled **G**.
   - ▸ Choose Sequence > Add Edit to All Tracks (Shift+Control/Command+K) **F**. Premiere Pro splits all clips on all tracks except for locked tracks **E**.

To enable the Through Edit indicator:

Click the Timeline's Settings button, and choose Show Through Edits **H**. Premiere Pro displays the Through Edit indicator.

Linking and Unlinking Clips

As we've discussed, Premiere Pro treats files that contain audio and video as a linked clip that stays together as the clip is moved or otherwise edited in a sequence. We've also discussed that by using the Alt (Windows) or Option (Mac OS) modifier, you can select and edit either component of a linked clip.

Once you're done with that edit, however, the link between the clip returns. To make the break permanent, you have to unlink the audio and video components, which you'll learn how to do in this section.

You can later relink the two components should the need arise. If the audio and video clips lose sync during the intervening edits, there's a fast and easy way to re-sync them. This technique is also useful if any linked clip loses sync due to other edits.

Just so you know, you can also link audio and video components that weren't originally part of the same clip. This is useful anytime you want to keep an audio file synchronized with a video file.

To unlink the audio and video components of a clip:

1. Select the clip.

2. Do one of the following:
   - Right-click and choose Unlink 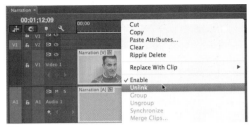.
   - Choose Clip > Unlink.

   Premiere Pro unlinks the clip components .

A To unlink a linked clip, right-click either element and choose Unlink.

B The two unlinked clips. Notice that the clip names no longer include the (V) and (A) labels **A**.

TIP You can tell when audio and video are unlinked, because the (V) and (A) track labels no longer appear.

TIP You can unlink multiple clips at one time, but can relink only one audio and one video clip at a time.

C To link two clips, select them both and choose Link. Note that these two appear to be out of sync.

D Oops—out of sync by 3:27. Since it's a talking-head clip, someone is sure to notice.

E I'm telling the video clip to move into sync with the audio clip.

F The video shifts to the right to regain sync. Had I clicked the audio track and chosen Move into Sync, it would have shifted to the left.

To relink the audio and video components of a clip:

1. Select the audio and video clips.
2. Do one of the following:
   - Right-click and choose Link C.
   - Choose Clip > Link.

   Premiere Pro links the clip components. If the clips are out of sync, you'll see a red timecode counter telling you how far out of sync the clips are D.

To synchronize out-of-sync clips:

1. Select the red timecode counter on either the video or audio track E. If you don't see the menu shown in E, it's because you have some other portion of the clip selected. Click an empty space in the Timeline to deselect the clip and try again
2. Right-click and choose one of the following:
   - Move into Sync. This moves the track you selected into sync with the other. This essentially gets you back to where you started but can result in clips being overwritten by the clip that moved. Assuming that you can avoid overwriting any adjacent clips, this is generally the preferred option F.
   - Slip into Sync. This slips the selected track to restore sync with the other. Both clips stay in the same location on the Timeline, and the content of the selected clip shifts to regain sync. This option is available only if there is sufficient content to make the slip edit. Note that this technique changes the content of the clip, so if the original clip was exactly what you wanted, you'll have some editing to do to restore that content.

Adding Markers on the Timeline

We discussed adding markers to clips in the Source Monitor in Chapter 4 (see "Working with markers in the Source Monitor"). You learned that you can insert a marker by pressing the M key, even when the clip is playing. You also learned that once you create a marker you can move it by dragging it, and that you can delete and perform other housekeeping and navigational functions via the right-click menu.

Most of the markers you insert in the Source Monitor direct some later editing function and are typically *comment markers*. While you can add these types of markers in the Timeline as well, there are also three markers that are inserted for some post-rendering function, often called *interactive markers*. These are *chapter markers*, which create chapter points for DVDs created in Encore; *web links*, which add a URL the video can link to when played back in QuickTime; and *Flash cue points*, which trigger events when the clips are played back within the Adobe Flash environment.

As you'll learn in these tasks, there are two ways to add markers on the Timeline. If you're adding comment markers that you don't need to immediately edit, you can use the keyboard shortcut M. For interactive markers, where you typically need to add some additional information in the Marker dialog, you'll use a different approach.

Premiere Pro stores all markers in the Markers panel, where you can perform basic edits and easily open the Markers dialog for more-comprehensive changes. If you're editing video or still images to music, using markers to automate the process can make you much more efficient.

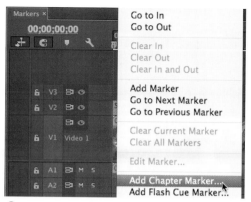

A The right-click menu is a convenient way to directly open the Marker dialog, even if you're not creating a chapter marker.

B You can also click here to add a marker.

C Double-click an existing marker to open the Marker dialog.

D Complete the necessary info for the comment marker and click OK.

E Comment markers are green.

To add markers via the Marker dialog:

1. Navigate to the target marker position on the Timeline. I'm adding a chapter marker to the start of this sequence.

2. Do one of the following:

   ▸ Right-click and choose Add Chapter Marker **A** (even if you want to add a different type of marker). Premiere Pro adds the marker and opens the Marker dialog.

   ▸ Choose Marker > Add Marker (or press M). Then double-click the marker over the time ruler in the Timeline or Program Monitor to open the Marker dialog.

   ▸ Click the Add Marker button on the Program Monitor ▮ or Timeline **B**. Then double-click the marker **C** over the time ruler in the Timeline or Program Monitor to open the Marker dialog.

3. Do one of the following:

   ▸ If you're creating a comment marker **D**, click the Comment Marker option and enter the name and any comments. Consider expanding the Timeline duration so that the comment name is legible in the Timeline. Click OK to close the dialog. Premiere Pro inserts a green comment marker on the Timeline **E**.

continues on next page

- If you're creating a chapter marker **F**, click the Chapter Marker option and enter the name and any necessary comments. Consider expanding the Timeline duration so that the comment name is legible in the Timeline. Click OK to close the dialog. Premiere Pro inserts a red chapter marker on the timeline **G**.

- If you're creating a web link **H**, click the Web Link option, enter the target URL, and enter the frame target if desired. Type the name and any comments. Consider expanding the Timeline duration so that the comment name is legible in the Timeline. Click OK to close the dialog. Premiere Pro inserts an orange web link marker on the Timeline **I**.

F Complete the necessary info for the chapter marker and click OK.

G Chapter markers are red.

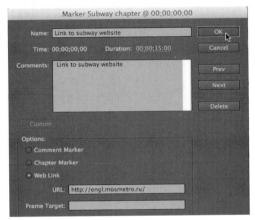

H Complete the necessary info for the web link and click OK.

I Web link markers are orange.

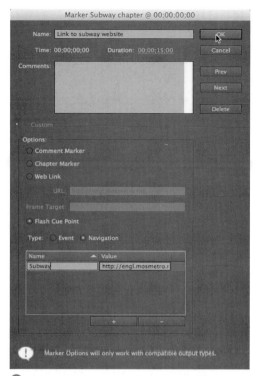

 Complete the necessary info for the Flash cue point and click OK.

 Flash cue point markers are yellow.

 Click the Markers panel tab to open the panel.

▶ If creating a Flash cue point marker **J**, click the Flash Cue Point option and add the required information. Type the name and any comments. Consider expanding the Timeline duration so that the comment name is legible in the Timeline. Click OK to close the dialog. Premiere Pro inserts a yellow Flash cue point marker on the Timeline **K**.

TIP If you want to add a Flash cue point marker, you can right-click and select that option directly from the menu.

To work with markers in the Markers panel:

1. To open the Markers panel, do one of the following:

   ▶ If the Markers panel tab is showing, click it **L**.

   ▶ If the Markers panel tab isn't showing (or you can't find it), choose Window > Markers.

continues on next page

2. Select the sequence containing the markers in the Timeline ⓜ. The sequence needs to be selected or the markers won't appear in the Marker panel.

   Premiere Pro opens the Markers panel ⓝ. The markers are color-coded, and only comment markers show any text, which you can edit by clicking the text box and making the desired changes ⓝ.

3. In the Markers panel, you can do the following:

   ▸ Click a marker to jump to that marker in the Timeline.

   ▸ Double-click a marker to open the Comments dialog and edit the marker.

   ▸ Edit the In and Out points by dragging the timecodes ⓞ or by clicking the timecode to make it active and typing in a new timecode ⓟ.

Automated editing using markers

When you're assembling multiple clips into a sequence, sometimes it's easier to arrange their order in the Project panel before dragging them into a sequence. We explored this technique in the Chapter 4 section "Storyboard Editing in the Project Panel." Now we'll take it one step further and automate to the sequence using

ⓜ Choose the sequence that contains the markers that you want to examine.

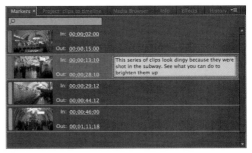

ⓝ The markers are color-coded, just like the Timeline markers. Red for chapter markers; green for comment markers; orange for web link markers; yellow for Flash cue point markers.

ⓞ You can drag the timecodes to a new In or Out point.

ⓟ Or enter the timecode directly (200 equals 2 seconds, 0 frames—or 00;00;02;00).

Marker-related Keyboard Shortcuts

Function	Windows	Mac OS
Add marker	M	M
Go to next marker	Shift+M	Shift+M
Go to previous marker	Control+Shift+M	Command+Shift+M
Clear current marker	Control+Alt+M	Option+M
Clear all markers	Control+Alt+Shift+M	Option+Command+M

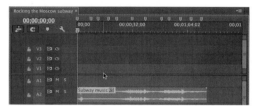

Q Make sure you include a marker at the start of the sequence.

R Play the sequence, pressing M at each beat.

S Arrange the clips and click Automate to Sequence.

markers. This technique is particularly useful when creating music videos or similar productions because you can insert your clips on a music beat. But it's also useful for general-purpose projects when you're trying to find the best order for clips, even if you don't use markers when inserting the clips.

The procedure takes two steps: adding markers to a music clip, then sorting your content and using the Automate to Sequence feature.

To add markers to clips during playback:

1. Create a new sequence Q.

2. Drag the background music clip to A2 or lower (assuming that you want to keep the original audio with the video clips deployed in the following edit) Q.

3. Press Home to return the playhead to the start of the clip Q.

4. Press M so you have a marker at the start of the clip Q.

5. Play the clip and press M at all major beats. Premiere Pro adds a marker at each click R.

To add clips to the sequence to the beat:

1. In the Project panel, drag the clips into the desired order. Remember that in Icon view, you can skim or play clips and watch them in the Source Monitor to get a better feel for their content. If you'd like, you can also mark In and Out points in the Project panel.

2. Once the clips are in the desired order, select the clips to include in the sequence S.

continues on next page

3. On the bottom right of the Project panel, click the Automate to Sequence ▦ button **S**. The Automate To Sequence dialog opens **T**.

4. In the Ordering menu, choose Sort Order **T**.

5. In the Placement menu, choose At Unnumbered Markers **U**.

6. In the Method menu, choose Overwrite Edit **V**.

7. If you don't want to insert audio or video during the edit, select the Ignore Audio and Ignore Video check boxes **T**. I recommend inserting the audio even if you don't plan to use it, just so it's available if you change your mind.

8. Click OK to close the dialog and complete the edit **T**. Premiere Pro inserts the clips at the markers **W**.

TIP If any clip is shorter than the gap between the markers that Premiere Pro inserted it into, it will leave a gap. So check for gaps after performing this edit.

TIP If you're using the Automate to Sequence tool without markers, select Sequentially in step 5. This will make the Clip Overlap and Transitions options available.

TIP Automate to Sequence is a great technique for setting slideshows to music.

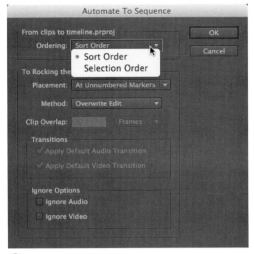

T Choose Sort Order if you sorted your clips in the Project panel, as we did.

U Telling Premiere Pro to use the markers.

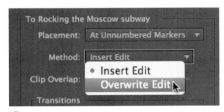

V Choose Overwrite Edit; otherwise, Premiere Pro will push the audio file back in a classic insert edit.

W Your music video, waiting for fine-tuning and MTV.

Advanced Timeline Techniques

By now you should be getting comfortable with the basics of editing. In this chapter, we'll address some advanced editing techniques, particularly trimming, which is a critical skill for all productions. We'll also look at changing the playback speed of your clips, nesting clips, finding clips and sequences in Premiere Pro, and several other topics.

In This Chapter

About the Trimming Modes

Premiere Pro offers five types of trims (regular, ripple, rolling, slip, slide) and three places to perform them (Timeline, Program Monitor, Trim Monitor). Within each interface, there are multiple ways to perform the different types of trims, including with your pointer or via keyboard shortcuts.

To put things in perspective, remember that *Gone with the Wind* editor Hal Kern edited with a razor blade or something similar. I edited for years using just a simple trim tool driven by my pointer. So when you're first starting out, you should look at the various trim tools as enhancements to be considered when needed, not skills you need to learn right away. As you gain experience and your projects get more complex—and the editing more finely tuned and the deadlines more onerous—you'll recognize that these advanced techniques enable you to edit faster and with more precision, which translates to better videos in less time.

Some additional thoughts and comments before getting started: First, unless you unlink the audio and video components of a clip, either permanently (via unlinking) or by pressing the Alt (Windows) or Option (Mac OS) key before selecting a clip, all trims affect both the audio and video components of a linked clip.

Second, while you can perform trims, ripple trims, and rolling trims in the Timeline and Program Monitor, you can perform only slip edits and slide edits on the Timeline. Third, for quick and simple edits, it's tough to beat the Timeline, though the Program Monitor provides superior visual feedback and you can hear the audio while you're trimming.

Finally, you can access many of the same keyboard shortcuts for switching trim modes and fine-tuning your edits when trimming in either the Timeline or Program Monitor. I'll cover editing on the Timeline via your pointer first, then I'll cover editing in the Program Monitor via your pointer, and then I'll address the efficiency and precision options afforded via your keyboard controls.

Regular trimming

The regular trim pointer ◀ is what you get when you hover your pointer near the edge of the beginning or end of a clip on the Timeline without clicking a special tool on the Tools panel or pressing the Control/Command modifier key. It's the basic tool that you'll use a gazillion times even with simple projects, trimming frames from the beginnings and ends of clips in the Timeline.

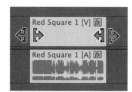

A The four faces of the regular (red) trim pointer.

B You get this error message a lot when editing between clips with the regular trim pointer.

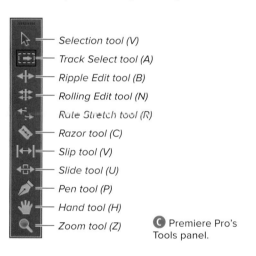

Selection tool (V)

Track Select tool (A)

Ripple Edit tool (B)

Rolling Edit tool (N)

Rate Stretch tool (R)

Razor tool (C)

Slip tool (V)

Slide tool (U)

Pen tool (P)

Hand tool (H)

Zoom tool (Z)

C Premiere Pro's Tools panel.

The first thing to note about the regular trim pointer is that it's red. The second thing is that its orientation changes according to the edit you're about to perform and whether the pointer is positioned at the start or end of the clip. Through the wonders of time-lapse photography, I captured the regular trim pointer in all four possible positions **A**. The two outside pointers point out and indicate that you can drag the edge outward. The two inner pointers point inward and indicate that you can drag the edge inward. As you'll see in many of the screens here, you don't always see the outward-facing pointers when dragging clips outward. Don't mind the pointer—just drag the edge outward. If it goes, it goes.

Although you can always drag edges inward, you can't always drag edges outward. For example, for audio, video, or linked clips, you can only drag outward to the edge of the clip in either direction. When you reach either the end (when trimming to the right) or the beginning (when trimming to the left) of the clip, you can't drag any farther. To make the clip longer, you have to slow playback speed, which you'll learn about later in this chapter. Notable exceptions include still images, titles, and other generated media that don't have a native length; those you can drag as far as you like.

Also, you can't use the regular trim pointer when the clip abuts other clips or the start of the sequence, or when applying the trim outward would move other clips. When this occurs, you'll see the error message "Trim blocked on [name of track]" **B**. When you're blocked in this fashion, you can convert to the Ripple Edit tool, either by pressing the Control/Command key or by choosing the Ripple Edit tool (or pressing B) in the Tools panel **C**. More on how to use the Ripple Edit tool in the next section following these tasks.

To trim a clip on the Timeline with your pointer:

1. Hover your pointer over the edge of the clip you intend to trim. The pointer changes to the appropriate trim pointer. In this case, I'm trimming inward, so the pointer faces in that direction ◀.

2. Drag the edge in the target direction. A yellow box **D** next to the pointer shows the length of the trim: a positive number if the trim is to the right, and a negative number if to the left. The box also shows the duration of the clip in the Timeline. At the same time, the Program Monitor **E** shows the length of the trim and clip duration, and also the original timecode of the frame shown in the Program Monitor. If you wanted to trim to a known frame in the source clip, this information makes it easy to do.

3. Release the pointer when you're done trimming.

> **TIP** The more you are zoomed in to the Timeline, the more precision you have while trimming. If you like to edit when zoomed out, you'll love Premiere Pro's trimming-related keyboard shortcuts, discussed later.

> **TIP** If snapping is making it tough to choose the desired location, you can disable snapping, even while dragging, by pressing the S key.

> **TIP** Sometimes it's useful to park the playhead at the desired trim point. With snapping enabled, it's easy to drag the clip edge to that point and complete the edit. If you use this approach, the trim will include the frame that the playhead is parked on.

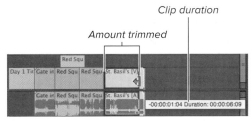

Clip duration

Amount trimmed

D Trimming a clip inward is probably the most frequent edit you'll perform with the regular trim pointer.

Timecode of trim location on the source clip

Amount trimmed

Clip duration on Timeline

E The frame in the Program Monitor is the new trim point, plus you get lots of extra information.

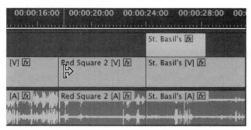

F Choosing the Ripple Edit tool.

G Hover your pointer over the edge of the clip, and the correct pointer will appear. Yellow means ripple trim.

Ripple trim

Whereas the regular trim is like the lift edit in that it affects no other content on any track, the ripple trim functions like the insert edit (when lengthening a clip) or the extract edit (when shortening a clip), either pushing content out of the way or closing any gaps, impacting the track upon which the edit is made and any synced tracks.

Most of the time, you want content to shift on all tracks, which is why you use the ripple trim pointer most frequently for editing between clips in the Timeline. But if you don't, you can disable Sync Lock on the tracks you don't want to ripple.

As you'll see, the ripple trim pointer has all the same shapes and directions as the regular trim pointer, but it's yellow, not red.

To ripple trim in the Timeline with your pointer:

1. Do one of the following:

    ▸ In the Tools panel, click the Ripple Edit tool ⊕⏘ **F**, or press B.

    ▸ With the normal selection pointer selected ⬉, press the Control (Windows) or Command (Mac OS) key before taking step 2 .

2. Hover your pointer over the edge of the clip you intend to trim. The pointer changes to the appropriate trim pointer **G** (and you can release the Control/Command key). In this case, I'm trimming inward so the pointer faces in that direction ⏵.

continues on next page

3. Drag the edge in the target direction.

A yellow box 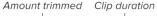 next to the pointer shows the length of the trim, showing a positive number if the trim is to the right and a negative number if the trim is to the left. The box also shows the duration of the clip in the Timeline. In addition, the Program Monitor **I** shows the length of the trim and the clip duration. Two frames are displayed, one showing the new trim point and the other the frame from the clip adjacent to the trim, both with source timecodes. The positioning of the frames will change depending on which side of the clip is being edited and in which direction.

4. Release the pointer when the trim is complete. Note that Premiere Pro closed the gap between the two clips and shifted the title on track V2 over **J**. That is the desired result in this case, but if it weren't, I would have disabled Sync Lock.

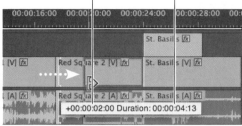

Amount trimmed   Clip duration

H Drag the edge (in this case, to the right).

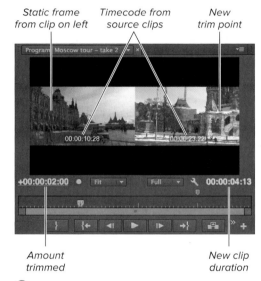

Static frame from clip on left   Timecode from source clips   New trim point

Amount trimmed   New clip duration

I Lots of information in the Program Monitor.

J Premiere Pro closed the gap on V1, and the title on V2 rippled as well.

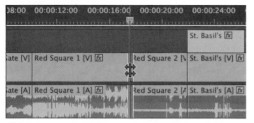

Ⓚ Choosing the Rolling Edit tool.

Ⓛ Hover your pointer between the two clips, and the rolling edit pointer will appear.

Rolling trim

Rolling trims adjust the meeting point between two adjacent clips while keeping the In point of the first clip and the Out point of the second clip static. One clip is shortened and the other lengthened by the same amount, so the overall length of the affected track doesn't change, and there is no rippling.

Use this edit when you want to change how the video flows from one clip to another.

To make a rolling trim in the Timeline with your pointer:

1. In the Tools panel, click the Rolling Edit tool ▦ Ⓚ, or press N.

2. Hover your pointer over the intersection between the two clips you intend to trim. The pointer changes to the rolling edit pointer ▦Ⓛ.

continues on next page

3. Drag the edge in the target direction.

A yellow box 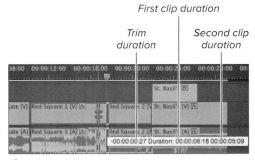 next to the pointer details the length of the trim, showing a positive number if the trim is to the right and a negative number if to the left. The box also shows the duration of the two clips in the Timeline. In addition, the Program Monitor **N** shows the duration of the trim and the clip duration of the second clip. Two frames are displayed, on the left the last frame from the first video (the Out point), and on the right the first frame from the second video (the In point), so you can visualize how the video will flow from one clip to the other. Timecodes for those frames from the source clips are also displayed.

4. Release the pointer when the trim is complete **O**. Compare **O** to **L** and you'll see that the only change was the intersection point between Red Square 1 and Red Square 2. No other In or Out point changed, and the title on V2 did not move.

Slip edit

A slip edit is probably the coolest edit that most new Premiere Pro users (and many experienced users) don't know about. Here's the setup: The source clip you're editing is about 30 seconds long. In the Source Monitor, you marked In and Out points identifying the 5 seconds from that clip you wanted in the project. Then you added the clip to the project.

Now you've decided that the 5 seconds you initially selected aren't the right 5 seconds; you want to move the In points and Out points back by about 6 seconds. You have many options, but the fastest one is to use the Slip tool to drag the content in the clip forward by 6 seconds. To be clear, you're not moving the clip in the Timeline— you're changing the section of the source clip that appears in that clip.

First clip duration

Trim duration | Second clip duration

M Drag the edge (in this case, to the left).

Last frame from first clip (Out point) | Timecode from source clips | First frame from second clip (In point)

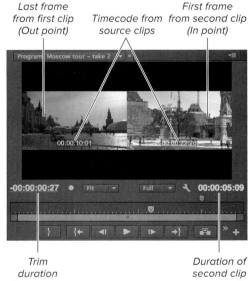

Trim duration | Duration of second clip

N Lots of information in the Program Monitor.

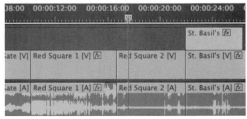

O The completed edit. Nothing shifted except the intersecting point between Red Square 1 and Red Square 2.

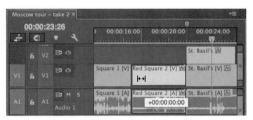

P Choosing the Slip tool.

Q I'm slipping the frames within Red Square 2 about 6 seconds to the right.

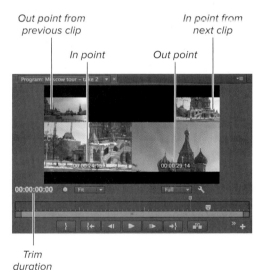

Out point from previous clip

In point from next clip

In point

Out point

Trim duration

R Here's the starting point in the Program Monitor.

In my project, I'm using Red Square 2 as a lead-in to the St. Basil's clip. But the clip ends with a shot of the Cathedral that is duplicative of the St. Basil's clip, which is a better shot. So I want to slip the video over about 6 seconds so it serves as a better lead-in to the St. Basil's clip.

To make a slip edit:

1. In the Tools panel, click the Slip tool ⬌ **P**, or press Y. The pointer changes to the slip pointer ⬌.

2. Click the clip you intend to trim **Q** and drag in the direction you wish to slip the clip.

Imagine the video were physically available in the clip on the Timeline. If you wanted to move to an earlier In and Out point, you would drag the video to the right, shifting the video shown in the Timeline to an earlier section. If you wanted to show a later portion, you would drag it to the left. The yellow box shows the duration of the trim, still at 00:00:00 because I haven't started dragging yet.

The Program Monitor shows the most valuable feedback **R**; in fact, nothing changes in the Timeline at all. The two largest frames in the Program Monitor are the In and Out points of the clip with source timecode shown. Doing the math, the portion of the clip in the Timeline is 5 seconds long (from 24:15 to 29:15). The smaller frames show the frames from the adjacent clips, which won't change during the edit. As you can see in **R**, the St. Basil's tower is visible on the lower right—I want to slip the clip about 6 seconds so that the entrance to the cathedral leads into the following clip of the cathedral itself.

continues on next page

In ⑤, I've shifted the clip forward by 6:10. Now the last frame in the clip is the entrance to St. Basil's, which is the perfect lead-in to the next clip. If you do the math again, you'll see that the portion on the Timeline is still 5 seconds; it's just a different 5 seconds.

3. Release the pointer when the trim is complete ①.

TIP You could always double-click the clip in the Timeline to perform the slip edit in the Source Monitor, but you wouldn't have the useful visualizations shown in the Program Monitor.

Slide edit

A slide edit is the toughest to explain and understand; fortunately, it's one that you'll use infrequently. A slide edit involves three clips on the Timeline ⑪. The In point of the first clip and the Out point of the third clip never change, so there is no ripple on any track.

New In point   New Out point

Trim duration

⑤ Here's the end point; I've dragged the clip by 6:10 to the right.

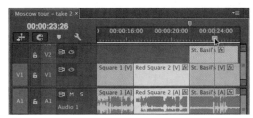

① The completed edit. Nothing has changed on the Timeline.

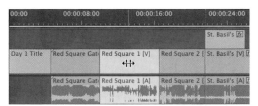

⑪ The starting point of the slide edit's three-clip edit. I'm moving Red Square 1 left and right.

Static frames

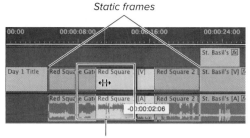

Red Square 1 shifted left

V Shifting Red Square 1 2:06 to the left. Note that the In point of Red Square Gate and the Out point of Red Square 2 don't change in any edits, nor do the duration or In and Out points of Red Square 1.

Static frames

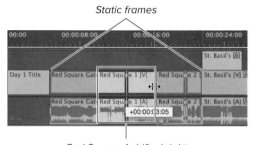

Red Square 1 shifted right

W Shifting Red Square 1 3:05 to the right. Static frames

X Choosing the Slide tool.

In addition, the middle clip doesn't change at all; basically, it's just like a rolling edit except that rather than dragging the intersection of the two clips to one side or the other, you drag the middle clip from one side to the other. Dragging to the left shortens the first clip and lengthens the third **V**; dragging to the right lengthens the first clip and shortens the third **W**, but the overall duration of the three clips never changes.

To make a slide edit in the Timeline:

1. In the Tools panel, click the Slide tool 🔲 **X**, or press U. The pointer changes to the slide pointer ⬌.

2. Click the middle clip of the three, and drag in the desired direction **V**. The yellow box shows the duration of the trim.

3. The Program Monitor again shows the most valuable feedback **Y**.

4. Release the pointer when the trim is complete.

Trim duration   In point middle clip   Out point middle clip

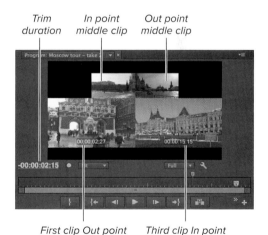

First clip Out point   Third clip In point

Y Again, lots of info in the Program Monitor.

Editing in the Program Monitor

While simple edits are most easily performed on the Timeline, the Program Monitor provides a much richer experience, particularly the ability to hear the audio while trimming your clips. However, only the first three trims—regular, ripple, and rolling—are available in the Program Monitor; you'll have to perform slip edits and slide edits on the Timeline.

Note that in Trim mode, the clip on the left is often referred to as the Out clip (for outgoing), while the clip on the right is the In clip (for incoming).

To access Trim mode:

Do one of the following:

- Press the T key. Premiere Pro moves the playhead to the nearest edit point and opens Trim mode in the Program Monitor.

- Double-click any edit point with the selection, ripple, or rolling edit pointer. As detailed later, your choice of pointer-and-click position will determine the initial mode that Trim mode opens into, though you can easily change editing mode once in Trim mode.

- With the ripple or rolling edit pointer, drag a marquee around an edit point . Trim mode opens to the mode of whatever pointer you used to open Trim mode Ⓑ.

Ⓐ Drag a marquee around the edit point with the ripple pointer or rolling edit pointer, and Trim mode opens in that mode.

Working in Trim mode

Trim mode is pretty straightforward, but let's review the major controls and operating modes. Here are the controls shown in **B**.

- Out Shift counter. How many frames the Out point of the first clip has been adjusted.

- Trim Backward Many (Control/Option+Shift+Left Arrow key). In the Trim tab of the Preferences dialog, which is accessed by choosing Edit > Preferences > Trim (Windows) or Premiere Pro > Preferences > Trim (Mac OS), you can set the Large Trim Offset preference, or how many frames each press of this button (and the corresponding forward button) adjusts the trim.

- Trim Backward (Control/Option+Left Arrow key). Trims backward a frame at a time.

- Apply Default Transition (Shift+D). Inserts the default transition (which starts out as a cross dissolve) between the clips.

- Trim Forward (Control/Option+Right Arrow key). Trims forward one frame.

- Trim Forward Many (Control/Option+Shift+Right Arrow key). Move trim forward by the number of frames specified in the Trim Preferences dialog.

- In Shift counter. How many frames the In point of the second clip has been adjusted.

- Trim mode indicator. The blue line beneath the preview windows indicates the mode. When the blue line is under both windows, it's a rolling edit, and the controls perform a rolling edit between the two clips. When the blue line is under one window, that clip is being edited in either normal or ripple edit mode.

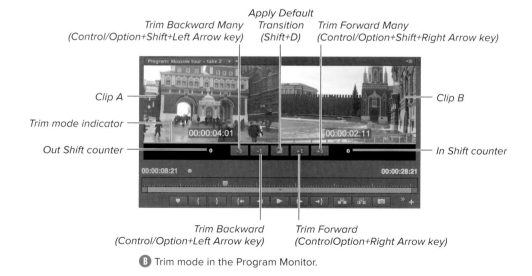

Apply Default
Trim Backward Many   Transition   Trim Forward Many
(Control/Option+Shift+Left Arrow key)   (Shift+D)   (Control/Option+Shift+Right Arrow key)

Clip A   *Clip B*

Trim mode indicator

Out Shift counter   *In Shift counter*

Trim Backward   *Trim Forward*
(Control/Option+Left Arrow key)   *(ControlOption+Right Arrow key)*

B Trim mode in the Program Monitor.

Choosing an editing mode in Trim mode

In Trim mode, you're either editing both clips (rolling edit) or editing one or the other in normal or ripple edit mode. This makes five potential editing modes 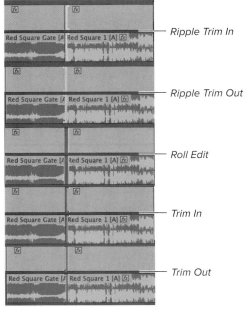, which you can access by right-clicking the intersection between two clips **D**. This looks complicated at first, but if you spend a moment thinking about it, it gets simple fast.

There are two clips at the edit point that you selected: the clip to the left of the edit point (the Out clip) and the clip to the right (the In clip). As you can see, when Ripple Trim Out is selected, you're performing a ripple edit on the clip on the left. Note that whichever direction the yellow bracket is pointing, this trim can go both ways. In contrast, a Trim In would be a normal trim on the clip on the right.

You don't have to use this menu to choose editing modes in Trim mode, but it's a useful tool for understanding the edits available. You should also know that the color and position of the highlight on the Timeline tells you which mode you're in even without right-clicking **C**.

Now that we know the basic editing modes that are available, it's easier to understand how to enter them and switch between them. We'll tackle this next using pointer controls and, later, keyboard shortcuts.

As mentioned, you control the mode you enter in Trim mode by the pointer you use when you click into Trim mode and where you click the edit point. Once you're in edit mode, it's easy enough to switch, but it's faster if you enter in the right mode.

Ripple Trim In

Ripple Trim Out

Roll Edit

Trim In

Trim Out

C Here's what the five editing modes look like on the Timeline, which is the easiest way to know which mode you are in.

D The five editing modes accessible in the Trim monitor (access this menu by right-clicking). You can toggle between them by pressing Shift+T (Windows) or Control+T (Mac OS).

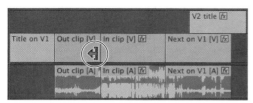

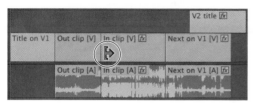

E Hovering over the right edge of the Out clip.

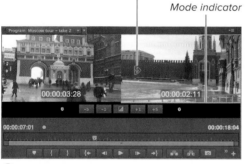

F Hovering over the left edge of the In clip. Then double-click...

Normal trim pointer (red)

Mode indicator

G ...to enter Trim mode in Trim In mode. You can tell this because the blue indicator is beneath the In clip and the trim pointer is red.

To enter Trim mode in normal edit mode:

With the selection pointer ▸ selected, do one of the following:

- Hover your pointer over the right edge of the Out clip **E** and double-click. You'll enter Trim mode in Trim Out mode (not shown).

- Hover your pointer over the left edge of the In clip **F** and double-click. You'll enter Trim mode in Trim In mode **G**.

TIP You can also enter Trim mode in normal edit mode if the Ripple Edit pointer is selected by pressing Control/Command while double-clicking.

To enter Trim mode in Ripple Edit mode:

1. In the Tools panel, click the Ripple Edit tool  **H**, or press B.

2. Do one of the following:

   ▶ Hover your pointer over the right edge of the Out clip **I** and double-click. You'll enter Trim mode in Ripple Trim Out mode **J**.

   ▶ Hover your pointer over the left edge of the In clip **K** and double-click. You'll enter Trim mode in Ripple Trim In mode (not shown).

> **TIP** You can also enter Ripple Trim mode in normal edit mode by pressing Control/Command before double-clicking.

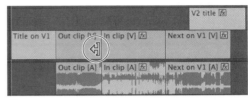

H Choosing the Ripple Edit tool.

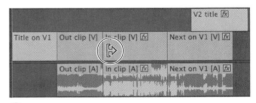

I Hovering over the right edge of the Out clip. Then double-click...

Ripple trim pointer (yellow)

Mode indicator

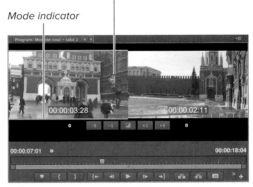

J ...to enter Trim mode in Ripple Trim Out mode.

K Hovering over the left edge of the In clip. If you double-clicked here, you'd enter Ripple Trim In mode.

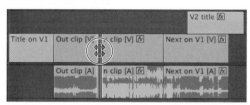

L Choosing the Rolling Edit tool.

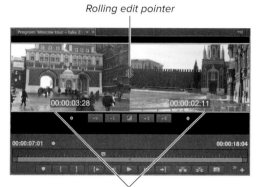

M With the rolling edit pointer, double-click the intersection of the two clips.

Rolling edit pointer

Trim Mode indicator

N Trim mode in Rolling Edit mode.

To enter Trim mode in Rolling Edit mode:

1. In the Tools panel, click the Rolling Edit tool ⊞ **L**, or press N. The pointer changes to the rolling edit pointer ⊞.

2. Double-click the intersection between the two clips you intend to trim **M**. The Trim monitor opens in Rolling Edit mode **N**.

Changing edit modes in the Trim Monitor

Changing edit modes in the Trim Monitor is simple: If you want to trim the In or Out clip, click that clip. If you want to perform a rolling edit, click the intersection between the clips.

Switching from normal edit mode to Ripple Edit mode can be a bit confusing because (at least in the beta versions of code that I used) there is a short time lag between when you press the Control/Command modifier key and when the pointer turns from red to yellow or vice versa. The easiest way to verify the mode you're in is to check the Timeline, since the bracket applied to and between the Out and In clips changes position and color immediately.

To change edit modes in the Trim Monitor via pointer controls:

Do one or more of the following:

- To change from Rolling Edit mode **O** to trim either the Out or In clip, click the desired clip **P**.

- To change into Rolling Edit mode, click the intersection between the clips **O**.

- If necessary, to change from normal edit mode to Ripple Edit mode, Control-click (Windows) or Command-click (Mac OS) the Out or In clip. The pointer will turn from red to yellow in the Trim Monitor and on the Timeline.

- To change from Ripple Edit mode to normal edit mode, Control-click (Windows) or Command-click (Mac OS) the Out or In clip. The pointer will turn from yellow to red in the Trim Monitor and on the Timeline.

Editing with your pointer in Trim mode

Whew! Lots of work to get to the point where we can actually edit in Trim mode. Again, in this section, I focus on editing with your pointer; later, I discuss keyboard shortcuts that apply to trimming in the Timeline and in Trim mode.

Once in Trim mode, you're going to choose your edit, and if it's not a rolling edit (which applies to both clips), you'll choose the clip to edit. Again, in all cases, it's one of the five edits shown in **C** and **D**.

O Trim mode in Rolling Edit mode.

P To edit either clip, just click target clip. Here, I'm in Trim Out mode since the mode indicator is on the Out clip and the pointer is red.

Q In Trim mode. You can tell it's either a Trim In edit or a Ripple Trim In edit because the mode indicator is on the In clip. But which is it?

R A quick glance at the Timeline tells you it's a Ripple Trim In, because yellow equals ripple edit.

Frames trimmed

S You can move the edit point with the controls beneath the preview windows, and the appropriate shift counter details the number of frames shifted.

T Or, you can just drag in the desired direction.

Once you've selected the edit, pressing any of the controls at the bottom of the Trim Monitor carries out the selected edit on the target clip or clips. In addition, you can drag the intersecting point (for rolling edits) or either clip (for normal or ripple edits) to carry out the trim.

One of the coolest features of the Trim Monitor is the ability to edit while previewing. The final task details how to move from edit point to edit point as you work your way through the project.

To edit with your pointer in Trim mode:

1. Select the edit and target clip. In this example, I'm performing a Ripple Trim In **Q**, which means a ripple edit on the incoming clip (on the right). You can't tell this by looking at the Trim Monitor (unless the pointer is hovering over either clip), but a quick glance at the Timeline **R** (yellow bracket on In clip) confirms this.

2. Do one or more of the following:
   ▶ Click the buttons beneath the preview windows to shift the edit point by the corresponding amounts. Note that the In Shift counter or Out Shift counter will show the number of frames trimmed **S**.
   ▶ Click the intersection between the two clips (for a rolling edit) or over either clip (for a normal or ripple edit) and drag in the direction of the edit **T**.

To edit while previewing in Trim mode:

1. In Trim mode, press the Program Monitor's Play-Stop toggle (or press the spacebar) **U**.

2. The Trim monitor enters preview mode **V** and loops playback around the edit point. You can adjust the edit point by using the controls beneath the preview window or their corresponding keyboard shortcuts.

3. To stop playback and return to Trim mode, press the Play-Stop toggle **W**. You'll notice that the appropriate shift counter is updated to reflect all edits performed in preview mode (compare **U** to **W**).

> **TIP** You can control the preroll and postroll time used by Premiere Pro in the Playback Preferences dialog, accessed by choosing Edit > Preferences > Playback (Windows) or Premiere Pro > Preferences > Playback (Mac OS). You can set the Large Trim Offset preference, or how many frames each press of this button (and the corresponding forward button) adjusts the trim.

To move from edit point to edit point:

Once you've completed a trim, do one of the following to move to a different edit point:

- Press the Up Arrow key to move to the previous edit point.

- Press the Down Arrow key to move the next edit point.

U Click Play or press the spacebar to enter preview mode.

V You can adjust the trim position while the video is looping and get instant feedback.

W Back in Trim mode. Note that both shift counters were updated.

A All set up to use keyboard commands to move the edit point.

Trimming with Keyboard Controls

Now that you know the basics, let's explore how to add precision to your edits via keyboard shortcuts and other keyboard commands in both the Timeline and Trim mode. When editing on the Timeline with keyboard shortcuts, it's useful to think about the edit point that you're editing. It's either the right edge (Out point) of the Out clip, the left edge (In point) of the In clip, or both edges (rolling edits).

For rolling edits, you'll choose the edit point with the rolling edit pointer. For trim edits, you'll choose the edit point with your pointer in either normal or Ripple Edit mode. For all edits, you'll use your arrow keys or the numeric keypad on an extended keyboard to move the edit point.

Although you can perform these edits in the Timeline, the Program Monitor doesn't update, so you're editing blind. The best way to use these keyboard techniques is by opening the Trim Monitor so you get the visual feedback.

We'll also look at how you can loop playback on the Timeline and adjust your trim live while the video is playing back.

To trim via keyboard shortcuts:

1. Choose the desired edge and trim mode, and double-click the edit point to open Trim mode. A shows a rolling edit.

continues on next page

2. Do any or all of the following:

▸ Press Control/Option+Left Arrow key to move the edit point a single frame to the left. Repeat as necessary.

▸ Press Control/Option+Right Arrow key to move the edit point a single frame to the right. Repeat as necessary.

▸ Press Control/Option+Shift+Left Arrow key to move the edit point backward by multiple frames. Repeat as necessary.

▸ Press Control/Option+Shift+Right Arrow key to move the edit point forward by multiple frames. Repeat as necessary.

Note that the shift counters **B** in Trim mode update with your edit.

To trim using the numeric keypad on an extended keyboard:

1. Choose the desired edge and trim mode, and double-click the edit point to open Trim mode. **C** shows a Ripple Trim Out.

2. Press the + key on the extended keyboard. Premiere Pro blanks out the timecode box on the upper left of the Timeline.

3. Type in the number of frames you'd like to shift the clip; use the − key to shift the clip to the left **D**.

4. Press Enter (Windows) or Return (Mac OS). Premiere Pro shifts the edit point by the specified duration **E**.

TIP Note that you don't need to enter the plus sign (+) first to enter a positive adjustment with the numeric keypad; you can just type in a number. You do have to enter a minus sign (−) first to enter a negative adjustment.

B Both shift counters were updated to reflect the edits, which totaled 46 frames to the right.

C Setting up for the Ripple Trim Out.

D Type the desired adjustment; use the minus sign key (−) to shift the edit point to the left.

E Mission accomplished: The Out point for the Out clip was adjusted 30 frames to the right, rippling the content on that track as well as on any synced tracks.

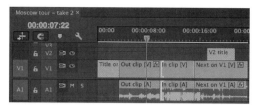

 You can trim and preview during playback by making sure that the playhead is in front of the edit point and pressing Shift+K.

To loop playback around the trim and edit while previewing on the Timeline:

1. Choose the desired edge and trim mode. **F** shows a Ripple Trim In.

2. Press Shift+K. If the Loop button is selected, Premiere Pro starts to loop video playback around the edit point.

3. Adjust the edit point during playback using the keyboard shortcuts detailed in the previous task. You can also use the pointer, though it's much more clunky.

Look Ma, No Pointer

Over the last few updates, Premiere Pro's ability to trim without the pointer has been significantly enhanced.

- Choose an edit point. Press T, and Premiere Pro chooses the closest editing point and enters Trim mode.

- Choose a trim mode. Toggle through the available modes by pressing Shift+T (Windows) or Control+T (Mac OS).

- Trim. Trim using the keyboard shortcuts identified in the tasks, or press Control+Left/ Right Arrow (Windows) or Option+Left/Right Arrow (Mac OS) (add the Shift key to edit multiple frames).

- Trim while previewing. You can do this with keyboard shortcuts both in Trim mode and on the Timeline.

- Trim via the JKL keys. In Trim mode, use the J, K, and L keys to trigger playback; choose the edit point by pressing K during playback. You can also keep the K key pressed and adjust the edit point forward and backward by pressing the J and L keys.

Producing Split Edits

Split edits, or L- and J-cuts, are popular techniques that involve transitions where the audio is heard before the video is seen (J-cut) or where the audio lingers after the video has changed to the next clip or scene (L-cut). The J-cut and L-cut designations come from what the Timeline looks like after the edit is performed.

For example, in my sequence on the Moscow subway, I want the sound of an incoming train to be heard before the train appears. Though the setup for the split edits will vary by type, you'll use the Rolling Edit tool on just the audio tracks to make it happen. Here's how.

To produce a rolling edit:

1. In the Tools panel, click the Rolling Edit tool ⊞ , or press N.

2. Hover your pointer over the intersection between the two audio clips you intend to trim. The pointer changes to the rolling edit pointer ⊞.

3. Alt-click (Windows) or Option-click (Mac OS) the intersection between the two video files. The rolling edit will be applied solely to the selected video tracks 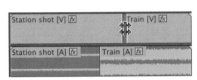.

4. Drag the edge in the target direction. Dragging the video to the right will create a J-cut 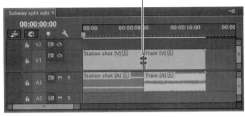; dragging to the left will create an L-cut 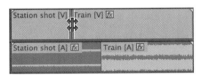.

   Typically, you'll have to fine-tune the edit to make it perfect, but this is the basic procedure.

Ⓐ Choosing the Rolling Edit tool.

Video only selected

Ⓑ Alt/Option-click just the intersection between the video clips.

Ⓒ Drag the video to the right to create the J-cut.

Ⓓ Or to the left to create the L-cut.

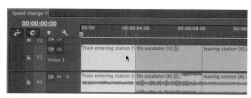

A The starting point. Note that the "Train entering station" clip is 4 seconds long.

B Right-click and choose Speed/Duration to open the Clip Speed/Duration dialog.

C The controls are straightforward.

Changing Clip Speed

Fast and slow motion are very common effects that are used frequently in many projects. There are at least four ways to change clip speed in Premiere Pro, one of which is outlined in the four-point edit task in Chapter 5.

In this section, we'll discuss two alternatives: the Clip Speed/Duration dialog and the Rate Stretch tool. These two tools are different means to get to a similar result, which is a clip with a uniform speed change throughout. That is, rather than playing at 100%, the clip plays at 200% speed (fast motion) or 50% speed (slow motion) through the entire clip.

There is one other technique, called time remapping, that lets you change the speed of a clip multiple times and transition the speed change in and out. That technique requires an understanding of how to create and adjust keyframes and is discussed in Chapter 8.

To change clip speed using the Clip Speed/Duration dialog:

1. Click the target clip **A**. In this case I'll be slowing down the "Train entering station" clip to 50% speed.

2. Right-click and choose Speed/Duration. The Clip Speed/Duration dialog opens **B**.

3. Type the desired speed or duration. (Duration is useful when you're trying to fill a specific duration **C**.)

continues on next page

4. Select the Reverse Speed check box to make the clip run in reverse **C**.

5. If the clip has audio that you intend to use in the project, select the Maintain Audio Pitch check box **C**.

6. Select the Ripple Edit check box to ripple the edit through other clips on that track and synced tracks. If you don't choose this option, Premiere Pro will either leave a gap (when making the clip faster) or won't extend the edit beyond the original Out point (when slowing the clip down) **C**.

7. Click OK to close the dialog.

As you can see **D**, the "Train entering station" clip is now 8 seconds long, and the clip speed indicator on the clip shows 50%.

Working with the Rate Stretch tool

While the Clip Speed/Duration dialog is ideal for simple, global changes to clip speed, sometimes you need to adjust the timing of a clip to match another clip. For these types of edits, the Rate Stretch tool is perfect.

Here's the setup **E**. In the narration on track V2, I'm talking about St. Basil's Cathedral through the position of the playhead at 20 seconds. Unfortunately, the St. Basil's clip that I'm describing is shorter than the description, so I want to extend the St. Basil's clip to the 20-second mark. I could do the math and use the Clip Speed/Duration dialog, but the Rate Stretch tool is faster and more intuitive.

D The clip is now 8 seconds long, and the speed indicator reads 50%.

E The narration talks about St. Basil's until 20 seconds in. I need to extend the St. Basil's clip to match.

F Choosing the Rate Stretch tool.

G Drag the clip to the desired length.

H Premiere Pro adjusts the clip speed so that the clip fills the designated gap.

To adjust clip speed with the Rate Stretch tool:

1. In the Tools panel, click the Rate Stretch tool ![icon] (or press R) **F**. The pointer changes to the rate stretch pointer ![icon].

2. Drag the edge of the target clip to the desired location **G**.

3. Release the pointer. Premiere Pro adjusts clip speed automatically to fit the dragged area **H**.

TIP After adjusting duration with the Rate Stretch tool, you can open the Clip Speed/Duration dialog and select the Maintain Audio Pitch check box to maintain the clip's audio pitch.

TIP The Rate Stretch tool won't push clips out of the way when extending in either direction. If you want to use it, you'll have to clear the track space first.

Working with Nested Clips

A nested sequence is when you insert one sequence into another. When you nest a sequence into another, the nested sequence looks like a single linked clip, even though there are multiple elements. For the most part, you can treat the nested sequence just like any other source clip, adding effects, trimming, changing speed, and the like.

For example, I built a short intro video for all Day 1 clips . There are three video tracks B, one containing the background title, one containing five 1-second high-lights of the videos from that day, and the title on V3 containing the picture-in-picture frame around the video. I created a nested sequence from this intro, called Day 1 intro, which I can insert it into other sequences, where it looks a single clip C.

Sometimes you'll use nested clips because it's required by the workflow. A good exam-ple is multicam editing, where you select camera angles in a sequence consisting of a nested sequence containing the synced camera angles.

Other times you'll use a nested sequence for convenience. When I produce a two-act ballet, it's easiest to edit each act sepa-rately and then nest them together into a single sequence to render.

The title in A is another good example; I'll be producing five separate videos from the first day in Moscow, and all will use the same intro. I could copy and paste the intro from video to video, but the nested clip is faster and easier to work with in the Timeline.

In addition, because the nested sequence is a single clip, you can apply the same effect to all clips and even adjust the

A The beautiful intro clip I want to insert into all my Day 1 videos. Nesting makes it simple.

Intro to be nested

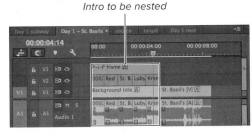

B These clips make up the intro I want to reuse, so I'll create a nested sequence from them and call it Day 1 Intro.

Nested intro

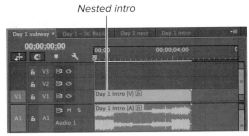

C When I nest the sequence it looks (and pretty much acts) just like a standard clip.

effect over time. For example, using the Color Balance effect, I converted the intro to black and white at the start, and then transitioned to full color over the 5-second clip. Doing this with the seven clips in the nested sequence is possible, but it would take many minutes of meticulous editing. With the nested sequence, it's a breeze.

Similarly, when you're working with stacked clips on a Timeline, as in Ⓑ, sometimes it's easier to apply a transition to a nested sequence rather than the individual clips, or to fade the stacked clips in and out. You'll see this in a task here.

Nesting clips has some consequences and limitations. (For the purposes of this discussion, the "source" sequence is the original sequence, and the "nested" sequence is the source sequence nested in another sequence.) First, and this is subtle, the video inserted into a sequence assumes the configuration of the sequence when that sequence is nested. So if you insert 1080p videos into a DV sequence (720x480) and then try to nest the DV sequence into a 1080p sequence, you have to zoom the sequence to fit and the HD resolution is gone, just as if you had rendered out at 720x480 and then reimported the rendered file. This dynamic complicates producing for DVD and Blu-ray, because DVDs look slightly sharper (in my experience) when produced at 720x480 rather than at full HD resolution and scaled down for export. See bit.ly/PP_preset for examples and optimal workflows for DVD/Blu-ray production.

The same holds true for high-resolution images. If you edit high-resolution images in a 720x480 sequence and then embed that sequence in a 1080p sequence, it's just as if your images were native 720x480.

Second, effects applied in the source sequence don't appear in the Effect Controls panel of the nested sequence. The effects are applied, but you don't have access to the controls from the nested sequence—again, just as if you had rendered the source sequence and reinserted it into the new sequence. This doesn't cause any problems—you can reapply the same effects to the nested sequence and adjust further. Or, you can adjust the effect in the source sequence, and all changes will automatically update where the sequence is nested. I just spent significant time scratching my head looking for the color correction I knew I had applied to the source sequences, and I don't want you doing the same.

Third, the duration of the nested clip is determined by the duration of the source clips within the nested clip. My 5-second nested intro is 5 seconds long because there are 5 seconds of content in the source sequence. I can't drag it to any greater length, though I could adjust the clip speed to make it longer.

You nest a sequence in one of two ways. Any time you drag a sequence into a sequence, you're nesting the sequence. You can also create a nested sequence on the Timeline, which lets you instantly harvest all the benefits of nested sequences.

Finally, in all pre-CS7 versions, the only way to add a nested sequence to a new sequence was as a single clip. With CS7, you can insert the nested clip as individual clips, which I demonstrate here.

Here's the workflow I demonstrate in the following tasks: I create a cool intro and think, "Hey, I could use this in all my Day 1 clips." So I create the nested sequence. Then, I drag the nested sequence into another Day 1 clip both as a single clip and by its components.

To create a nested sequence on the Timeline:

1. Select the clips to insert into the sequence.

   In the figure I'm dragging a marquee around the selected clips  **D**.

2. Right-click any of the selected clips, and choose Nest **E**. The Nested Sequence Name dialog opens **F**.

3. Type the desired name and click OK. Premiere Pro creates the sequence in the Project panel **G** and replaces the clips on the Timeline with the nested sequence.

> **TIP** To access the original clips in the new sequence (Day 1 Intro), double-click the sequence to open it in the Timeline.

> **TIP** To access the original frame from the source clip, press **Control+Shift+F (Windows)** or **Shift+T (Mac OS)**.

D Dragging to select the clips to nest.

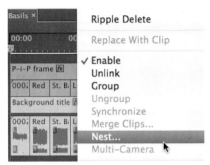

E Right-click and choose Nest.

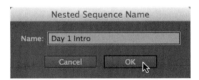

F Name the new sequence.

The new nested sequence

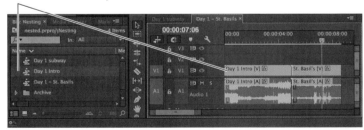

G Premiere Pro creates the new sequence and inserts it into the original sequence, replacing the source clips.

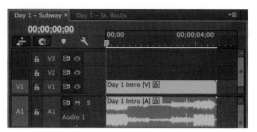

H Drag the sequence from the Project panel to the target clip.

I Premiere Pro inserts the sequence, creating a nested sequence.

To nest a sequence in a sequence:

1. Open the target sequence in the Timeline. Here I'm reusing the new intro in the Day 1 Subway video.

2. Drag the sequence into the target sequence and release **H**. Premiere Pro nests the sequence into the target **I**.

TIP Note that you can load a sequence into the Source Monitor by dragging it from the Project panel to the Source Monitor. From there, you can use either buttons or keyboard shortcuts to insert the sequence into the sequence.

Chapter Points and Waveforms

For me, one of the most welcome nesting-related new features of Premiere Pro is that waveforms now appear under nested sequences. In CS6 and previous versions, the audio files came through (of course), but there were no waveforms, so you were working blind from an audio perspective. Given that waveforms were the best clue as to when a song or act finished (applause and silence are always easy to find), this will make it much simpler to add chapter points with nested sequences.

In addition, chapter points also carry over from the original source sequence, but only when you drag the original sequence into another sequence. If you create a separate nested sequence, the chapter points won't follow. In most longform productions where you're likely to insert chapter points, this doesn't matter, because there's typically no reason to create a separate nested sequence. But if your chapter points disappear unexpectedly, now you know why.

To insert a sequence as original clips:

1. In the Project panel, click the sequence to nest **J**.

2. Open the target sequence in the Timeline. Again, I'm reusing the new intro in the Day 1 Subway video.

3. On the top left of the Timeline, toggle the "Insert and overwrite sequences as nests or individual clips" button ![button] to the up position (the lighter color) **K**.

4. Note that all the video tracks in the track targeting area of the Timeline become active **L**. If desired, you can change the track targeting. I'm inserting the title on V3 of the source sequence on V4 in the target.

5. Drag the sequence into the target sequence and release **M**. Premiere Pro inserts the individual clips into the sequence, placing the "P-i-P frame" title on V4.

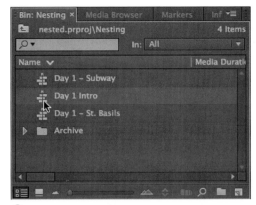

J Click the sequence to insert.

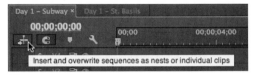

K Toggle this (new in CS7) button to the up position.

L This activates track targeting. I'll move the title on V3 in the source clip to V4 in the target.

M Drag the source clip over and release, and Premiere Pro inserts the individual clips, not the nested sequence.

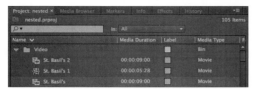

A Right-click the clip and choose Reveal in Project.

B St. Basil's in the Project panel.

C To find the match frame, choose the frame in the Timeline or Program Monitor and press F.

D Premiere Pro opens the clip to that frame in the Source Monitor.

Finding Stuff

Projects involve multiple files from multiple places stored in multiple bins, and it's important to know how and where to find things when you need them. Here are the ways you can locate content and other project elements from Premiere Pro.

Finding match frames

When you've deployed content in the Timeline, often you may want to locate the source clip or find the "match frame" within the source clip, which is the frame then showing in the Program Monitor.

To find a clip on the Timeline in the Project panel:

Right-click the clip and choose Reveal in Project **A**. Premiere Pro highlights the clip in the Project panel **B**.

To find a clip's match frame:

Move the playhead to the desired frame in the Timeline or Program Monitor **C**, and press F. Premiere Pro opens the source clip in the Source Monitor, with the playhead on the match frame **D**.

Finding other project elements

Here are ways to find project elements in the Project panel or on your hard drive.

To find a sequence in the Project panel:

In the Timeline, right-click the sequence tab and choose Reveal Sequence in Project 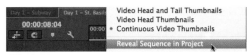. Premiere Pro highlights the sequence in the Project panel.

To find a source file on your hard drive:

In the Project panel, right-click the clip and choose Properties . Premiere Pro opens the Properties window , which shows the file location.

To reveal the clip in Adobe Bridge or Windows Explorer (Windows)/Finder (Mac OS):

In the Project panel, right-click the clip and choose Reveal in Adobe Bridge, Reveal in Windows Explorer (Windows), or Reveal in Finder (Mac OS) . The program runs and shows the file location.

To reveal the project file in Windows Explorer (Windows) or Finder (Mac OS):

In the Project panel, right-click any clip and choose Reveal Project in Windows Explorer (Windows) or Reveal Project in Finder (Mac OS) . The program runs and shows the file location.

E Can't find your sequence in the Project panel? Try this.

F Right-click the target clip (St. Basil's 2 in this case) and choose Properties.

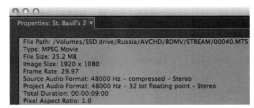

G The Properties window opens, showing the file's location.

H Right-click, and choose the program to reveal the file in.

I Here's how you find the project file on your hard drive.

8

Adding Motion to Clips

You've got your rough cut in place; it's time to start refining and polishing. In this chapter, you learn about Premiere Pro's Motion controls, which are critical to the resizing and reframing that accompany all video projects, but especially those involving HD video produced for lower-resolution playback like DVD and streaming.

You'll also learn about keyframes, which unlock a world of animated effects. Keyframes seem hard to grasp at first, but once you get them, you get them, and your creative capabilities skyrocket. Once you've got keyframes under your belt, you can address time remapping, which is the most polished technique for changing the speed of your clips on the Timeline.

Not to gush, but it's exciting to think how much better an editor you'll be after you work through this chapter.

In This Chapter

Working with Premiere Pro's Motion Controls

Premiere Pro's Motion controls are fixed effects, meaning they're applied to every clip automatically; you don't have to apply them manually like other effects. Besides the Motion adjustments, there are five other fixed effects: Opacity and Time Remapping for video, and Volume, Channel Volume, and Panner for audio.

To view Motion controls:

1. Click the target clip in the Timeline.

2. Do one of the following:

   ▸ Click the Effect Controls tab Ⓐ.

   ▸ Choose Window > Effect Controls (or press Shift+5).

   The Effect Controls panel opens Ⓑ.

3. In the Effect Controls panel, click the Motion disclosure triangle to open those controls Ⓑ.

4. In the upper right of the Effect Controls panel, click the Show/Hide Timeline View triangle to close the Effect Controls Timeline Ⓑ, which we'll return to later in the chapter. This leaves the Motion controls open without the Timeline Ⓒ.

Scaling and reframing an HD clip using the Motion controls

Scaling and reframing using Motion controls is a very common task when using digital pictures in projects or when you shoot in HD for deployment at a smaller resolution. I'll demonstrate how to work with a 1080p video edited in a 720p sequence, which is how I produce most of

Ⓐ One way to open the Effect Controls panel.

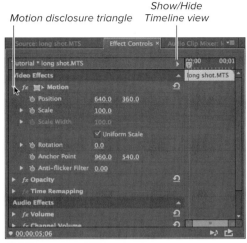

Motion disclosure triangle   *Show/Hide Timeline view*

Ⓑ The Effect Controls panel.

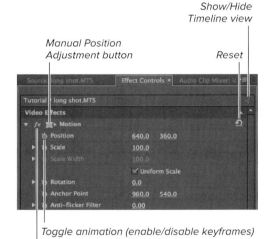

Manual Position Adjustment button   *Show/Hide Timeline view*   *Reset*

Toggle animation (enable/disable keyframes)

Toggle the effect on or off

Ⓒ Some of the unlabeled moving parts in the Effect Controls panel.

my tutorials, but the issues would be the same for high-res digital photos. Either way, you have to adjust the size and position of the high-resolution video or image within the smaller-resolution sequence.

I detail why I prefer to edit in a sequence setting that matches my target in the "Choosing Project Resolution" sidebar. For a 720p tutorial, I would create a 720p sequence, and click No when Premiere Pro asks if I want to change the sequence settings to match the HD clip I insert.

Depending on how you set your preferences, you may need to perform one additional task to access the full resolution of your video or your digital pictures. In the General Preferences (Edit > Preferences > General [Windows] or Premiere Pro > Preferences > General [Mac OS]), there's a Scale to Frame Size setting.

When Scale to Frame Size is enabled, as it is by default, Premiere Pro automatically scales inserted videos and still images to the sequence resolution when they're inserted into a Timeline. It's actually a convenient feature much of the time, but it can be confusing. When it's enabled, your content is scaled to the sequence resolution. In the case of the example I'll be demonstrating, this means that the 1080p video inserted into the 720p sequence looks and acts like a 720p video. Fortunately, there's a quick fix, which I'll detail in a second.

The Most Critical Motion Controls

Let's identify the most relevant configuration options in the Motion controls.

- Manual Position Adjustment. Click this button, and Premiere Pro places a bounding box around the video in the Program Monitor, which you can use to manually position the video.

- Position adjustments. Horizontal (x) and vertical (y) adjustments. Coordinates are based on the position of the middle pixel from the upper-left corner.

- Scale. This controls the size of the video, which by default is 100%, or full size. When you deselect the Uniform Scale check box, enabling separate adjustments for height and width, the Scale label changes to Scale Height and the Scale Width control becomes active. Obviously, adjusting height and width separately can distort the image.

- Rotation. Enables rotating the image around the z-axis. This value can extend beyond plus or minus 360 degrees to enable motion effects where, for example, you rotate the clip four times during playback.

- Anchor Point. Defines the point around which the clip rotates. By default, it's the center of the frame (the video clip used in this task is 1080p) so the video rotates in place.

- Anti-flicker filter. Useful for images with fine lines and other detail; applies a slight blur filter. Use when you see flickering in your images, but watch for excessive blurriness.

- Toggle the effect on or off. Does what the name suggests, allowing you to preview with and without the filter applied.

- Reset. Resets all configuration options to their default.

- Toggle animation (enable/disable keyframes). As you'll learn, keyframes let you animate the effects you apply.

For example, in ⓓ, the video is scaled to 100%. I've clicked the Manual Position Adjustment button, so there's a bounding box around the video in the Program Monitor on the right. Even though the video is 1080p and the sequence 720p, the video is 100% of the sequence resolution because it was automatically scaled to the frame size.

I detail how to fix the problem in the next task. Once the issue resolved, Premiere Pro should look like ⓔ. Now the bounding box shows the full resolution of the video, and you've got room to pan around the image and to make the adjustments you'll be performing in the tasks to come.

While we have both these views in front of us, let's explore what's ahead in the tasks. As you can see in ⓓ, I framed the video loosely in this shot, which was filmed from a tripod without a camera operator. So, I want to use Premiere Pro's Motion controls to zoom in.

On the other hand, at a true 100% scaling ⓔ, the image is too close and improperly framed. So, I want to change both the scaling and the positioning.

One final point before we attack the specific tasks: 100% is the magic number when scaling your video. As long as the value is 100% or less, you have actual pixels behind every pixel of output, which means quality is high. Once you go beyond 100%, Premiere Pro has to make the detail up. While Premiere Pro has great algorithms for doing so, once you go beyond 120% or so, pixelation, or a blocky appearance, can become a problem.

ⓓ In this screen, the 1080p file in the Timeline is the same size as the Program Monitor preview for the 720p sequence. Where's the extra resolution?

ⓔ Here it is. After disabling Scale to Frame Size, the 1080 video looks larger than the 720p sequence.

F Here's how to change **D** to **E**.

G Drag the numbers to a different value.

H Or you can click the coordinate box to make it active and type a new number.

I That's better.

To disable Scale to Frame Size:

Right-click the video and choose Scale to Frame Size **F** so that the check mark disappears. Premiere Pro scales the image to its full resolution.

TIP This works the same way with still images, and you'll use this a lot when working with high-resolution source images.

To reframe the video via the position controls:

In the Effect Controls panel, do one of the following:

- Hover your pointer over the horizontal or vertical adjustment until it becomes a two-headed drag pointer ![icon]. Drag the coordinates to the desired values **G**.

- Click the horizontal or vertical coordinate to make it active. Then type the desired value and press Enter (Windows) or Return (Mac OS) **H**.

Premiere Pro adjusts the frame to the new position. Compare **I** with **E**.

TIP The bounding box appears only when you've clicked the Manual Position Adjustment button, as shown in the next task.

TIP You can use the Tab key to move from the horizontal to the vertical adjustment.

TIP Note that I'm working in a cramped space to make the screenshots look better. In real editing, on my 31" screen, I would adjust the resolution shown in the Program Monitor and the Program Monitor's size to show the complete bounding box (if I needed to see it).

To reframe the video using manual position adjustment:

1. In the Effect Controls panel, to the left of the Motion label, click the Manual Position Adjustment ▦ button ⓙ.

   Premiere Pro presents the bounding box around the video, and the anchor point icon appears in the middle of the frame.

2. Click anywhere within the frame and drag the video to the desired position ⓚ. The horizontal and vertical coordinates update as you position the video.

   Premiere Pro adjusts the frame to the new positioning. Compare ⓚ with ⓔ.

   TIP In all these screens, the Program Monitor resolution is set to 25% because I wanted to show the bounding box, which helps demonstrate the principles discussed. If you don't have sufficient space around the Program Monitor, as when resolution is set to Fit, the bounding box won't appear, though the anchor point icon in the middle always will.

ⓙ Click here to show the bounding box.

ⓚ Click the anchor point icon in the middle, and drag the frame to the right location.

L Drag the scale to the desired value.

M Click and enter the number directly.

N If you deselect the Uniform Scale check box, you can adjust Height and Width separately. Note the disclosure triangles that open sliders if you prefer using them to the other techniques.

To adjust scale via the Scale controls:

In the Effect Controls panel, do one of the following:

- Hover your pointer over the Scale adjustment until it becomes a two-headed drag pointer. Drag the coordinate to the desired value **L**.

- Click the Scale coordinate to make it active. Then type the desired value and press Enter (Windows) or Return (Mac OS) **M**.

- In the Effect Controls panel, to the left of the Motion Label, click the Manual Position Adjustment button . Then drag any corner of the bounding box until the scale is correct.

TIP To scale the video disproportionately, deselect the Uniform Scale check box **N**. Adjusting the Height and Width separately has occasionally been useful in some of my projects to correct aspect ratio distortion present in source footage, but try adjusting the aspect ratio in the Interpret Footage dialog first (right-click the video in the Project panel and choose Modify > Interpret Footage).

TIP In addition to dragging the coordinates directly or typing in the desired value, you can click the disclosure triangle to expose a slider that allows you to make the same adjustment **N**.

To adjust scale using manual position adjustment:

1. In the Effect Controls panel, to the left of the Motion label, click the Manual Position Adjustment ▦ button ①. Premiere Pro presents the bounding box around the video, and the anchor point icon appears in the middle of the frame.

2. Click any box in the bounding box and the pointer becomes the double-headed drag icon ▦. Drag the box to the desired scale ①. With the Uniform Scale check box selected, you can adjust height and width using any box. When it's deselected, you can adjust width with boxes on the sides, height with boxes on the bottom and top, and both axes with boxes in the corners; press the Shift key to make the adjustment proportional.

Adjusting rotation and opacity

Let's segue to two other fixed effects: Rotation (which is one of the Motion controls) and Opacity. Here we'll be working with the venerable Peachpit logo.

Normally, you'd shrink the logo and place it unobtrusively in one of the lower corners, but that would make for a challenging screenshot. But to enhance the learning experience, I'll work with the logo at full size for the next few tasks. We'll rotate the logo a bit, and then adjust its opacity so that it's less jarring.

In addition to configuring effects in the Effect Controls panel, you can also configure them in the Timeline, as you'll see in the third and final task.

① To adjust clip scale, drag a box inward or outward as necessary.

Choosing Project Resolution

By now you're starting to see some of the benefits of editing in a sequence that matches your target output resolution, particularly when shooting in HD. As an example, let's discuss a project shot at 1080p for distribution at 720p.

If you edit in a 720p sequence and need to reframe for any reason, you have the pixels and so won't need to scale beyond 100% (which degrades quality) to accomplish this. In fact, one of the editors of this book, Stephen Nathans-Kelly, wrote a great tutorial on this—"Creating a Two-Camera Interview from a One-Camera Shoot," which you can find at bit.ly/twocamera. It details how to create a two-camera look from a single HD camera shoot by using a 640x360 sequence setting. When you shoot at high resolution and edit at your target, you get much more editing flexibility.

As mentioned, I've also found that producing video bound for DVD in a 720x480 sequence produces slightly higher quality than producing using a 1080 sequence (see bit.ly/PP_preset). Shooting big and editing at your target enables better quality and more editing flexibility. Need I say more?

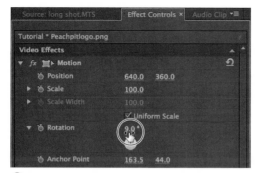

P Dragging the Rotation value to the desired value.

Q Or click to make it active and type the desired value.

R You can rotate up to 90 times for creating rotating effects.

Anchor point

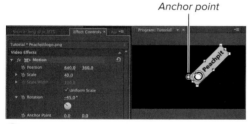

S Changing the anchor point lets you rotate the clip around a different axis.

To rotate a clip:

1. Click to select the clip in the Timeline.

2. In the Effect Controls panel, do one of the following:

   ▸ Hover your pointer over the Rotation coordinate until it becomes a two-headed drag pointer ██. Drag the coordinate to the desired value P.

   ▸ Click the Rotation coordinate to make it active. Then type the desired value and press Enter (Windows) or Return (Mac OS) Q.

TIP The rotation adjustment works great to fix video that was shot slightly off-kilter (usually because the tripod was improperly adjusted at the shoot). Just adjust rotation by one or two degrees in the right direction, and the tilt is gone. Note that if your sequence setting matches your camera resolution, you'll have to zoom the video slightly to make this adjustment.

TIP In the context of a static rotation adjustment, it never makes sense to adjust more than + or – 359 degrees. If you're trying to create a spinning effect with keyframes, however, you can adjust rotation up to 90 times + or – R.

TIP You can adjust the anchor point to create custom rotation effects. In S I've set the anchor point at 0,0—the upper-left corner of the logo. This lets me rotate the logo around that anchor point rather than simply spinning it around the center.

To adjust opacity in the Effect Controls panel:

1. Click to select the clip in the Timeline.

2. In the Effect Controls panel, click the disclosure triangle next to Opacity to open those controls 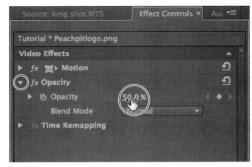.

3. Do one of the following:

   ▶ Hover your pointer over the Opacity coordinate until it becomes a two-headed drag pointer. Drag the coordinate to the desired value.

   ▶ Click the Opacity coordinate to make it active. Then type the desired value and press Enter (Windows) or Return (Mac OS) .

4. Make sure the Blend Mode menu is set to Normal.

T Click the disclosure triangle to open the Opacity controls, then drag to the desired value.

U Or click the coordinate to make it active, and type the desired value.

(A) Showing keyframes in the Timeline.

Keyframe graph

(B) Click the target track in the track header, and increase the size with your scroll wheel until you can see the keyframe graph.

Adjusting Effects in the Timeline

In addition to configuring effects in the Effect Controls panel, you can also adjust effects in the Timeline. As you'll learn as you get more projects under your belt, some effects are easier to adjust in the Timeline, while others are better configured in the Effect Controls panel. Opacity is one effect I almost exclusively adjust in the Timeline, so let's explore how that works.

First we'll have to get the Timeline ready for effect configuration, then we'll choose and set the Opacity adjustment.

To show keyframes on the Timeline:

1. In the Timeline, click the Timeline Display Settings icon 🔧 , and choose Show Video Keyframes (A)

2. Let's make the track we'll be adjusting bigger. Click the track header (B), and use the scroll wheel on your mouse to expand the track until you see the line that represents the effect configuration value. This is called the keyframe graph.

> **TIP** I've got thumbnails disabled because it makes the screenshots clearer, but I usually work with them showing.

To adjust opacity on the Timeline:

1. Click the FX icon 🎬 on the video track **C**, which opens a menu that lets you choose which effect to configure. Choose Opacity > Opacity **C**.

2. Hover your pointer over the keyframe graph until the two-headed drag vertical pointer 🔼 appears **D**.

   A yellow box beneath the pointer displays the timecode at the pointer position, identifies the effect being configured (Opacity:Opacity), and indicates the current value. The value is 50 because of the adjustment made two tasks ago in the Effect Controls panel. Whether you configure the effect in the Timeline or in the Effect Controls panel, there's just one value **D**.

3. Drag the graph to the desired value, and Premiere Pro adjusts the value for the entire clip.

C Choosing the Opacity effect to edit via the keyframe graph.

D Note that the Opacity value on the Timeline matches that in the Effect Controls panel.

A Setting up to create a keyframe at the one-second mark.

Peachpitlogo.png [fx]

B Press the Control/Command key to convert the pointer to a cross.

Working with Keyframes

Keyframes are an incredibly powerful feature in Premiere Pro. They allow you to animate a range of effects, from motion to opacity to audio volume. Simply stated, a keyframe is a point where you set a value.

Say you want to fade-in a clip from black over one second. You set a keyframe at the very start of the clip, with the Opacity value at 0 for completely dark. One second in, you set a keyframe with an Opacity value of 100. Premiere Pro automatically interpolates the appropriate Opacity value over the intervening frames, so at frame 15 (in a 30p sequence), the Opacity value will be 50%.

Since we've been working with opacity, let's fade in a clip using keyframes in the Timeline. If you haven't read the section "Adjusting Effects in the Timeline," please do so, and zoom in to your Timeline so you can comfortably see and edit the first few seconds.

Once we accomplish the fade in, we'll return to the Effect Controls panel and add motion to a clip there.

To fade-in a clip from black using keyframes on the Timeline:

1. Navigate the playhead to one second in the Timeline **A**.

2. Position your pointer over the keyframe graph at the one-second mark, and it will convert to the two-headed vertical drag pointer **A**.

3. Press the Control (Windows) or Command (Mac OS) key to convert the pointer to a small cross icon **B**.

continues on next page

4. Click the keyframe graph to create a keyframe at that location **C**.

5. Create a keyframe at the very start of the clip by hovering your pointer over the keyframe graph at that location and Control/Command-clicking the keyframe graph **D**.

6. Drag the keyframe at the start of the clip down until it reaches an Opacity value of 0, as shown in the yellow box **E**.

To complete the fade-in, you'd have to work through the same process on all video tracks **F**. You could also use the same process on the audio volume graphs to fade audio in.

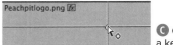

C Click to create a keyframe.

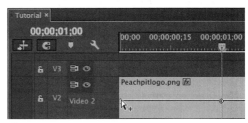

D Repeat at the start of the clip to create a keyframe there.

TIP Technically, you don't have to perform step 1; you can create a keyframe at any location on the keyframe graph without the playhead being there (as you discovered in step 5). I just like the precision afforded by having the playhead at the target keyframe location.

TIP You can also create keyframes with the Pen tool, but the Control/Command modifier with the regular pointer is faster for most users.

TIP You'll use the same basic procedure in reverse to fade to black at the end of a clip. At the end of the clip, sometimes you'll have to create a separate Opacity keyframe a few frames before the final keyframe to get to a true black by the end of the video **G**.

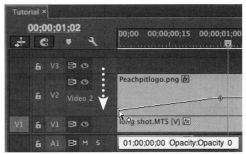

E Drag the new keyframe to an Opacity value of 0.

F Repeat for all video tracks on the Timeline.

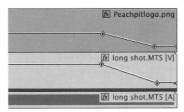

G Sometimes to get to true black when fading to black at the end of a clip, you have to add an Opacity keyframe with a zero value a few frames before the end of the clip.

Working with Keyframes in the Effect Controls Panel

As we saw in the last task, the basic work-flow for animating effects with keyframes is to create a keyframe, configure the relevant options, and then choose the next keyframe and configure those options. Premiere Pro then interpolates the values for all frames between the keyframes.

Beyond setting the keyframes themselves, you can also set the technique used by Premiere Pro for creating the interpolated frames. In these next two tasks, we'll zoom in to our video via keyframes and then explore the interpolation options. We'll be working with the same tutorial video, zooming from the long shot the video actually captured to a closer-up view that shows more detail.

About the Effect Controls Timeline

Before we get started, let's take a closer look at the Effect Controls panel and Timeline and some basic controls therein **A**. The Effect Controls Timeline (in essence) shows the Timeline from the location of the clip in the sequence. So if the selected clip is located 20 minutes into the project, the timecode in the Effect Controls panel will be at 00;20;00;00. Similarly, the playhead in both Timelines is always in the same location; if you move one playhead, it moves in the other. As with the regular Timeline, you can zoom in to and move around in the Effect Controls Timeline via the zoom bar on the bottom.

The Toggle Animation button has to be depressed to create keyframes for that particular effect, and once you create a keyframe, it will appear in the Timeline. You can precisely navigate to the keyframes using the Go to Previous Keyframe and Go to Next Keyframe buttons.

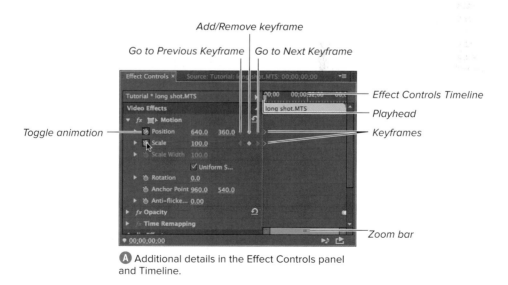

A Additional details in the Effect Controls panel and Timeline.

To add motion to video using keyframes:

1. Click the clip you're editing on the Timeline to select it.

2. Open the Effect Controls panel.

3. If the Effect Controls Timeline isn't open, click the Show/Hide Timeline View icon on the upper right of the Effect Controls panel to open it .

   We'll adjust two effects, Position and Scale, to create the effect. We'll begin by creating and configuring keyframes at the start of the clip.

4. With the playhead at the start of the clip, click the Toggle Animation buttons to the left of each effect , creating a keyframe for each effect. As you can see, because Scale is set to 100, the complete 1080p video does not show in the 720p frame.

5. Now configure the values for the first keyframe. In this project, the values for Position are fine, but I'll have to adjust the Scale value to 67  to show the full 1080p video in the 720p frame.

6. Move the playhead to the location of the next keyframe, in this case one second in from the start of the video . If necessary, adjust the zoom bar  on the bottom of the Effect Controls Timeline so you can see the playhead location.

7. Once the playhead is in the desired location, configure the Position and Scale values as necessary . Whenever you change the value of an effect configuration at a new location, Premiere Pro automatically creates a new keyframe. If you compare the Program Monitor in  to , you'll see the beginning and end points of the zoom.

B Opening the Effect Controls Timeline.

C With Scale at 100, we're already zoomed in.

D Adjusting the Scale to 67 fits the 1080p video into the 720p frame size shown in the Program Monitor.

E Move the playhead to the next keyframe location—in this case, one second in.

F Now we're at 100% but with better framing. The zoom is from what you see in the Program Monitor in D to what you see here.

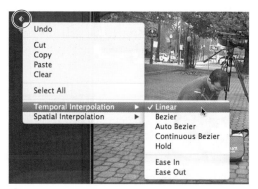

G Right-click a keyframe to view your interpolation options.

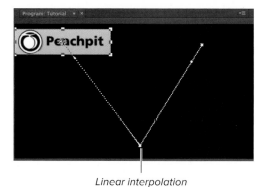

Linear interpolation

H Linear interpolation can look mechanical.

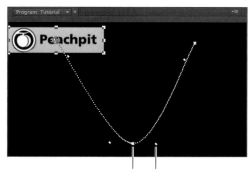

Auto Bezier   Control handles

I Auto Bezier simulates real-world motion, and you can customize the effect via the control handles.

Using keyframe interpolation techniques

You're in charge of creating and configuring keyframes, and then Premiere Pro fills in the blanks between frames via a technique called interpolation. Premiere Pro offers multiple interpolation techniques, for both temporal and spatial interpolation, that you can access by right-clicking any keyframe G. Note that not all keyframes offer both techniques; for example, scaling offers only temporal interpolation.

Temporal interpolation involves changes in speed, and its default interpolation technique is Linear, which means that the speed of the motion is identical in all frames. That's neat and tidy, but it's not how nature works, so it can make your motion look overly mechanical. For example, imagine a horse galloping from start to stop. It starts out slow, reaches maximum speed after a moment or two, and then slows down before reaching the stopping point.

The easy way to make your speed-related keyframes simulate this reality is to right-click the first keyframe in a motion-related effect and choose Temporal Interpolation > Ease In; right-click the last keyframe and choose Temporal Interpolation > Ease Out; and choose both for any keyframes in the middle.

Spatial interpolation involves how an object moves along a motion path. The default spatial interpolation changes; sometimes it's Linear H (which produces the perfect 90-degree turn), and sometime it's Auto Bezier I (which smooths the 90-degree turn considerably). If the motion in your keyframe looks too mechanical, consider changing or even customizing the interpolation technique applied to that keyframe.

The Premiere Pro Help file contains comprehensive definitions of the various interpolation techniques. For temporal interpolation, Ease In and Ease Out generally get the job done. For spatial interpolation, Linear is seldom the desired option. The three Bezier options allow you to customize the settings of the interpolation; if you're looking for a no-muss, no-fuss approach, use Auto Bezier and leave it at that.

The Hold interpolation command is useful when you want the motion to occur all at once. For example, in some tutorials, I use keyframed motion to move an arrow from topic to topic in the agenda. I don't want gradual movement; I want an instantaneous move from topic A to topic B when the topic changes. The Hold command is ideal for this.

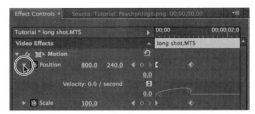

J Click the disclosure triangle to reveal the velocity graphs and control handles.

K Customize the interpolation with these control handles.

To choose and customize an interpolation technique:

1. To choose an interpolation technique, right-click the keyframe and choose the technique **G**. Note that the keyframe icon changes when you change the interpolation technique.

2. To customize the selected interpolation technique **J**, right-click the disclosure triangle next to the effect name to reveal the velocity graph and control handles.

3. Adjust the control handles to the desired values **K**.

4. Repeat as necessary for all keyframes.

A You have to enable keyframes before you can add them.

B Once you've enabled keyframes, you can add more with this button.

Customizing Keyframes

Now that you know what a keyframe is, there are a number of keyframe-related skills you need to acquire.

To add a keyframe in the Effect Controls panel:

1. Move the playhead to the desired location.

2. If necessary, click the Toggle Animation button for the effect to enable keyframes A. If keyframes weren't enabled, this creates a keyframe at that location.

3. If keyframes are already enabled, do one of the following:

   ▸ Change any of the configuration options. Premiere Pro automatically creates a keyframe.

   ▸ Click the Add/Remove Keyframe button B.

To move keyframes:

To move a keyframe, click it **C** and then drag it to the new location **D**.

To select keyframes:

1. To select a single keyframe, click it. The keyframe turns yellow **E**.
2. To select multiple keyframes, do one of the following:
   - Shift-click multiple keyframes **F**.
   - Click an empty area in the Effect Controls Timeline, and drag a marquee around the keyframes **G**.

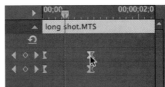

C Moving a keyframe is as simple as click...

D ...and drag.

E Click to select a keyframe, and it turns yellow.

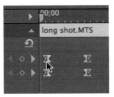

F Shift-click to select multiple keyframes.

The selected keyframes

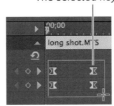

G Or drag a marquee around the target keyframes.

H To delete a keyframe, right-click it and choose Clear.

I Click the Toggle Animation button to delete all keyframes for a particular effect.

J Press OK.

K And the keyframes are gone.

To delete keyframes:

1. To remove one or more selected keyframes, choose the keyframes, right-click, and choose Clear **H**. Premiere Pro deletes the keyframe or keyframes.

2. To remove all keyframes for a particular effect, click the Toggle Animation button **I** for that effect and then click OK in the Warning dialog that appears **J**. Premiere Pro removes all keyframes for that effect **K**.

Copying and pasting keyframes

Whoever said, "Consistency is the last refuge of the unimaginative" never edited video (actually, it was Oscar Wilde, and I'm pretty sure he never used a non-linear editor). When I'm editing video—particularly when framing and reframing—I want to return to the exact same scale and position that I used previously. The easy way to do this is to copy and paste the related keyframes. For example, if I wanted to return to the same long shot view that I started with a few tasks ago, I would copy and paste those keyframes. It's straightforward, but let's run through it.

To copy and paste keyframes:

1. Choose the target keyframes .

2. Right-click the keyframes and choose Copy .

3. Move the playhead to the new location.

4. Right-click anywhere in the Effect Controls Timeline and choose Paste . Premiere Pro pastes the keyframes at that location .

5. Preview to make sure that the interpolation technique you copied over works in the new location.

 To copy keyframes, begin by selecting them.

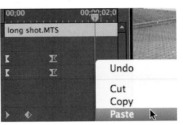

 Then right-click and choose Copy.

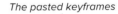

 Move the playhead to the new location; then right-click and choose Paste.

The pasted keyframes

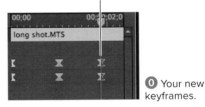

 Your new keyframes.

A Click the track header, and expand the track with your scroll wheel.

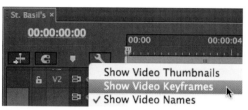

B If necessary, expose the video keyframes in the settings menu.

C Choose Speed for the keyframe graph.

Time Remapping via Keyframes

In Chapter 7 you learned two options for changing the speed of a clip: the Clip Speed/Duration dialog and the Rate Stretch tool. Although highly functional in many instances, both of these approaches share a key limitation: They change the speed of the entire clip. The third alternative, called time remapping, allows you to change the speed multiple times in a clip and ramp the speed adjustments in and out. This makes it the most desirable technique in many instances.

While you can use this technique in the Effect Controls panel and Timeline, I prefer the Timeline. Note that this effect ignores audio, so you'll have to address that separately, which usually means deleting the audio clip and substituting background music or narration.

In this task I'll be slowing a tilt shot of the St. Basil's Cathedral to 50% speed one second into the shot, and transitioning the speed change over one second.

To apply time remapping in the Timeline:

1. You'll need room to work, so start by clicking the track header and increasing the size of the track with your scroll wheel **A**.

2. If necessary, click the Timeline Display Settings icon ![wrench icon], and choose Show Video Keyframes **B**.

3. Click the FX icon ![fx icon] on the video track **C**, which opens a menu that lets you choose which effect to configure. Choose Time Remapping > Speed **C**.

continues on next page

4. Move the playhead to the keyframe position.

5. Press the Control (Windows) or Command (Mac OS) key to convert the pointer to a small cross icon 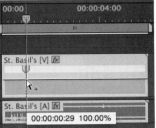 **D** 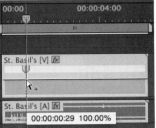, and click the keyframe graph to create a keyframe. Note that the speed keyframe has two parts, which represent the In and Out points of the speed transition.

D Control/ Command-click the keyframe graph to create the speed keyframe.

6. Click the keyframe graph to the right of the new keyframe and drag it down, watching the yellow speed box until you reach the desired speed, in this case 50% **E**. Premiere Pro lengthens the video component of the clip **F**.

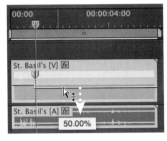

E Drag the keyframe graph down to the desired speed.

7. Drag the right, Out point, component of the speed keyframe to the desired location **F**. The yellow box indicates the location of the Out point in the Timeline and the average speed of the transition.

F Drag the speed transition Out point to the desired position.

8. If desired, adjust the control handles to customize the transition **G** (you'll have to expand the size of the track significantly to do so).

9. Repeat the procedure as necessary throughout the clip.

> **TIP** Time remapping doesn't "ripple," so it won't push video located to the right of the target clip back to accommodate any slow motion. Nor will it delete any gaps caused by increasing the overall speed of a clip.

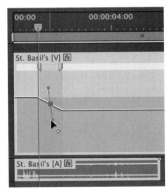

G Adjust the control handles to customize the transition.

9

Working with Video Effects

I remember a vague feeling of letdown when I first opened the effects bin of a long-forgotten video editor, oh so long ago. Where, I wondered, were the effects that would let me part the Red Sea, blow up buildings and jet fighters, or simulate gunshot wounds? You know—all the special effects you see in the movies.

I quickly learned that, these deficits notwithstanding, effects play a critical role in several areas, including color and brightness correction, which we'll address in Chapter 11. Effects also polish and tweak your movie with different looks, and let you produce overlay, or greenscreen effects, that let you combine two or more videos in very creative ways. We'll cover these last two types of effects here here.

In this chapter, you'll learn where to find Premiere Pro's effects and how to apply, customize, and animate them for application to one or more clips on the Timeline. You'll learn how to produce a greenscreen effect, and some similar effects, and we'll conclude with a look at rendering the Timeline, which may be necessary to preview your effects at full frame rate.

About Premiere Pro Effects

Premiere Pro has a special workspace for editing effects, so let's start there.

A Switching to the Effects workspace.

To enter the Effects workspace:

To enter the Effects Workspace, do one of the following:

- In the Premiere Pro menu, choose Window > Workspace > Effects **A**.

- Press Alt/Option+Shift+6.

    Premiere Pro enters the Effects workspace **B**.

The three panels shown in **B** are the Effects panel, where all audio and video transitions and effects are stored; the Effect Controls panel, where you can configure all effects; and the Program Monitor, where you can preview your effects. As you learned in Chapter 8, you can also configure effects in the Timeline, though you'll do the bulk of your effects configuration in the Effect Controls panel.

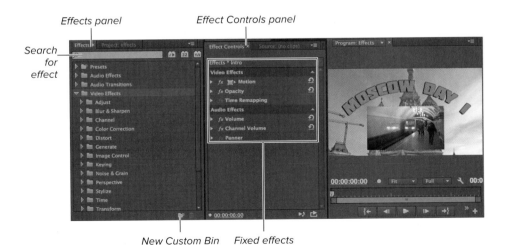

Effects panel *Effect Controls panel*

Search for effect

New Custom Bin *Fixed effects*

B The top half of the Effects workspace.

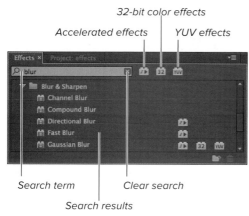

32-bit color effects

Accelerated effects   *YUV effects*

Search term   *Clear search*

Search results

Ⓒ Searching for a Blur effect.

Premiere Pro has multiple categories for its effects. The highest level is between fixed and standard effects. Fixed effects, shown at the top of the Effect Controls panel, are applied to every clip you add to the Timeline. Standard effects are those in the Effects panel that you have to apply manually.

There are 16 categories of effects, with self-descriptive names. Though you can't move effects from one bin to another, you can create your own custom bin and drag effects into that. You can also search for effects, which has proven surprisingly useful to me over the course of many projects.

To search for effects in the effects panel:

1. Click the Effects tab to select it, or press Shift+7.

2. In the Effects panel search field, type the first few letters of the effect name Ⓒ. Premiere Pro displays all effects with names starting with those letters Ⓒ.

3. Click the close icon in the search field to clear the search.

TIP If after searching for an effect, it appears that some or all of your effects are missing, it's likely because you forgot step 3. If you don't clear the search, you'll see only a partial listing of your effects.

Other effects categories

C also shows three other categories of effects: GPU-accelerated, 32-bit color, and YUV effects.

- GPU-accelerated effects. Accelerated by compatible graphics cards, these effects preview in real time (within limits) and render faster than non-GPU compatible effects.

- 32-bit color effects. These are processed in 32-bit floating point color rather than 8-bit color, for the highest possible color processing, though you need to enable Maximum Bit Depth in your sequence settings. I also recommend optimizing performance for memory in your memory preferences.

- YUV effects. These are processed in the YUV color space, which is used in most acquisition formats (like AVCHD, AVC-Intra, and MPEG-2). Non-YUV effects are processed in RGB color space, which can cause conversion errors.

How should you work with these categories of effects? In some cases, you'll have the option to use different effects to accomplish the same general function. For example, we'll be adding a blur filter to a clip in an upcoming task. C shows many blur effects, several of which could get the job done, though all have slightly different features. In this case, I would use the Gaussian Blur filter.

As a general rule, I prefer accelerated and YUV effects. Whether you limit yourself to 32-bit color effects depends on your source footage and computer system. If you are working with video shot with 10- or 12-bits-per-channel codecs (like RED or ARRI) and have lots of memory in your system, you may wish to use only 32-bit effects. If you're working with DSLR or AVCHD input on a notebook, you may see no qualitative benefit, and performance will likely suffer. So limiting yourself to 32-bit effects and using the memory-optimized settings described here may not be worth it, particularly if you're not seeing banding or other obvious color-related problems. For more on this topic, check out the article at bit.ly/32-bitcolor.

Note that you can limit the effects shown in the Effect panel to any or all of the three categories by pressing the badge atop the panel C.

TIP Note that if you use any 8-bit effects on a clip, it will force 8-bit processing, which can degrade overall quality.

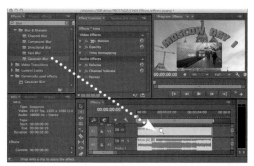

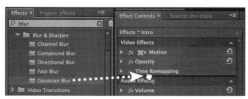

(A) You can drag an effect from the Effects panel onto a clip in the Timeline.

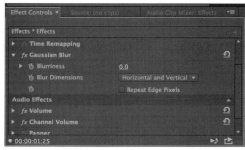

(B) Or drag the clip from the Effects panel directly into the Effect Controls panel, which gives you precise control over the order when multiple standard effects have been applied.

(C) The Gaussian Blur effect, ready to be configured.

The Effects Workflow

Let's tackle some of the nuts and bolts of applying and configuring effects. Most of these are straightforward, but pay attention to the "To toggle an effect on and off" task.

Toggling an effect on and off in the Program Monitor allows you to gauge the impact of the effect. For many effects, this is the most valuable tool for perfecting your settings, kind of like the optometrist asking, "Is it clearer here, or here?"

To add an effect to a single clip:

Do one of the following:

- Drag the effect onto the clip in the Timeline (A).

- With a clip selected in the Timeline, double-click the target effect.

- Drag the effect into the desired order in the Effect Controls panel (B). This approach is best when you need to control the rendering order of the standard effects applied to a clip (see the "Order Matters" sidebar for more details).

  Premiere Pro adds the effect to the clip (C).

TIP You can use the first two techniques to add an effect to multiple clips; just select them on the Timeline before you drag or double-click. Since it's easier to configure an effect and then add it to multiple clips, you may want to check out the section "Applying Effects to Multiple Clips" for efficient techniques for doing so.

To customize an effect:

To customize an effect, change any or all of the effect configuration options in the Effect Controls panel. The Program Monitor will update in real time as you change the parameters. Note that you can change most numeric parameters using one of these three techniques:

- Hover your pointer over any numeric value until it becomes the two-headed drag pointer ![icon]. Then drag to the desired value ⓓ.

- Click the disclosure triangle to the left of the configuration option to reveal a slider that you can drag to the desired value ⓓ.

- Click the numeric value to make it active, and type the desired value. Press Enter/Return ⓔ.

TIP Most effects have very different controls, and beyond popular effects like the Warp Stabilizer or Ultra Key, there's little documentation anywhere about how to use them. Sometimes you just have to wiggle the controls to see what happens.

TIP If things get irreparably hosed, click the Restart button and begin again ⓓ.

TIP You can also configure effects on the Timeline. See "Adjusting Effects in the Timeline," in Chapter 8, for the detailed procedure.

Toggle the effect on and off

Show/Hide Timeline view

Toggle animation (enable/disable keyframes)

Reset

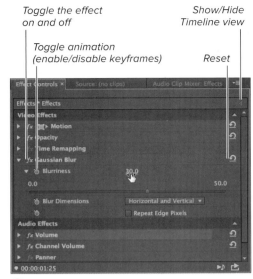

ⓓ Dragging the Blurriness adjustment to the desired level.

ⓔ Click the numerical field to make it active, then type in the desired value and press Enter/Return.

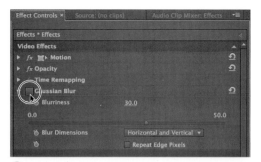

F Click this icon to enable or disable the effect.

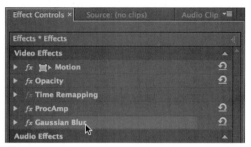

G We're going to move the Gaussian Blur effect above the ProcAmp effect.

Position bar

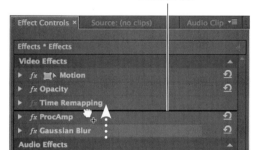

H Drag to the desired location.

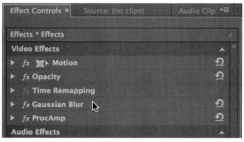

I Premiere Pro rearranges the effect order.

To toggle an effect on and off:

1. To toggle an effect off, click the fx icon [fx] to the left of the effect name so the icon disappears **F**. In this mode, the effect is disabled for preview and output.

2. To toggle the effect back on, click the button again; when the icon reappears, the effect is active.

To change the order of an effect:

Drag **G** the effect up or down to the desired position **H**. Premiere Pro will display a black horizontal position bar in the drop position at each possible location. When the effect is in the desired position, release the pointer and Premiere Pro will change the order **I**. Note that you can't drag standard effects above fixed effects, or fixed effects below the standard effects.

Order Matters

Premiere Pro renders fixed effects only after rendering the standard effects in order, from the top down. If you change the order of your standard effects, you may see a subtle or dramatic difference in the output, or no difference at all. Be aware of this when you're applying the same effect to multiple clips, hoping to achieve a consistent look.

I've never seen this happen, but if you're getting an anomalous result that you think is the result of the fixed effects being rendered last, you can substitute a standard effect for a fixed effect. Specifically, you can substitute the Transform effect for the Motion effects, and the Alpha Adjust effect for the Opacity effect. Then set the rendering order manually, and see if that resolves your problem.

To remove an effect in the Effect Controls panel:

1. Select the clip in the Timeline, and open the Effect Controls panel.

2. Click to select a single standard effect, or Control/Command-click to select multiple effects .

3. Do one of the following:

   ▸ Press the Backspace/Delete key.

   ▸ Right-click any of the selected effects, and choose Clear .

   Premiere Pro deletes the effects .

Selected clips

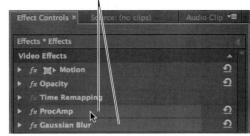

 Choose the target effects.

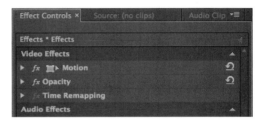

 Right-click and choose Clear.

 Premiere Pro removes the effects.

Choosing multiple clips.

Right-click and choose Remove Effects.

Choosing which effects to remove.

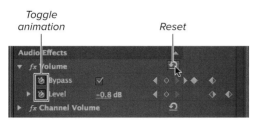

Resetting and removing keyframes manually.

To remove effects from one or more clips in the Timeline:

1. Select the clip or clips in the Timeline. Here I'm drawing a marquee around four clips in the Timeline .

2. Right-click any of the selected clips and choose Remove Effects . The Remove Effects dialog opens .

3. Click the check box of each effect that you want to remove .

   Intrinsic effects are the fixed effects for Motion, Opacity, and Volume (but not Time Remapping, Channel Volume, and Panner). Video effects are the standard effects applied to the clip, and removing any effect resets the parameters and removes all keyframes.

4. Click OK to remove the effects . Premiere Pro removes the selected effects.

> **TIP** Obviously, the key benefit of this approach is the ability to remove effects from multiple clips simultaneously. Equally obvious is that this technique is a blunt instrument for standard effects, because it's all or nothing.

> **TIP** To remove the Time Remapping, Channel Volume, and Panner effects, click the Reset button , and if keyframes were applied, click the "Toggle animation" buttons for all keyframed effect configurations.

Animate an Effect with Keyframes

I detailed what keyframes are and how to work with them in the Chapter 8 section "Working with Keyframes." There, we used keyframes to animate a motion effect, zooming into a clip that was shot very wide.

Now we'll use keyframes to animate effects applied to a clip in the Timeline—specifically, the Gaussian Blur and ProcAmp effects.

This is the five-second nested intro clip that I created in Chapter 7. The clip will start blurry and in black and white, and will transition to its clear, full-color state over the five-second duration. Since I've already applied the effects, I'll start work in the Effect Controls panel.

To add motion to effects via keyframes:

1. If necessary, in the Effect Controls panel, click the Show/Hide Timeline View triangle to open the Timeline **A**. Note that the clip in the Program Monitor is clear and in full color. We'll fix that soon enough.

2. Navigate the playhead to the start of the clip **B**.

3. Click the disclosure triangle next to the effect to reveal the configuration options **B**.

4. To enable keyframes, click the "Toggle animation" button to the left of the effect that you'll configure **B**. Premiere Pro inserts a keyframe at that location.

5. Adjust the configuration option to the desired value **C**. Here I'm dragging Saturation to 0 to convert the video to black and white.

A Our starting point. Click Show/Hide Timeline View to open the Effect Controls Timeline.

Disclosure triangle   *Keyframe*

Toggle animation button   *Playhead to start of clip*

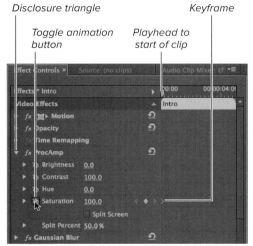

B Creating our first keyframe at the start of the clip.

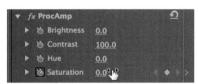

C Configuring the initial value for the first keyframe. Saturation of 0 takes the full-color video to black and white.

Initial value   Keyframe

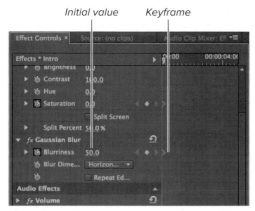

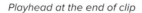

D Setting the keyframe for the second effect. This is what the video will look like when it starts to play.

Playhead at the end of clip

New keyframe

E Configuring one keyframe at the end of the clip. Saturation of 100 restores full color.

Final values

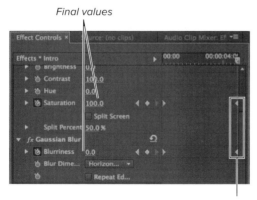

New keyframes

F Here's what the video will look like at the end of the effect.

6. Repeat as necessary for any other keyframes at that location D. I've added and configured the Blur effect, delivering the promised blurry, black and white video the viewer will see once the video starts playing.

7. Move the playhead to the next location E. If that's the end of the clip, press the Down Arrow key to move to the next edit point, then the Left Arrow key to move to the last frame of the clip we're editing.

8. Change the value of any keyframed configuration option, and Premiere Pro creates another keyframe at that value at the new location E.

9. Repeat as necessary. F shows our clip, fully restored to clarity and color over the course of the five-second intro.

10. Check to make sure that your interpolation options (also discussed in Chapter 8) are optimized. For these effects, Linear is fine.

Applying Effects to Multiple Clips

If you're applying effects *without* keyframes to multiple clips, save yourself some time and jump straight to the tasks. If you're using keyframes, you should read this section.

Here's the setup. You just spent two hours creating the perfect intro that combined just the right combination of keyframe-animated effects. Now you want to apply that same combination to other sequences, in this project and in others. What are your options? Well, you have a bunch.

If you just have just one effect to copy to one other clip, you can do just that. If you have multiple targets, you can use the Paste Attributes function to paste all the effects to multiple clips, a fantastically useful technique.

If you want to use the effect combination in later projects, you can create presets that you drag onto one or more clips in later projects. Note that all these techniques copy the effect values and any associated keyframes to the target clips.

Working with keyframes

Speaking of keyframes, let's focus on them a bit. In a previous task, we created a five-second transition from blurry grayscale to clear full color. For this discussion, I've created a similar effect on a five-second clip, except that I shortened the transition in to one second and added a one-second transition out to blurry black and white at the end of the clip. You can see the Effect Controls Timeline in Ⓐ. This is the effect I want to apply to other clips.

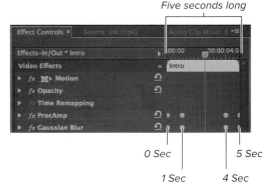

Five seconds long

0 Sec

1 Sec

4 Sec

5 Sec

Ⓐ Here's our starting point: a five-second clip with a one-second transition in and a one-second transition out.

Ten seconds long

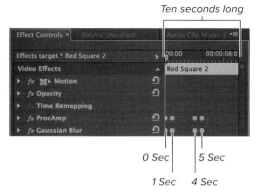

0 Sec | 5 Sec

1 Sec | 4 Sec

B If you copy and paste an effect or effects, Premiere Pro takes a literal approach.

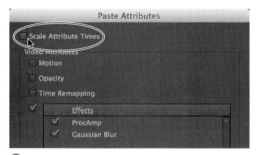

C To scale or not to scale, that is the question.

Ten seconds long

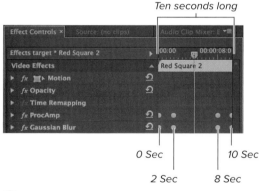

0 Sec | 10 Sec

2 Sec | 8 Sec

D If you scale, Premiere Pro spreads your keyframes proportionately through the clip.

There are multiple elements to consider when copying and pasting the effects from one clip to other clips. For example, the source clip is five seconds long. The first effect stops one second in, and the second effect starts four seconds in and finishes at the five-second mark. So what happens when you paste this combination of effects on another clip that's, say, ten seconds long? Here, you'd want Premiere Pro to apply a one-second transition at both ends of the clip.

Unfortunately, Premiere Pro can't read minds. When you copy and paste effects in the Effect Controls panel, Premiere Pro pastes the keyframes at the exact same location as the original clip, ignoring the time difference **B**. You can fix this by dragging the two sets of keyframes on the right to the end of the clip, but if you're wondering why the second transition starts in the middle of the clip, now you know.

In the Paste Attributes dialog, you have a choice: you can elect to scale attributes **C**, which spreads the keyframes proportionately over the duration of the clip **D**, or you can elect not to scale them. Scaling attributes probably isn't what you want in this case, though it is also easy to fix. If you choose not to scale attributes, you get the result shown in **B**.

When you create a preset, you get three choices . If you scale, you get the result shown in ⒟, if you Anchor to In Point, Premiere Pro applies the effect to the first five seconds of the target clip, producing the result shown in ⒝. If you choose Anchor to Out Point, Premiere Pro applies the effect to the last five seconds of the target clip, producing the result shown in ⒡.

What to do? Well, you could create two presets—one for the transition in, and one for the transition out. The transition in preset would Anchor to In Point, and the transition out preset would Anchor to Out Point. Then you could apply both presets to any target clip and get the result shown in ⒢.

Overall, these techniques are wonderfully functional, but things quickly get complicated once you start to use keyframes. Understanding how these techniques work will help you use them more efficiently and effectively. Now that you know the implications of these keyframe-related issues, I'll happily ignore them as much as possible in the following tasks.

TIP Adjustment layers are another technique for sharing effects over multiple clips (see Chapter 11).

ⓔ Your keyframe-related choices when you save a preset.

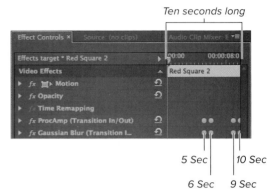

ⓕ Here's what happens if you Anchor to Out Point.

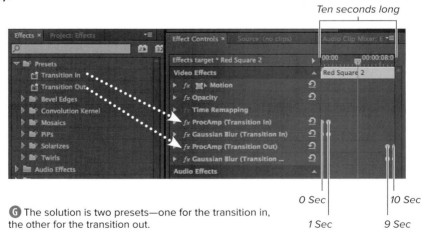

ⓖ The solution is two presets—one for the transition in, the other for the transition out.

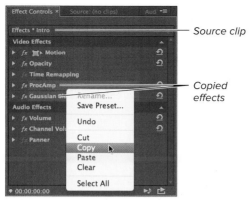

Source clip

Copied effects

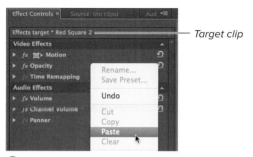

H Select the effects to copy, right-click, and choose Copy.

Target clip

I In the Effect Controls panel of the target clip, right-click and choose Paste.

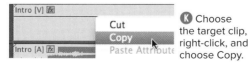

Pasted effects

J Premiere Pro pastes the effects into the Effect Controls panel of the target clip.

K Choose the target clip, right-click, and choose Copy.

To copy and paste effects from one clip to another:

1. In the Timeline, click the clip that contains the effects to copy, and open the Effect Controls panel **H**.

2. Click a single effect, or Control/Command-click multiple effects to select them **H**.

3. Right-click and choose Copy **H**.

4. In the Timeline, click the target clip to select it.

5. In the Effect Controls panel, right-click anywhere and choose Paste **I**. Premiere Pro pastes the effects into the Effect Controls panel of the target clip **J**.

> **TIP** If there are keyframes in the source effects, Premiere Pro applies them to the target in the same temporal locations without considering any duration differences between the source and target clips.

To copy and paste effects to one or more clips via the Paste Attributes function:

1. Select the target clip in the Timeline.

2. Right-click and choose Copy **K**.

continues on next page

3. Select one or more target clips in the Timeline. Here I'm drawing a marquee around four target clips .

4. Right-click any selected clip and choose Paste Attributes . The Paste Attributes dialog opens ⓝ.

5. Choose the effects to apply to the target clips ⓝ.

6. Select the Scale Attribute Times ⓝ check box to scale keyframes in the source clip over the duration of the target clips ⓓ. If this check box is unselected, Premiere Pro will insert the keyframes at the same temporal location in the target clip as they are in the source clip ⓑ.

7. Click OK ⓝ to close the dialog and paste the effects onto the target.

TIP Every once in a while, when you think you're performing step 4, you'll choose Paste instead of Paste Attributes, and the target clips will be replaced by the source. Just press Control/Command+Z to undo, and then choose Paste Attributes instead of Paste.

To create an effect preset:

1. In the Timeline, click the clip that contains the effects to copy, and open the Effect Controls panel ⓞ.

2. Click a single effect, or Control/Command+click multiple effects to select them ⓞ. Note that this is a Transition In effect, with keyframes at the start of the clip and one second in.

ⓛ Select the target or targets.

ⓜ Right-click any clip and choose Paste Attributes.

ⓝ Configure the Paste Attributes dialog, and click OK.

Selected effects

ⓞ Select the effects to include in the preset, right-click, and choose Save Preset.

P Make your selection, complete the information, and click OK to create the preset.

Q Premiere Pro saves the preset in a folder at the top of the Effects panel.

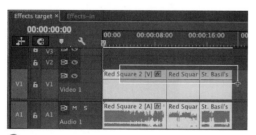

R Choose the target clip or clips on the Timeline.

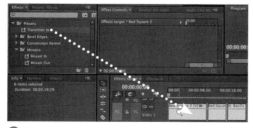

S Drag the preset onto any of the target clips.

3. Right-click any selected effect and choose Save Preset **O**. The Save Preset dialog opens **P**.

4. Type the desired preset name **P**.

5. Choose one of the following **P**:

   ▸ Scale. Scales the source keyframes proportionally over the length of the target clip and deletes existing keyframes on the target **D**.

   ▸ Anchor to In Point. Applies the source keyframes to the start of the target clip with no adjustment for differences in duration **B**.

   ▸ Anchor to Out Point. Applies the source keyframes to the end of the target clip with no adjustment for differences in duration **F**.

   I'm selecting Anchor to In Point because the source effect was a Transition In effect.

6. Click OK to close the dialog and save the preset **P**. Premiere Pro saves the preset in the top folder in the Effects panel **Q**.

TIP Premiere Pro comes with multiple presets in the Preset subfolders—primarily Transition In and Transition Out presets. Double-click any preset to open the Preset Properties dialog (essentially the same as **P**). In the next task, you'll learn how to apply them.

To apply an effect preset:

1. In the Timeline, select the clip or clips to apply the preset to **R**.

2. In the Effects panel, choose the preset to apply, and do one of the following:

   ▸ Double-click the preset.

   ▸ Drag the preset onto any of the selected clips **S**. Premiere Pro applies the preset to all selected clips.

Previewing Effects

After applying effects, you may wish to preview your work, which you can easily accomplish by pressing the spacebar or using any of the controls in the Program Monitor. Premiere Pro will attempt to play the video in real time, but if you're working on an older computer or a computer without a Mercury Engine-compatible graphics card—or if you simply have too many effects on a particular clip—Premiere Pro will drop frames, with an indicator on the Program Monitor to let you know ⓣ.

Premiere Pro also includes a clue on the Timeline: the colored bar beneath the time ruler. When the line is yellow, preview should occur in real time; when it's red, you'll probably drop frames.

What do you do? If you need to see a full-frame preview of the effects, you'll need to render the Timeline, which you can do by pressing Enter/Return or by choosing Sequence > Render Effects In to Out.

When you choose this option, however, Premiere Pro renders the entire Timeline, which can be time consuming, particularly when the clip that you're working on is near the end of the project. To render just a particular area of the Timeline, mark In and Out points around the target clip ⓤ, and when you press Enter/Return to render, Premiere Pro will render just the selected region.

To clear the In and Out points, right-click the time ruler and choose Clear In and Out ⓥ.

Dropped-frame indicator   *Potential problem areas*

ⓣ Red regions on the Timeline usually mean that Premiere Pro can't preview the clip in real time.

Mark In   Mark Out

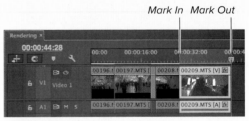

ⓤ Mark the region that you want to render.

ⓥ To clear the In and Out markers, right-click the time ruler and choose Clear In and Out.

Keying and Greenscreen Basics

Keying and compositing are two essential functions of any professional video editor, and Premiere Pro offers capabilities that can handle almost any project, given footage that's properly produced. *Compositing* is combining two separate images in a single scene so that they appear to have been shot together. *Keying*, also known as chromakeying, greenscreening, and bluescreening, involves replacing one narrowly defined ("keyed") color in an image with parts from a second background image.

TV weather broadcasts and movie action scenes often use greenscreens. Technically, any color can be used for chromakeying, but blue and green are the most common because they are furthest away from skin tones. Green is especially effective because the green channel in digital video cameras contains the least amount of noise and green is a less common color in clothing. It is important to avoid having a color in the scene (whether in your subject's clothing or in on-screen objects) be the same as the screen color. Keying involves removing everything that's the same color as the screen, and anything in your foreground image that contains the screen color will become transparent, and in its place you'll see the image from the background scene.

Requirements for high-quality keying

Thanks to the Ultra Key effect, Premiere Pro makes keying easy, but all good keys require great source material. Here are a few tips for achieving a great key.

Shoot with a video camera that has a full-raster sensor and doesn't interpolate to attain HD resolution, as HDV cameras do. Select a video camera with a high ISO starting value, and use it with no gain; add additional lights if necessary. Record in progressive, not interlaced, format so you're recording full frames instead of fields.

Record at the highest bitrate your camera can handle, and consider using an external HDMI or HD-SDI recorder to record with an intraframe codec, not an interframe or Long-GOP codec (like the highly compressed signal your AVCHD camera automatically records to a Secure Digital or CompactFlash card).

Evenly light your background, and make sure the screen material is ironed or taut to avoid wrinkles and shadows.

Don't film with too shallow a depth of field with a large-sensor camera, but do put some distance between your subject and the background.

When you're filming a single subject who is standing, consider using a tripod L bracket to mount your camera vertically. This will result in a higher resolution, a higher pixel density around your edges, and a better key.

Applying and Configuring the Ultra Key Effect

The Ultra Key effect is the most popular and effective way to pull a key in Premiere Pro. You'll want to do most, if not all, of your keying using this effect.

To add the Ultra Key effect:

1. Create a new sequence with your greenscreen footage by dragging it onto the New Item icon in the Project panel **A**. Your greenscreen footage will appear in the Program Monitor **B**.

    In this example, I filmed the greenscreen footage with the video camera turned 90 degrees to increase pixel density. I'll rotate the footage in a later step.

2. Rename the new sequence, and optionally organize it in a bin **C**.

3. Select the Effects tab, and type **ultra** into the Effects search box. The Ultra Key effect will be visible **D**. Alternatively, you can choose Video Effects > Keying to reveal the Ultra Key effect.

4. Drag the Ultra Key effect from the Effects panel to the clip on the sequence you created in step 1, and release **E**.

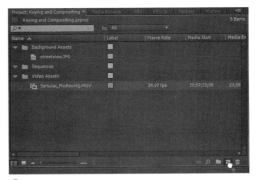

A Selecting a greenscreen clip.

B The clip we'll be keying, shot vertically for higher pixel density.

C Renaming the sequence.

D Our keyer of choice: the Ultra Key Effect.

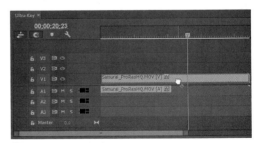

E Drag the Ultra Key effect onto the clip.

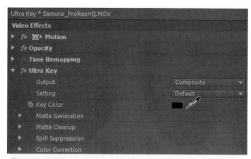

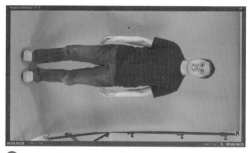

F Selecting the eyedropper.

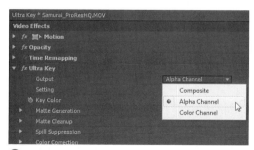

G Choosing a color to key out.

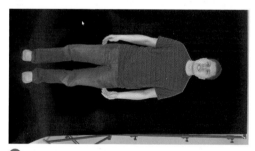

H The background turns (mostly) black—it's the gray areas we need to fix.

I Choosing Alpha Channel output.

To key out a color:

1. Select the Effect Controls tab, and the Ultra Key effect will be visible F. Hover over the eyedropper 🖋 until the pointer changes to an eyedropper tool, and then select the eyedropper.

2. Select the background color on your video clip in the Program Monitor G. Your background color changes to black, but the key needs more work H.

To customize and clean up your key:

1. In the Effect Controls panel, choose Alpha Channel from the Output menu I.

   Your video clip converts to a black-and-white clip J. In the next steps, we will adjust the key setting so that the black is solid black, the white is solid white, and the only areas with gray are around fine edges (like hair). Throughout the next steps you will want to toggle between the Alpha Channel and Composite views to compare the effects of the various settings.

continues on next page

J The image turns black, white, and (unfortunately) gray.

The composite output shows the keyed channel and the channel below it; the alpha channel shows the video clip converted to a binary 1-and-0 channel, displaying white for areas that will remain and black for areas that will appear transparent; and the color channel shows the original video clip before the key was applied.

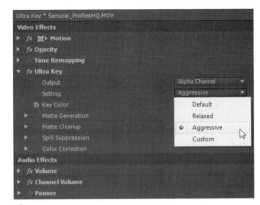

2. Select a Setting preset. The options include three presets—Default, Relaxed, and Aggressive—and a Custom option **K**. The presets can serve as a good starting point from which to begin adjusting settings. I'll select Aggressive **L** and adjust the settings to deal with the shadow around the feet **B**.

3. Click the Matte Generation disclosure triangle to reveal the Transparency, Highlight, Shadow, Tolerance, and Pedestal controls **M**. These controls adjust how the matte is interpreted. Repeat for the Matte Cleanup, Spill Suppression, and Color Correction controls.

K Ultra Key's preset options.

L Here's what Aggressive looks like.

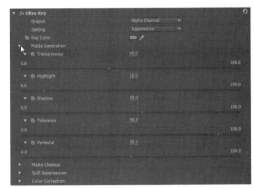

M Matte Generation parameters revealed.

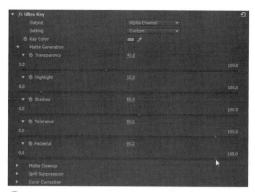

Make adjustments using the sliders.

Or enter a custom value.

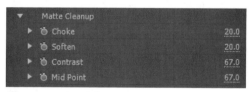

Pedestal adjustments get us closer to clearing up the issues in the feet area.

Matte Cleanup

▶ Choke		20.0
▶ Soften		20.0
▶ Contrast		67.0
▶ Mid Point		67.0

Adjusting the Matte Cleanup values to clean up the matte we defined.

4. Drag the slider right or left to increase or decrease, respectively, the effect of the adjustments . Alternatively, enter a custom value in the corresponding field. I'll increase the Pedestal amount to 90, which will bring more of the shadow area into the black part of the alpha channel .

5. Under Matte Cleanup, you can access the Choke, Soften, Contrast, and Mid Point controls and adjust them as described in step 4. The Matte Cleanup controls adjust the matte that you defined . I'll increase both Choke and Soften to 20 and both Contrast and Mid Point to 67 . Experiment with the controls until the muddy areas of your key look clean.

continues on next page

6. Under Spill Suppression, you can access the Desaturate, Range, Spill, and Luma controls. Spill Suppression controls help remove color that reflects off the backdrop (or from colored lighting) onto your subject. I don't have any spill in this shot, so I'm not going to make any adjustments here ⓡ.

7. Under Color Correction, you can access the Saturation, Hue, and Luminance controls. These controls affect the white part of the alpha channel—that is, your subject and not your background—so they won't affect your key. I'm not going to make any color correction adjustments here ⓡ.

To composite your video:

1. Choose Composite from the Output menu Ⓢ to display the resulting key in the Program Monitor Ⓣ.

2. Move your keyed video clip to Track V2 if it isn't already there, and drag your background clip onto V1 ⓤ.

The greenscreen footage is now keyed and composited with the background photo, although both need adjustments: the background photo is too large for the HD video frame, and the video footage still needs to be rotated and is showing part of the backdrop stand Ⓥ.

ⓡ Adjust Spill Suppression and Color Correction as needed to clean up any remaining issues.

Ⓢ Choose Composite output to see your cleaned-up key.

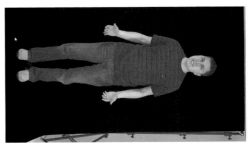

Ⓣ The resulting key.

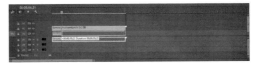

ⓤ Drag your background clip to V1 (or at least one track lower than your foreground clip).

Ⓥ The composited image with the new background.

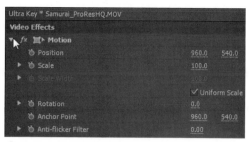

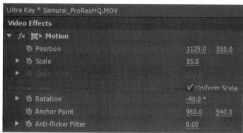

W Scaling the background image to the size of the video frame.

X Now to re-position and re-orient the image.

Y Position, Scale, and Rotation parameters entered.

3. Right-click the background, and select Scale to Frame Size **W**.

4. Select the video clip in the Timeline, and in the Effect Controls panel, click the Motion disclosure triangle to reveal the Position, Scale, and Rotation controls **X**.

5. To position this vertically shot image properly with respect to the background, I'm going to change the horizontal position to 1125, the vertical position to 555, the scale to 55, and the rotation to –90° **Y**. Make adjustments to the motion of the background, if needed, and your key should be done. In this case, though, I'll need to use a garbage matte to clean up the edges of the greenscreen backdrop stand **Z**.

Z The composited image looks good—except for the greenscreen frame artifacts.

Cleaning Up Edges with Garbage Mattes

To remove unwanted edges around a greenscreen key, you need to use a garbage matte. A simple crop applied to the green-screen footage can also work, but if the area to be cropped doesn't have four right angles, then the solution is a garbage matte, accessed via the same Keying folder in the Effects panel where you found Ultra Key.

To apply a garbage matte:

1. Select the Effects panel, and type **gar-bage** into the search bar. Premiere Pro's three garbage matte effects—Eight-Point Garbage Matte, Four-Point Gar-bage Matte, and Sixteen-Point Garbage Matte—appear. Alternatively, you can select Video Effects > Keying to reveal the garbage matte options .

2. Drag and drop one of the garbage mattes onto the keyed greenscreen foot-age . I'll use the Eight-Point Garbage Matte. The Eight-Point Garbage Matte effect appears in the Effect Controls panel, with eight horizontal and vertical position controls 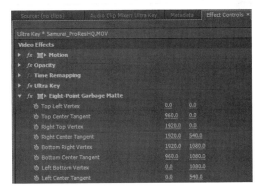. You can manually input values for each of these position controls, but there's a faster way.

A Garbage matte options.

B Dragging the Eight-Point Garbage Matte onto the foreground clip.

C Adjustable position controls.

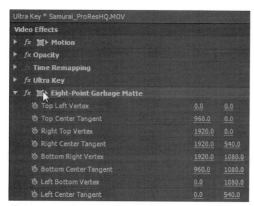

D Click the effect to make eight handles appear.

E Handles allow you to adjust the matte visually.

3. Click the Eight-Point Garbage Matte effect in the Effect Controls panel **D**. Eight handles appear around the green-screen footage **E**.

To adjust the garbage matte:

1. One at a time, grab the handles and bring them in **F**, being careful to ensure that your talent does not leave the area within the matte, and that you exclude anything that you don't want to end up in the final key (like the backdrop stands you can see in **E**).

2. My finished matte cuts out the backdrop but leaves room for the hand motions **G** (which will disappear into the composited background if I make the garbage matte too narrow in that part of the image).

3. Click an empty space in the Timeline or the Effect Controls panel to deselect the Eight-Point Garbage Matte handles, and your keying, compositing, and garbage matte are complete **H**.

F Moving the garbage matte handles to remove the greenscreen stand from the composited image.

G Handles pulled in; hand gestures intact.

H The final composited image.

Working with Transitions

Transitions are effects placed between clips on the Timeline to smooth the flow from clip to clip. Because transitions are so easy to apply, and available in such plentiful supply, they tend to be misused—variety is good, right?

Actually, no. In fact, transitions are best used only when they're "motivated." The concept of motivated transitions means to never use one unless it solves a problem, smooths the flow from clip to clip, or sends a necessary message to the viewer that something is changing.

In addition to when to use transitions, in this chapter you'll also learn how they work and how to apply them—singly and en masse—to both audio and video tracks.

One final note before we jump in: Make sure your project is very close to final form before you start adding transitions, since they complicate trimming and, particularly, motion-related effects.

In This Chapter

About Transitions

Transitions live in the Effects panel, in separate folders for audio and video 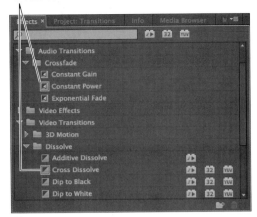. To find transitions, click the disclosure triangle to open a folder. To use them, simply drag the transition between the two target clips. Transitions marked in yellow are the default transitions applied when you use menu controls or keyboard shortcuts to insert them; you'll learn how to change the default in these tasks.

Technically, transitions are effects—that's why they're in the Effects panel. As you can see in **A**, transitions fall into the same three classes as effects: GPU-accelerated, 32-bit color, and YUV. You can read more about these categories, the differences between them, and when to choose among them in the "About Premiere Pro Effects" section of Chapter 9. To search for transitions, use the same procedure demonstrated in the task "To search for effects in the Effects panel" (also in Chapter 9).

The default duration for video and audio transitions is one second **B**, though you can change this in the General Preferences dialog (Edit > Preferences > General [Windows] or Premiere Pro > Preferences > General [Mac OS]).

The mechanics of transitions

When two clips abut each other on the Timeline, the transition between them is called a *cut*. Cuts (transitions without a transition effect) constitute the vast majority of transitions used in movies, television, and well-edited business and family videos.

Default transitions

A Transitions are in the Effects panel. Transitions marked in yellow are the defaults.

B Here's where you set the default transition duration.

When you apply a transition effect between two clips, Premiere Pro uses frames from the two clips to create the transition. When they're available, Premiere Pro uses frames trimmed from the end of the first clip (called the tail) and start of the second clip (called the head) to create the transition. When these frames aren't available, you'll see an error message **C**, and the transition will appear in the Timeline with zebra stripes **D**. These zebra stripes indicate that Premiere Pro used a static frame in the transition, which could be the last frame of the first clip, the first frame of the second clip, or both, depending upon whether the source clips had trimmed frames.

C You'll see this error message when you don't have trimmed frames available to create the transition.

In most projects, most clips will have trimmed frames on both ends, so this is seldom a problem. Even when it does occur, it's usually unnoticeable to all but the most discriminating viewers (like instructors and some bosses and clients). The only fix is to trim frames from the problem clip, but if you've already trimmed all you can, this isn't possible.

D Zebra stripes in your transitions mean that repeated frames are being used.

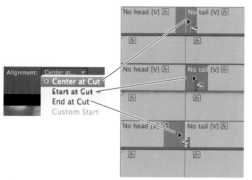

E The three alignments for transitions.

Premiere Pro will attempt to limit the impact of this problem. If both clips involved in the transition have available frames, or if neither does, you can choose Center at Cut (preferred), Start at Cut, or End at Cut **E**.

However, when one clip has trimmed frames available for the transition and the other doesn't, Premiere Pro will force you to insert the transition so that no frames are repeated **F**. In **F**, the first clip ("No tail") has no frames trimmed from the end of the clip, but the next clip ("head and tails") does. You can tell that a clip does not have trimmed frames available because its corner will display a small triangle, which indicates the end of the clip (or the start, when the triangle is at the front of the clip).

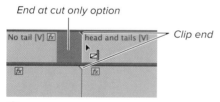

F I can't choose Center at Cut or Begin at Cut for this transition because the first clip has no trimmed frames from the end (hence the name "No tail").

So if you manually drag the transition to the intersection, your only choice will be End at Cut, since this uses no duplicated frames. Similarly, if you apply transitions automatically to a number of clips, Premiere Pro will choose this position. Though you can manually change the alignment of any of the three positions, you shouldn't, since this will force Premiere Pro to use a static frame that will be way more noticeable than the fact that the transition isn't centered.

As you'll see near the end of the chapter, Premiere Pro deals with clips without trimmed audio in a similar fashion.

The art of transitions

Time for the lecture. If you're an experienced editor, feel free to jump ahead.

For most producers, the best transitions are the ones that viewers never notice, or ones that they notice only because you want them to. Pay attention to how transitions are used in the next movie you watch, and you'll typically notice a fade-in at the start of the movie, transitions between major scenes, and a fade-out at the end. Clearly, transitions are not mandatory between every pair of clips on the Timeline.

As discussed in the introduction to this chapter, transitions are best used when they're motivated. For me, this includes several classes of transitions and several general rules.

Transitions signal major scene changes. Most movies or television shows don't use transitions between cuts within a scene. But when the scene changes from day to night, from one location to another, from one time to another, a transition lets the viewer know that something is changing.

The simplest way to convey change is the familiar fade in and fade out. Many videos fade in from black at the start and fade to black at the end. When you're producing for the web, on the other hand, if the first frame is displayed on the website, a visible frame with a title or other information may be preferable to a black frame. Similarly, if the last frame stays visible after playback, you may wish to leave a call to action or logo on that frame.

Transitions should match the mood of the project. If you're producing a kids' show or a home movie about your kids, wild and wacky transitions are almost *de rigueur*, though you'll have to find a third-party library for them since Premiere Pro's transitions are pretty businesslike. Adobe lists third-party libraries of transitions and effects at bit.ly/moreeffects. If you're producing a business video or something with a more serious tone, limit yourself to transitions that match the mood. In this regard, my motto is, "when in doubt, dissolve."

Cube Spin transition

I inserted this Cube Spin transition to make it clear to the viewer that there was a transition between the two adjacent clips.

You can also use transitions to smooth the flow from one clip to another. Though I'm probably in the minority, I prefer very short (three to five frames) transitions between switched camera angles in my multicamera projects. These are short cross-dissolve transitions that smooth the hard cut from camera to camera.

The other scenario that I smooth with transitions is the jump-cut, where the footage in the two clips involved is so similar that it's tough to see that a transition occurred—it just looks like the speaker jumped a bit. You see this in ⒢, where I'm editing a tutorial video. Because the two clips are visually identical, I inserted a Cube Spin transition between the first and second clip, which makes the transition obvious to the viewer. Other techniques I've seen include a fast Dip to White transition.

Long transitions look ugly when compressed. If you're producing video for streaming, try to keep transitions around half a second or less, since longer transitions can appear noticeably blocky.

OK, lecture over. Let's learn how to apply and customize transitions.

Working with Transitions

As with all effects, transitions are first applied and then customized as desired. You can also change the default transition used when inserting transitions via keyboard shortcuts or menu commands. We'll start there.

Then we'll look at two ways to add a transition between clips (manually and via keyboard shortcuts), cover some basic transition-related housekeeping functions, and look at how to customize a transition. Next, you'll learn how to insert a single-sided transition to the start and end of the video on the Timeline and to fade in from black and out to black. The final task will teach you how to add audio and video transitions to multiple clips on the Timeline.

If you plan to add and configure multiple transitions, you might consider entering the Effects workspace by choosing Window > Workspace > Effects. Typically, however, inserting and configuring transitions is so fast and easy that I stay in the Editing workspace.

To set the default video or audio transition:

Right-click the target transition and choose Set Selected as Default Transition **Ⓐ**. Premiere Pro sets that transition as the new default **Ⓑ**.

Current default

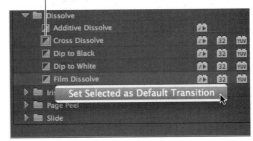

Ⓐ Choosing a new default transition.

New default

Ⓑ The yellow box around the transition identifies the default.

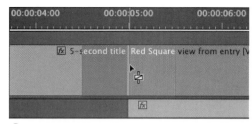

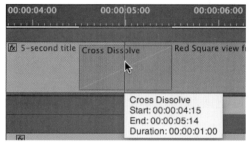

C Drag the transition to the intersection between the two clips, and choose the alignment (Center at Cut shown here).

Cross Dissolve
Start: 00:00:04:15
End: 00:00:05:14
Duration: 00:00:01:00

D The name is clearly visible, and you can get more information by hovering your pointer over the transition.

To manually add a video transition between two clips:

1. Drag the transition from the Effects panel to the intersection between the two target clips.

2. Do one of the following:

   ▸ If all alignment positions are available (Center at Cut, Start at Cut, and End at Cut), choose the desired alignment. Generally, Center at Cut works and looks best **C**.

   ▸ If there are insufficient trimmed frames on both clips, Premiere Pro will force you to choose either Start at Cut or End at Cut (whichever will result in the fewest number of repeated frames). You can change this when configuring the transition, but the alignment Premiere Pro forces you into is generally the best choice.

   Premiere Pro inserts the transition with the name visible **D**; learn more about the transition by hovering your pointer over it.

To add a video transition via a keyboard shortcut:

1. Position the playhead between the two target clips .

2. Do one of the following:

   ▸ Press Control/Command+D.

   ▸ Choose Sequence > Apply Video Transition.

   Premiere Pro inserts the default transition into the selected intersection . If heads and tails exist, or if neither clip has trimmed frames, Premiere Pro will choose the Center at Cut alignment. If trimmed frames are available on one clip but not the other, Premiere Pro will choose the alignment that produces the fewest repeated frames. For example, since there were plenty of frames trimmed from the end of the first clip (named "Plenty of tails") and none trimmed from the start of the second clip ("No head"), Premiere Pro started the transition at the cut, since that would use no duplicate frames (the transition would use 30 trimmed frames from the first clip and the first 30 frames of the second).

To delete a transition:

Do one of the following:

- Click the transition and press Backspace (Windows) or Delete (Mac OS).

- Right-click the transition and choose Clear 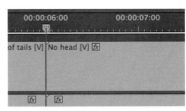.

Premiere Pro deletes the transition .

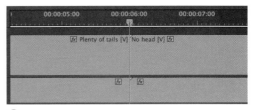

E To use a keyboard shortcut to insert a transition, place the playhead at the target intersection.

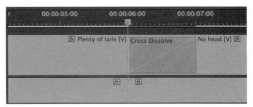

F Premiere Pro started the transition at the cut because there were no trimmed frames from the start of the second clip.

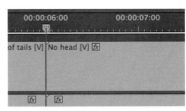

G To delete a transition, right-click it and choose Clear.

H Premiere Pro deletes the transition.

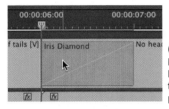

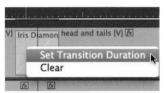

I To replace this Cross Dissolve transition, drag another transition onto it and release.

J Premiere Pro inserts the Iris Diamond transition it its place.

K Opening the Set Transition Duration dialog.

L Type in the new duration and click OK.

M The one-second transition is now two seconds long.

To replace a transition:

Drag a transition from the Effects panel and drop it on the existing transition **I**. Premiere Pro replaces the transition **J**.

To change transition duration in the Set Transition Duration dialog:

1. Do one of the following:

   ▸ Double-click the transition.

   ▸ Right-click the transition and choose Set Transition Duration **K**.

   The Set Transition Duration dialog opens.

2. Enter the desired transition duration and click OK **L**. Premiere Pro changes the transition duration **M**.

To adjust transition duration by dragging in the Timeline:

1. Hover your pointer over one edge of the transition. Your pointer changes to the transition drag pointer ⬛.

2. Drag to the desired duration . A yellow box beneath the pointer displays the distance dragged and the new transition duration. As the start position for the transition updates, the Program Monitor displays the frame and timecode of the start frame ⓞ.

> **TIP** To adjust one side or the other (and not both), hold the Shift key while dragging ⓟ.

> **TIP** If you have insufficient frames in either clip, Premiere Pro won't let you adjust duration proportionately, or on the side that has insufficient frames. To adjust the other side, press the Shift key.

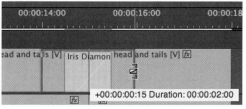

Ⓝ Dragging the transition to the new duration.

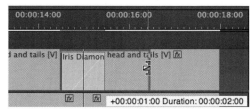

Ⓞ The Program Monitor provides visual feedback.

Ⓟ You can drag one side or the other by pressing the Shift key while dragging.

Effect Controls Timeline

Play the transition

Show/Hide Timeline View

A Open the Effect Controls panel, and click Show/Hide Timeline View to open the Effect Controls Timeline.

B The big-picture view of the Effect Controls panel. Note the tiny preview function on the upper left.

C Entering a new duration.

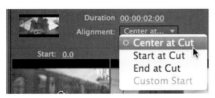

D Choosing an alignment.

Customizing Transitions

Like effects, transitions are unique and have different configuration options. Duration is one of the few options that is available for all transitions. As you'll see, you customize transitions in the Effect Controls panel while previewing in the Program Monitor.

To customize a transition:

1. Click the transition in the Timeline to select it.

2. Open the Effect Controls panel to access the configuration options **A**.

3. If necessary, click Show/Hide Timeline View to open the Effect Controls Timeline **A**.

4. At the top of the Effect Controls panel, click the Play button to see a (very tiny) preview of the transition. Select the Show Actual Sources check box to replace the A B slates **B**.

5. If desired, click the Duration field to make it active, and type a new duration (200 = 00:00:02:00) **C**.

6. If desired, choose a different alignment from the Alignment menu **D**. Unlike when you're dragging the transition into the Timeline, Premiere Pro will let you choose an alignment that produces repeated frames, though you'll see the zebra-stripe warnings.

continues on next page

7. If desired, drag the sliders beneath the preview windows to different starting and ending positions **E**.

8. To configure the transition using the A B slates, deselect the Show Actual Sources check box **F**.

9. To create a border, do one of the following:

- ▸ Hover your pointer over the Border Width field. Your pointer becomes the two-headed drag pointer ![drag pointer icon]. Drag to the desired value.

- ▸ Click the Border Width field to make it active, and type the desired border value **G**.

10. To change the border color, click the Border Color color chip **H**, which opens the Color Picker dialog **I**.

11. If you're producing a video for web distribution, select the Only Web Colors check box on the lower left of the Color Picker **I**.

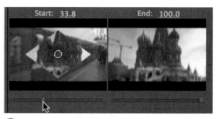

E Choosing a new start frame for the transition.

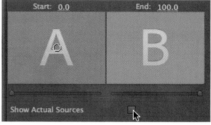

F You can preview using the A B slates, or select the Show Actual Sources check box to preview with the actual sources.

G Creating a border for the transition.

H Click the color chip.

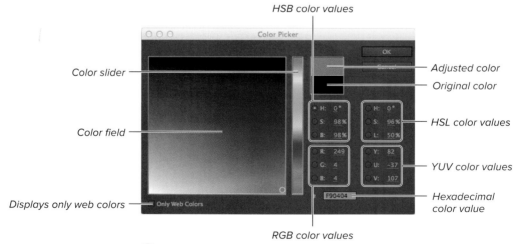

HSB color values

Color slider

Color field

Displays only web colors

RGB color values

Adjusted color

Original color

HSL color values

YUV color values

Hexadecimal color value

I Choose a color.

J Here's the spiffy border.

K Select the Reverse check box to reverse the effect—just another creative option.

L If your transition has sharp edges (particularly borders), you should choose the highest anti-aliasing quality.

12. To choose the color for the matte, do one of the following I:

- ▸ Click the color slider in the center to select a color for the Color field. Finalize your selection by clicking in the Color field.

- ▸ Directly enter Hue, Saturation, and Brightness (HSB) values by clicking the text field and typing the desired value.

- ▸ Directly enter Hue, Saturation, and Lightness (HSL) values by clicking the text field and typing the desired value.

- ▸ Directly enter Red, Green, and Blue (RGB) values by clicking the text field and typing the desired value.

- ▸ Directly enter Y, U, and V values by clicking the text field and typing the desired value.

- ▸ On the bottom right, directly enter the Hexadecimal color value.

13. Click OK I to close the Color Picker, and preview the border and color in the Program Monitor J.

14. If desired, select the Reverse check box to reverse the transition K. In this case, it would reverse the transition from a small diamond within clip A opening up to clip B, to a large diamond closing down on clip A to reveal clip B.

15. Choose a quality from the Anti-aliasing Quality menu L. When the transition has a border, particularly with diagonal lines, you should select High.

16. Preview the transition a few times in real time (after rendering, if necessary) to gauge final quality.

Fading In from and Out to Black

Fading from black at the start of the clip and to black at the end used to be almost a stylistic necessity. As mentioned, however, if the video is bound for web delivery, you need to ascertain whether the first frame will be shown within the video frame on the webpage, and whether the final frame (which may contain some kind of call to action, contact information, or logo) will remain onscreen after playback. If the answer to either of these questions is yes, you probably don't want to fade in or fade out.

If no, you probably do, and here are the simple procedures.

To fade in from black:

Do one of the following:

- Drag the Cross Dissolve transition from the Effects panel to the start of the video on the Timeline Ⓐ.

- Press the Home key to navigate the playhead to the start of video and (with Cross Dissolve as the default transition), press Control/Command+D.

  Premiere Pro inserts the Cross Dissolve transition at the start of the video Ⓑ.

Ⓐ To fade in from black, drag the Cross Dissolve transition from the Effects panel to the start of the video.

Ⓑ The inserted Cross Dissolve will fade the clip in from black.

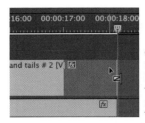

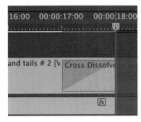

C To fade out to black, drag the Cross Dissolve transition from the Effects panel to the end of the video.

D The inserted Cross Dissolve will fade the clip out to black.

To fade out to black:

Do one of the following:

- Drag the Cross Dissolve transition from the Effects panel to the end of the video on the Timeline **C**.

- Press the End key to navigate the play-head to the end of the video and (with Cross Dissolve as the Default transition), press Control/Command+D.

  Premiere Pro inserts the Cross Dissolve transition at the end of the video **D**.

TIP Although using the Cross Dissolve to fade in from black works well, sometimes fading to black using this transition doesn't go to full black quickly enough for me. In these cases, I prefer to use the Opacity controls to fade to black, as discussed in "Working with Keyframes" in Chapter 8.

Transitions and Titles

I'm a stickler for inserting short transitions (like five to seven frames) at the beginning and end of all titles used in the Timeline; it's a nice touch of polish. The procedure outlined here will also work to insert these transitions; just substitute the start and end of the title for the start and end of the video in the tasks.

What slows you down is navigating to the individual titles, which are typically on track V2 or higher ⒠. You can use the Down Arrow key to navigate from edit point to edit point, but if you're using the default settings, you'll stop at every edit point on all tracks.

The simple answer is to disable track targeting on V1 and A1 by clicking the Toggle Track Targeting header. When the track gets darker, targeting is off. With V1/A1 off, the Down Arrow key will take you to the next edit point on V2 (or whichever track is enabled).

Using the keyboard shortcut for inserting the default transition (Control/Command+D), you can add transitions into and out of each title with four keystrokes:

- Down Arrow (to get to the start of the transition)
- Control/Command+D to insert a transition there
- Down Arrow again to get to the end of the title
- Control/Command+D to insert a transition there

Just remember to first change the default transition duration to five to seven frames, or you'll be changing all those transitions manually after you insert them.

The other, even faster, alternative is discussed later in this chapter in "Adding the Default Transitions to Multiple Clips."

TIP I discuss track targeting in general in "Working with Track Targeting" in Chapter 6.

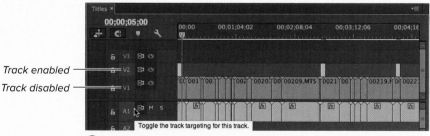

Track enabled
Track disabled

⒠ Disable track targeting on V1 and A1, and the Down Arrow key will navigate directly to all titles on V2.

A Your three audio transitions.

Audio Transitions

Just as video clips need transitions to ease the flow from clip to clip, so do audio clips. For this reason, Premiere Pro includes three audio transitions in a separate folder in the Effects panel **A**. For a technical description as to why Constant Power is the default transition, search for "audio crossfade transitions" in the Premiere Pro Help file.

Audio transitions operate very similarly to video transitions: You add them the same way, you can stretch them to the desired duration, you edit them the same way, and you can use them to fade in and fade out at the start and end of your videos (or the audio files within your videos).

Audio transitions work with trimmed audio, just like video transitions work with trimmed video. So if there isn't trimmed audio available, Premiere Pro makes certain adjustments, as you'll learn.

Here I'll show you how to add an audio transition manually and via keyboard shortcuts. You can figure out the rest by referring to the video-related transition tasks.

To manually add an audio transition between two clips:

1. Drag the transition from the Effects panel to the intersection between the two target clips.

2. Do one of the following:

   ▸ If all alignment positions are available (Center at Cut, Start at Cut, End at Cut), choose the desired alignment. This happens only when you have sufficient trimmed audio on both clips. Generally, Center at Cut is the preferred alignment **B**.

   ▸ If sufficient trimmed audio is available on one clip but not the other, Premiere Pro will force you to the side that enables the transition without repeated audio **C**.

   ▸ If there is insufficient trimmed audio on either clip, Premiere Pro will force you into either the Start at Cut or End at Cut alignment. You can change this when configuring the transition, but the alignment Premiere Pro forces you into is generally the best choice.

   Premiere Pro inserts the transition.

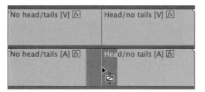

B Drag the transition to the intersection between the two clips, and choose the alignment (Center at Cut shown here).

C Premiere Pro forces the Start at Cut alignment because there is trimmed audio in the first clip ("No head/tails") but not the second ("No head/tail").

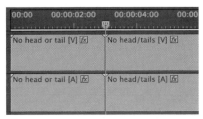

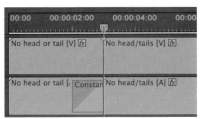

D To insert the default transition using keyboard shortcuts, navigate the playhead to the target insertion point.

E Since there were no heads or tails on these clips, Premiere Pro inserted the transition in the End at Cut alignment.

To add an audio transition via a keyboard shortcut:

1. Position the playhead between the two target clips **D**.

2. Do one of the following:

   ▸ Press Control/Command+Shift+D.

   ▸ Choose Sequence > Apply Audio Transition.

   Premiere Pro inserts the default transition into the selected intersection. If sufficient trimmed audio exists on both clips, Premiere Pro will choose the Center at Cut alignment **B**. If trimmed frames are available on one clip but not the other, Premiere Pro will choose the alignment that uses the available trimmed audio **C**. If neither clip has trimmed audio, Premiere Pro will use the End at Cut alignment **E**.

Adding the Default Transitions to Multiple Clips

Premiere Pro makes it easy to add the default audio and video transitions, including audio and video fade-ins and fade-outs, via one menu command.

I'm going to make life easy on all of us and perform this task on clips with plenty of video and audio heads and tails. If there weren't sufficient heads or tails, Premiere Pro would take the actions described in the tasks "To add a video transition via a keyboard shortcut" and "To add an audio transition via a keyboard shortcut."

Note that you can easily add transitions in and out to all titles in a project by selecting all the titles and following the procedure.

To add the default transitions to multiple clips:

1. In the Timeline, select the target clips. Here, I'm drawing a marquee around the five clips in my opening sequence .

2. Do one of the following:
   ▸ Choose Sequence > Apply Default Transitions to Selection.
   ▸ Press Shift+D.

   Premiere Pro inserts the default audio and video transitions, including fade-ins and fade-outs .

TIP Note that I shortened the default transitions to five frames and .25 of a second, respectively, before applying them.

 I'm dragging a marquee to select all content in the Timeline.

 One keystroke combination later (Shift+D), I'm all set.

Color and Brightness Correction

Few shoots go perfectly outside of a studio setting. In 15 years of shooting and editing video, I can remember only three or four projects where I didn't adjust brightness, color, or both. Fortunately, Premiere Pro makes these adjustments easy, with multiple tools of varying complexity levels and scopes to help add objectivity to an otherwise subjective function.

In this chapter, we'll tackle two basic adjustments: first, brightness and contrast; then color correction. The goal of these adjustments is to optimize the exposure and color of the video as if you had captured it perfectly at the shoot.

The final topic involves applying a Lumetri look to your video. Rather than addressing a correction function, the goal of this exercise is to give your video a different look and feel.

This chapter is toward the end of the book because it covers fairly advanced topics that require several skills addressed earlier in the book. In terms of project workflow, I recommend adjusting exposure and color as soon as you're sure the clip will remain in the project.

In This Chapter

Working in Color Correction Mode

All of the brightness and color correction effects discussed in this chapter are just that: effects found in the Effects panel, and configured in the Effect Controls panel. When adjusting these effects, you'll want easy access to the Effect Controls panel and the ability to access any number of video scopes. Premiere Pro has a special workspace called the Color Correction workspace, which accomplishes both of these functions.

To enter the Color Correction workspace:

Do one of the following:

- Choose Window > Workspace > Color Correction **A**.

- Press Alt/Option+Shift+3.

    Premiere Pro enters the Color Correction workspace **B**.

A Entering the Color Correction workspace.

Effect Controls panel   *Timeline*   *Program Monitor in Tonal Range mode*

Reference Monitor

Waveform Monitor scope

B The Color Correction workspace . Note that you won't see color wheels if you haven't already added color correction effects.

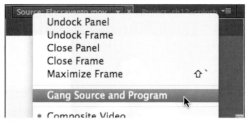

C Ganging the Source Monitor and Program Monitor to get the before-and-after view.

Midtones   *Highlights*   *Shadows*

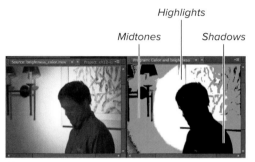

D Composite (full-color) view on the left in the Source Monitor; Tonal Range view on the right in the Program Monitor.

E The three tonal ranges adjusted by the Three-way Color Corrector.

The Color Correction workspace provides up to three views of your video. If you "gang" the Source Monitor and Program Monitor via the Source Monitor panel menu **C**, you see two views of the same video. Since the Program Monitor displays the video after you apply effects, and the Source Monitor before effects, you get the before and after view, supplemented by whichever scope you have configured into the Reference Monitor. Note that the Reference Monitor should automatically gang with the Program Monitor, but if it doesn't, there's a similar gang menu option in its panel menu.

Understanding tonal ranges

In **B**, the Program Monitor is in Tonal Range view, which helps illustrate one of the fundamental concepts underlying both exposure and color correction. When making certain brightness and contrast adjustments, Premiere Pro divides the video into three tonal ranges based upon brightness: shadows, midtones, and highlights. On the right in **D**, you see blacks, grays, and whites, which correspond to these values.

Several effects, like the Three-Way Color Corrector **E**, have specific controls that target one of these regions. For example, the Highlights color wheel **E** will adjust only the colors in the white regions in the Program Monitor in **D**. These tools are configured in this manner because sometimes color issues occur in one tonal range but not the others.

Similarly, to correct exposure issues, often you want to adjust one tonal range. For example, when a backlight condition occurs, the face—which is often in the midtones or shadows regions—is too dark. Meanwhile, other regions—typically the highlights—are fine. To correct this, you usually need to adjust only the shadows and midtones without boosting the highlights. Though there are some caveats I'll discuss later, the ability to adjust primarily the shadows is what makes the Shadow/Highlight effect  so effective at correcting backlighting; you can boost the brightness in the shadows without boosting the highlights.

When you're diagnosing a brightness- or color-related issue, one of the most important questions to ask is whether the problem affects all tonal ranges evenly. If so, you can use general-purpose tools—like the Brightness & Contrast and Fast Color Corrector effects—that adjust all tonal ranges equally.

If the problem is specific to a tonal range, like backlighting, you'll need a tool that lets you address the tonal ranges separately. For exposure, you would use the Shadow/Highlight or Gamma Correction effect—or, in the color realm, the Three-Way Color Corrector.

Later in the chapter, we'll spend more time adjusting brightness and color using many of these tools. But since tonal range is a foundational concept, I wanted to cover that up front.

Incidentally, to show the tonal ranges you must apply the Luma Corrector effect and choose Tonal Range output . This is not an effect that we will otherwise discuss.

F The Shadow/Highlight effect lets you adjust the brightness of the shadows and highlights separately.

G To generate the Tonal Range view, apply the Luma Corrector and choose Tonal Range.

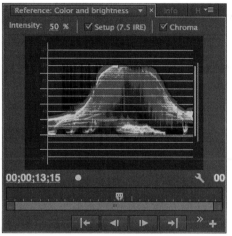

Using the Waveform Monitor

I identify the scopes available in all monitors in the Chapter 4 section "Choosing Display Modes"; you can find a thorough description there. The scope that's most useful for brightness and contrast adjustments is the Waveform Monitor, which you can open in any monitor—not just the Reference Monitor.

Note that you don't have to enter the Color Correction workspace to open the Reference Monitor. You can do that in any workspace by choosing Window > Reference Monitor.

To choose the Waveform Monitor:

Click the Settings button 🔧, and choose YC Waveform Ⓐ. Premiere Pro opens the YC waveform in the selected monitor Ⓑ.

To configure the Waveform Monitor:

1. Deselect the Chroma check box Ⓒ. This removes the chroma (color) values from the scope, which aren't that helpful.

2. Deselect the Setup (7.5 IRE) check box. This sets the scope's black level to 0 Ⓒ.

3. Set the Intensity value to 100%, which makes the scope easier to read Ⓒ.

Ⓐ Choosing the YC waveform.

Ⓑ Here it is; now let's configure it.

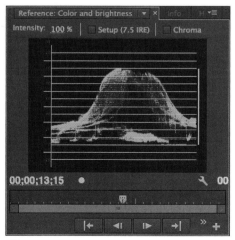

Ⓒ The preferred configuration for the YC waveform.

Interpreting the Waveform Monitor

D shows the Waveform Monitor within the Program Monitor, next to the same video in the Source panel. Briefly, the Waveform Monitor displays the brightness of pixels in the frame in a range from −20 to +120 on the IRE (Institute of Radio Engineers) scale. All pixels with values lower than 0 or higher than 100 start to lose detail, which is called clipping or crushing.

In a perfectly exposed shot, the whitest highlights would be at 100 IRE, the blackest shadows would be at 0 IRE, and the average pixels in the face would be around 70 IRE.

In **D**, we see that the highlights are in good shape, pushing against 100 IRE. The shadows are also in good shape, with many reaching down to 0 IRE. But the midtones are a mess, with the face averaging around 35 IRE, which is way too low.

To fix these issues, you boost the shadows until the bulk of the pixels in the face are in the 70 IRE range. You do this without pushing the highlights much higher or pulling the darkest shadows off the 0 IRE value, which causes fading.

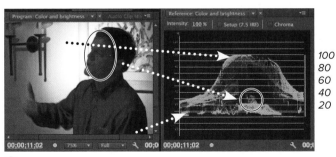

D The highlights are fine, as are the darkest shadows, but the face is way below the target.

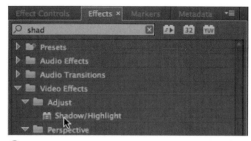

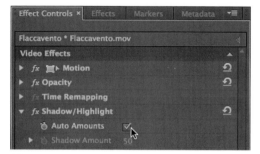

E Finding the Shadow/Highlight effect in the Effects panel.

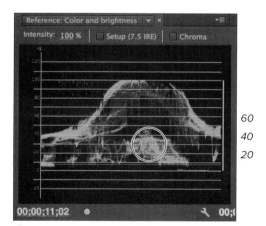

F By default, Premiere Pro enables Auto Amounts.

G The face is brighter, but not nearly enough.

This is the classic backlight situation, which we'll resolve in a moment. Although space doesn't allow us to examine every problem that you might have to address, the waveform gives you three objective reference points—0, 70, and 100—that should let you diagnose whether the problem is universal (too bright, too dark) or specific to a single tonal range, as it is here. If universal, the Brightness & Contrast adjustment should work well; if specific to a tonal range, my favorites are the Shadow/Highlight and Gamma Correction effects, which I'll demonstrate.

To adjust exposure with the Shadow/Highlight effect:

1. In the Effects panel, locate the Shadow/Highlight effect E. I did so by typing "shad" in the search field. Apply the effect to the target clip. Premiere Pro applies the effect with Auto Amounts enabled F, which brightens the face significantly G but not to the target of 70 IRE. Let's see if we can improve that result.

continues on next page

2. Deselect the Auto Amounts check box to shift into manual mode.

3. Adjust the Shadow Amount value until the face is within the target range. Watch for a halo effect if the adjustment is too severe. For this video, a value of 85 is about right ⒣. This adjustment boosts the highlights as well, which I'll reduce by dragging the Highlight Amount value to 50. Unfortunately, this pulls the darkest shadows far from 0 IRE ⒤, causing a slight fading.

4. To counteract the fading, apply the Brightness & Contrast effect and adjust the controls to bring the shadows closer to 0 IRE, while keeping the face as close to 70 IRE as possible. With this clip, a configuration of 0 for Brightness and 8.0 for Contrast worked for me ⒥.

5. To gauge the impact of the effect, click the "Toggle the effect on or off" button 🔲 to preview with and without the effect ⒦.

   The improvement is striking ⒧ because the problem was very significant to begin with. With most footage, a similar exercise would produce much less noticeable results, but at the very least, you should be able to brighten the face and improve contrast.

6. Render and preview. This is particularly important with the Shadow/Highlight effect, which has had problems with causing flickering (Google "Shadow/Highlight flicker" to see what I mean). If the flicker is unacceptable, try using the Gamma Correction effect.

TIP Note in ⒣ that once you disable Auto Amounts, Temporal Smoothing, which has been promoted as one potential cure for the flicker described in step 6, is grayed out and disabled.

⒣ Deselect the Auto Amounts check box and try your own settings.

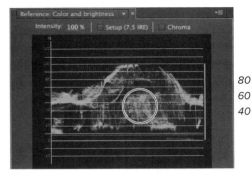

⒤ The face is much brighter, but some of the darker shadows have been pulled from 0 IRE.

⒥ I added the Brightness & Contrast effect to correct this.

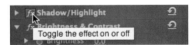

⒦ Toggle the effect on and off to gauge the result.

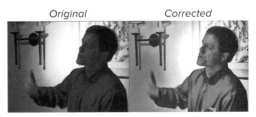

Original   *Corrected*

⒧ Pretty striking results. Though it's not perfect, at least you can recognize the speaker.

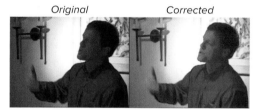
The Gamma Correction effect adjusts only the midtones, so I needed the Brightness & Contrast effect to finish the job.

Original   *Corrected*

The effects again brightened the face and enhanced the overall color.

Working with the Gamma Correction effect

Again, the problem with this video is that the issue isn't universal; the highlights are clearly bright enough, but we need to boost the midtones and shadows. If the Shadow/Highlight effect causes flicker or haloing, try Gamma Correction.

Here's the description of the Gamma Correction effect from the Premiere Pro online Help file: "The Gamma Correction effect lightens or darkens a clip without substantially changing the shadows and highlights. It does this by changing the brightness levels of the midtones (the middle-gray levels), while leaving the dark and light areas unaffected. The default gamma setting is 10. In the effect's Settings dialog box, you can adjust the gamma from 1 to 28."

Since you already know how to apply and configure an effect and read a waveform, I'll cut to the chase and show the final settings and the comparison. As you can see, I applied the Brightness & Contrast effect again to finalize the overall results. The face background is significantly brighter, but the Gamma Correction effect lacks the ability to reduce the highlights, which the Shadow/Highlight effect offers.

Fixing Dingy Clips (and the Essence of Contrast)

Few clips that you have to fix will be as bad as the clip shown in this task. But many clips will appear dingy, like the clip we'll color-correct in the next set of tasks **O**. The clip has a bluish tinge, and overall looks gloomy and drab. Since you should always fix brightness before color, let's do that.

Looking at the frame, you can see sun streaming on the ground, and clear whites in the frame. In the waveform, however, the brightest highlights are well below 100 IRE. So we definitely need to brighten all the tonal modes—shadows, midtones, and highlights—of the video.

In addition, the bulk of the pixels are clumped within a very limited range. The term *contrast* refers to the separation between the brightest and darkest pixels in the frame. When there is little separation, as there is here, the video lacks contrast.

Sounds like the perfect job for the Brightness & Contrast effect. With these values **P**, you get the results in **Q**; the Brightness adjustment boosted the IRE level of all pixels evenly, while the Contrast adjustment pushed the brightest and darkest pixels farther apart.

It's very rare that a video can't benefit at least a little bit from some tweaking of contrast and brightness.

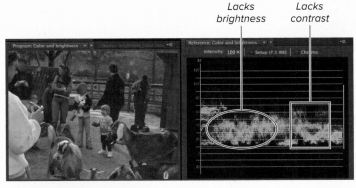

Lacks brightness *Lacks contrast*

O Oops, first day with a new camera, and it shows. Both exposure and color are hosed.

P I used the Brightness & Contrast effect with these settings.

fx Brightness & Contrast	
Brightness	35.0
Contrast	39.0

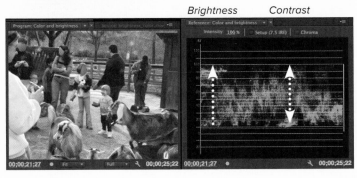

Brightness *Contrast*

Q The Brightness adjustment boosted the brightness of all pixels in the video. The Contrast adjustment increased the spread between the darkest and lightest pixels.

A Our starting point for the color correction. Someone was having a blue day.

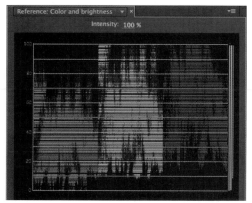

B The RGB Parade scope. There's lots of green in the scene, so that makes sense, but blue is clearly dominant over red—that's the bluish cast.

Color-Correcting Your Video

To me, color correction means adjusting the color of a video so that it matches the precise reality of the colors at the actual shoot. It conforms the video to that reality. For important shoots, it's always a good idea to bring a DSLR camera to capture a high-quality image, just so you know what the reality was.

In contrast, color grading goes beyond conforming to reality; instead, you're trying to create an alternate look for the video. We'll look at the color grading side later in this chapter when we apply a Lumetri look to several clips via an adjustment layer.

Like many things in editing, color correction can be short and sweet or it can take forever. You can use tools like the Fast Color Corrector for both exposure correction and color correction, or just for the latter. I prefer using these tools because they make sense to me, which is 99 percent of the battle.

Color-related scopes

The scope I find most valuable when correcting color is the RGB parade. The usual process is that I'll look at a clip, like the zoo clip in **A**, and think, "Man, that clip looks blue—did I hose the white balance?" Then I check the RGB parade **B**, which shows a blue/green dominance over red, and say, "Yup, I sure did." The scope is also helpful in confirming corrective adjustments, and especially when trying to match the color characteristics of clips in a multiple-camera shoot.

To choose the RGB parade:

Click the Settings button ![wrench icon], and choose RGB Parade **C**. Premiere Pro opens the RGB parade in the selected monitor **B**.

Interpreting the RGB Parade scope

The RGB Parade scope displays the comparative levels of the red, green, and blue pixels in a frame. Obviously, you have to take into account the content in the footage in this analysis; if the video is of a man in a blue suit on a blue couch in a blue room, blue will appropriately predominate. In **A**, however, we don't have that; we have a natural scene that shouldn't be dominated by one color over another. A quick look at **B** confirms that blue and green are dominating over red. Let's fix that with the Fast Color Corrector.

Using the Fast Color Corrector effect

When you adjust the white balance of your camera at a shoot, you point the camera at a white object and push the white balance button, essentially telling the camera, "Hey, this is white." With the Fast Color Corrector, you do pretty much the same thing.

To correct color using the Fast Color Corrector effect:

1. In the Effects panel, locate the Fast Color Corrector effect, and apply it to your target clip. If you've already adjusted color and brightness with a separate effect, make sure the Fast Color Corrector is beneath that effect **D** in the Effect Controls panel.

2. If necessary, click the disclosure triangle to the left of the Fast Color Corrector effect to reveal its configurable properties **E**.

C Opening the RGB Parade scope.

D Dragging the Fast Color Corrector beneath the Brightness & Contrast effect.

E Click a known white object in the frame.

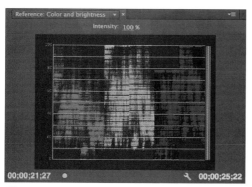

Balance magnitude

Balance angle

Balance gain

F Drag the color correction widget for gross adjustments, and fine-tune with the numerical adjustments below.

Intensity: 100 %

00;00;21;27

00;00;25;22

G Red and blue are now about equal.

3. If desired, select the Show Split View check box and choose Layout and Percentage **E**.

4. Click the eyedropper next to the White Balance chip, and Control/Command-click a spot in the frame that's supposed to be white **E**. Sample a few areas to see which provides the best overall result. The color chip assumes the selected color, which sets the initial value for the correction.

5. If necessary, drag the outside color wheel, the color correction widget, or both to optimize the correction, and then fine-tune with the numerical controls **F**.

Pulling the widget away from center strengthens the adjustment, and rotating the widget changes the color adjusted. Often it helps to view the RGB parade; here, in this green-dominated scene, I'm trying to get the reds and blues fairly close **G**.

continues on next page

6. Experiment by boosting the Saturation value to see if this improves the look **H**.

7. To gauge the impact of the effect, click the "Toggle the effect on or off" button **fx** to preview with and without the effect. In just a few moments, we turned a dingy blue memory into a sunny, colorful day **I**.

8. Once you've finalized your adjustments, remember to deselect the Show Split View check box; otherwise, Premiere Pro will render the split into your video.

TIP If there's no white in the frame, change to a frame with white in it. If there are no frames with white, pull the widget away from the dominant color as shown in the RGB parade.

TIP You can check for the precise definitions of the Fast Color Corrector adjustments in the Premiere Pro Help file. I typically adjust intensity by dragging the widget farther from or closer to the center, and I adjust the color by dragging the widget around the wheel.

▶ ⊙ Saturation   120.00

H While you're here, try boosting Saturation a bit to make your color pop.

Original   Corrected

I I can get pretty excited about this kind of improvement, particularly since it takes five minutes or less.

Applying Lumetri Effects with Adjustment Layers

OK, we've learned how to correct brightness and color issues, restoring our videos to the reality of the day and maybe adding a touch of extra saturation. Once this is done, you may want to apply a Lumetri look to your videos to create a certain look or feel.

SpeedGrade is the color-grading component of the Creative Suite. One of SpeedGrade's outputs is a LUT (lookup table) that contains canned instructions for color and exposure adjustments to achieve a certain look. You can make your own LUTs in SpeedGrade and deploy them in Premiere Pro, and Premiere Pro comes with pre-baked looks that you can apply to your videos.

If you're going to apply a Lumetri look to a video, the best approach is to use an adjustment layer, which is a special kind of layer that you can position over other clips in the Timeline. Any standard effects applied to the adjustment layer are added to the clips below it. Not only do adjustment layers save time over other techniques for applying effects to multiple clips simultaneously, but they also provide one centralized location for making any changes.

In the next two tasks, you'll learn to apply an adjustment layer and then add a canned Lumetri look from the Effects panel.

To add an adjustment layer to a sequence:

1. Open the sequence that you want to add the adjustment layer to.

2. On the bottom right of the Project panel, click the New Item button , and choose Adjustment Layer ⑧. The Adjustment Layer dialog opens ⓒ.

3. The configuration shown in the Adjustment Layer dialog matches the open sequence. To create an adjustment layer using that configuration, click OK ⓒ. Premiere Pro creates the adjustment layer and adds it to the Project panel ⑩. You can rename the adjustment layer and otherwise treat it like any other clip.

4. Add the adjustment layer to the sequence, and drag it over the target clips Ⓔ.

Ⓐ Click the New Item icon to add an adjustment layer.

Ⓑ Choose Adjustment Layer.

Ⓒ The specs match that of the open sequence; click OK to create the adjustment layer.

Ⓓ Premiere Pro inserts the adjustment layer in the Project panel.

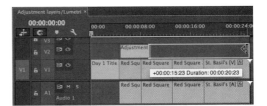

Ⓔ Add it to the sequence and spread it over the clips, and you're all set.

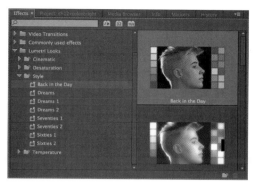

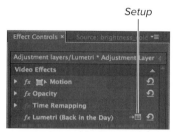

F You'll find the Lumetri looks in the Effects panel. Just drag one onto the adjustment layer.

Setup

G Here's the Lumetri look in the Effect Controls panel. Click Setup to load your own look or LUT.

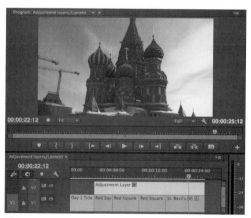

H The look applies to all clips under the adjustment layer.

To add a Lumetri look to an adjustment layer:

1. In the Effects panel, locate the Lumetri Looks folder, which should be at or near the bottom **F**.

2. Click the disclosure triangle to reveal the subfolders, and again to view looks within the folders. View the looks in the Effects panel, and choose a look. I'll go with Back in the Day for a sepia feel **G**.

3. Add the Lumetri look to the adjustment layer like any other effect (dragging is fine). The look will appear in the Effect Controls panel, where you can toggle the effect on and off to preview it, but you can't configure or keyframe it **G**. Premiere Pro will apply the look to any clip located under the adjustment layer **H**.

TIP You can choose a look or LUT file on your hard drive by clicking the Setup icon **G**. In the Select a Look/LUT dialog that appears, navigate to and load the LUT.

Multi-Camera Editing

Just as a technical director switches live camera feeds on a video switcher, a Premiere Pro editor can view and choose from multiple camera angles. The Multi-Camera Monitor provides significant time savings compared to viewing one video angle at a time in the single-view Program Monitor.

As with any media mixed in Premiere Pro sequences, the camera angles don't all need to be recorded in the same codec, but as the number of camera angles increases, so will the CPU, GPU, and hard drive requirements. You can edit as many camera angles in the Multi-Camera Monitor as your editing hardware can support.

When you're filming multi-camera content that you plan to edit in post (rather than switch live), an important consideration is the creation of synchronization points that you can use to align the camera angles when you edit your footage in Premiere Pro.

In This Chapter

Syncing Clips from Multiple Cameras

Let's start with some of the features you can use to synchronize multiple video clips 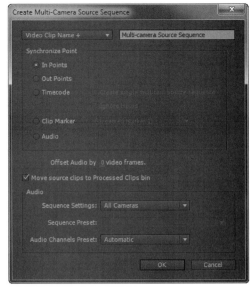. Not all will be available, depending on the video cameras that you utilize.

- Timecode: Useful only if your cameras are jam-synced with SMPTE timecode, a feature available only on some professional video cameras.

- In Points: These require the editor to manually insert In Point markers on each camera angle, typically using a clapper board, camera flash, or simple hand clap to create a point from which to sync.

- Out Points: These are similar to In Point markers, but they're used at the end of the recording rather than at the beginning.

- Clip Marker: If you don't have an opening or closing slate, you can find a suitable cue in the audio or video and insert a Clip marker. It can take a bit longer, but you can use either the video or the audio to look for an easily identifiable point that is common to all the camera angles.

A Name your sequence and choose your sync method in this dialog.

Maintaining Synchronization Accuracy

Light and sound travel at different speeds, and this can result in audio and video that are out of sync. The difference is especially noticeable when audio is recorded at a distance from the original source, such as a video camera at the back of a theater recording from its internal microphone or a camera-mounted shotgun microphone. The difference may be only two to four frames and not too noticeable at regular playback speed, but in a multi-camera edit, the difference can be more noticeable both visually and aurally.

The speed of light and the speed of sound aren't the only factors to contend with; when audio is processed through a soundboard and video through an HDMI-to-HD-SDI or other converter, they can both cause additional delays. It's important to adjust the audio on each camera angle in order to match the video, as this will result in a better multi-camera sync. You can adjust the audio track by Alt-dragging (Windows) or Control-dragging (Mac OS) it to the left or right by the number of frames required.

- Audio: This feature offers functionality unavailable in previous versions of Premiere Pro. You can synchronize multiple clips using only the audio, which is especially useful in event videography when synced timecode and clapper boards are not possible, and especially when using DSLRs, some of which have limited recording times. This method requires that both cameras record audio and that the audio they're capturing is similar. Audio syncing is available only when using a multi-camera source sequence and not when using a nested timeline.

When working with any of these synchronization techniques and tools, keep in mind that they work only if all cameras are timecode-synced, see the same slate or visual cue, or can capture the same audio cue, although it's possible to use a combination of sync techniques when these conditions aren't in place.

Premiere Pro offers two workflows for synchronizing multi-camera video footage. One involves creating a multi-camera source sequence from within the Project panel. The other requires starting from a normal sequence containing all the multi-camera video clips and then creating a second, nested sequence with multi-camera enabled. In the next three sections, we'll look at the multi-camera source sequence approach for each synchronization method.

Identifying Sync Points Using a Multi-Camera Source Sequence

Each of the three types of sync points—audio, timecode, and markers—can be used to synchronize your multi-camera clips using a multi-camera source sequence in the Project panel. We'll deal with each in turn, starting with audio.

Syncing with audio

Using audio to synchronize multiple camera angles is a new feature that offers functionality unavailable in previous versions of Premiere Pro. You can synchronize multiple clips using only the audio, which is especially useful in event videography when synced timecode and clapper boards are not possible, and especially when using DSLRs, some of which have limited recording times. This method requires that both cameras record audio and that the audio they're capturing is similar. Audio syncing is available only when using a multi-camera source sequence and not when using a nested timeline.

To synchronize multi-camera clips using audio in the Project panel:

1. Select the video clips to be synced Ⓐ by Control/Command-clicking each clip in the Project panel.

2. While still holding the Control/Command key, right-click any selected video clip and select Create Multi-Camera Source Sequence Ⓑ. The Multi-Camera Source Sequence dialog opens.

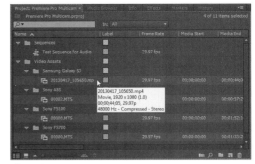

Ⓐ Select multiple video clips in the Project panel.

Ⓑ Select Create Multi-Camera Source Sequence to create the sequence.

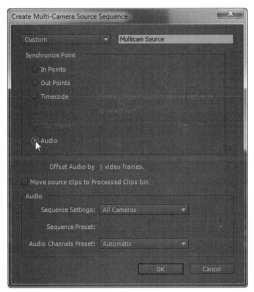

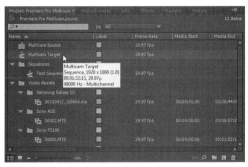

C Name your sequence and select a synchronization point.

D Note the icon on the Multicam Source sequence—it differentiates a multi-camera sequence from a single-camera sequence.

3. At the top of the Multi-Camera Source Sequence dialog, select Custom, if it's not already selected, and enter a name in the sequence name field C.

4. For your Synchronize Point, choose Audio C. Then click OK, unless you want to select any of the advanced options, as discussed in the sidebar "Multi-Camera Source Sequence Advanced Options."

Premiere Pro creates a new multi-camera source sequence in the Project panel D. Its icon looks similar to a sequence icon ![icon] except that its tracks are aligned ![icon].

Syncing with timecode

Using timecode to identify sync points is similar to the audio-based method described in the previous task. The difference is that it synchronizes your clips by using timecode data embedded in the video footage rather than analyzing the audio. There are two ways to sync clips using timecode: by creating a multi-camera source sequence in the Project panel, and by using a nested sequence. In this section, we'll look at the multi-camera source sequence method.

Multi-Camera Source Sequence Advanced Options

There are several advanced parameters in the Create Multi-Camera Source Sequence dialog 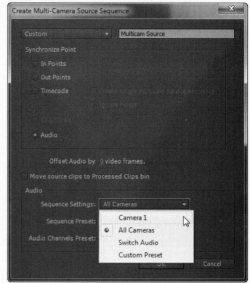 that you might want to consider, depending on the particulars of your project.

- Offset Audio: This adjustment allows the editor to compensate for audio and video that are out of sync, and allows for values from –100 to +100 frames. The compensation will apply to all selected video clips.

- Move source clips to Processed Clips bin: This selection moves the source clips to a newly created Processed Clips bin within the Project folder.

- Audio – Sequence Settings: Available options are Camera 1, All Cameras, Switch Audio, and Custom Preset ⓔ. If you choose Camera 1, Premiere Pro will copy only the audio from camera angle 1 to audio track 1 of the new multi-camera source sequence. If you choose All Cameras, the audio from each camera angle will be copied as individual audio tracks to the multi-camera source sequence. If you choose Switch Audio, Premiere Pro will create a single multi-audio track, and the audio will follow the video switches. If you choose Custom Preset, Premiere Pro will present you with options to match the audio settings from available sequence presets.

- Audio Channels Preset: From the drop-down menu, choose the type of audio channels your multi-camera sequence will use ⓕ.

ⓔ Tell Premiere Pro which audio track(s) to use in the new multi-camera source sequence.

ⓕ Choose the type of audio channels your multi-camera sequence will have.

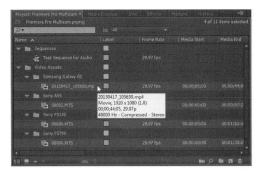

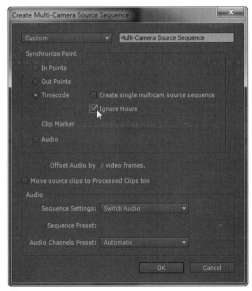

G Selecting clips to sync in the Project panel.

H Creating a multi-camera source sequence.

I Enter a name for your multi-camera sequence, and choose your sync options.

To sync clips using timecode in the Project panel:

1. Select the multi-camera video clips to be synchronized in the Project panel by Control/Command-clicking each clip G.

2. While still holding the Control/Command key, right-click any selected video clip and select Create Multi-Camera Source Sequence H.

3. Select Custom, and enter a sequence name I.

continues on next page

4. Select Timecode. If you use different hours on each camera to denote different camera angles, select the Ignore Hours check box. Click OK, unless you want to select any of the advanced options described in the "Multi-Camera Source Sequence Advanced Options" sidebar .

Premiere Pro creates a new multi-camera source sequence in the Project panel. Its icon looks similar to a sequence icon ▦ except that its tracks are aligned ▦ .

Identifying sync points using markers

As with timecode, there are two methods for identifying sync points with markers. We'll look at the multi-camera source sequence method in the Project panel here.

This method is similar to the audio workflow, but you'll need to add markers.

To create a synced multi-camera source sequence using markers in the Project panel:

1. Add the video clip from the first camera angle to the Source Monitor . You can do this by double-clicking the clip in the Project panel, or you can drag the video clip from the Project panel and drop it into the Source Monitor.

2. If you're using an In Point marker, you'll need to locate the cue point at the beginning of the video clip (it's usually a slate or a simple hand clap) . If you're using an Out Point marker, locate the cue point at the end of the video clip. If you're using a Clip marker, locate a visual or aural cue.

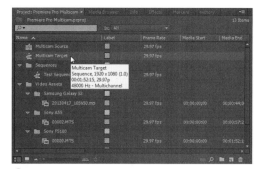

J Your multi-camera source sequence appears in the Project panel.

K Selecting the appropriate marker in the Source Monitor.

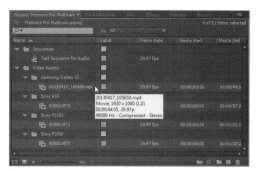

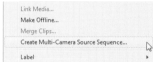

L Selecting the clips to synchronize.

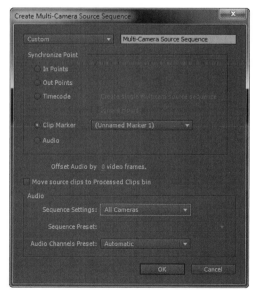

M Creating a multi-camera source sequence.

N Naming your multi-camera source sequence and choosing parameters.

O Your multi-camera source sequence and a regular sequence in the Project panel.

3. Move the Source Monitor playhead to the exact frame where the cue point occurs. Then select the appropriate marker by pressing I for In Point marker, O for Out Point marker, or M for Clip marker **K**; or you can click the appropriate icon ♥ { } below the Source Monitor.

4. Repeat steps 1–3 for each multi-camera video clip.

5. To select the multi-camera video clips in the Project panel that are to be synchronized, Control/Command-click each clip **L**.

6. While still holding the Control/Command key, right-click any selected video clip and select Create Multi-Camera Source Sequence **M**.

7. Select Custom, and enter a sequence name **N**

8. Select In Points, Out Points, or Clip Marker, depending on the type of marker you selected in step 3 **N**. Then click OK, unless you want to select any of the advanced options discussed in the sidebar "Multi-Camera Source Sequence Advanced Options."

   Premiere Pro creates a new multi-camera source sequence in the Project panel **O**. Its icon looks similar to a sequence icon 🎞 except that its tracks are aligned 🎞.

Accessing the Multi-Camera Source Sequence in the Timeline

Once you have created a synchronized multi-camera source sequence using audio, markers, or timecode, you are ready to access this sequence in the Timeline.

To open the multi-camera source sequence in the Timeline:

1. Right-click the multi-camera source sequence, and choose Open in Timeline .

   The multi-camera source sequence opens 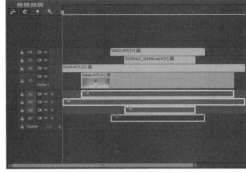, and the multi-camera clips are aligned using the audio.

2. To open the tracks, press Shift++. Premiere Pro displays the video thumbnail and audio waveform for each track 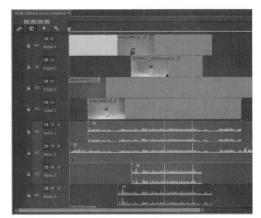.

Ⓐ Opening the sequence in the Timeline.

Ⓑ Multi-camera source sequence tracks are closed by default.

Ⓒ The peaks in the waveforms show that the audio is in sync.

D Choose New Sequence From Clip to create the new sequence.

E Renaming the sequence.

F Adding the Toggle Multi-Camera View button to the Program Monitor's button toolbar.

G Adding the Multi-Camera Record On/Off Toggle button.

3. In the Project panel, right-click the multi-camera source sequence and choose New Sequence From Clip **D**. Rename this sequence "Multi-camera Target" **E**.

4. In the Program Monitor, click the + button. The Button Editor launches **F**.

5. Drag the Toggle Multi-Camera View button [icon] to the Program Monitor's button toolbar **F**.

6. Drag the Multi-Camera Record On/Off Toggle button [icon] to the Program Monitor's button toolbar **G**.

7. Click the Toggle Multi-Camera View button [icon], and the Multi-Camera View Monitor will display a grid containing four previews and the Program Monitor **H**.

   If you have more than four camera angles, Premiere Pro increases the grid from a 2x2 grid to a 3x3 grid and beyond, as required.

   Now that your video tracks are synced with one another by audio cues, only one step remains before you're ready to edit: making sure the audio and video are still in sync within each track.

H The default 2x2 grid for up to four camera angles.

To confirm and fine-tune video/audio sync:

1. Check to see if your video is synchronized to the audio in the Multi-Camera Monitor by looking for a visual cue . If any video tracks are out of sync, you will need to make adjustments.

2. In the multi-camera source sequence, locate a visual cue. Select the Razor tool . The pointer converts to the razor pointer. Use it to split the top clip at the cue point .

3. Hide the top video track by clicking the Toggle Track Output button (it will change to the "on" position). Continue with the next video track by finding the same visual cue and razor-cutting that track .

 Checking video/audio sync.

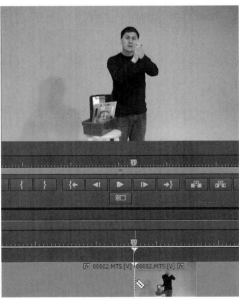

 Use the Razor tool to split the clip at the cue point.

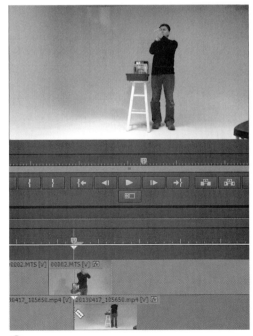

 Repeat on the next video track.

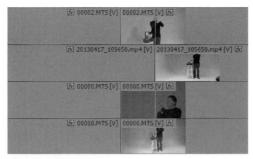

L Off by two frames.

 M The Selection tool.

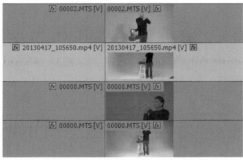

N Video and audio are now in sync.

4. Continue for each remaining video track. In L you can see that one of the video tracks is out of sync by two frames, because the razor cuts don't align.

5. Select the Selection tool M.

6. Shift-click both portions of the video track that is out of sync. Then Alt-drag (Windows) or Control-drag (Mac OS) the out-of-sync video track so that the razor cut aligns with the other video tracks—two frames, in this example N.

The Nested Sequence Method

As mentioned, Premiere Pro supports two methods of synchronizing multi-camera angles, and in this section we will explore using the nested sequence method with timecode and markers. Audio synchronization is not available in the nested sequence method.

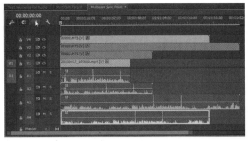

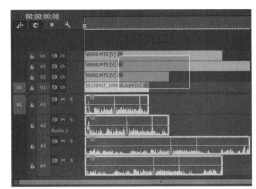

 Your new sequence, with discrete video and audio tracks for each source clip.

To sync clips using timecode via the nested sequence method:

1. To begin, create a new sequence and add the multi-camera video clips to it, being careful to place each camera angle on its own video and audio track **A**.

2. Select all the tracks by Shift-clicking the footage in each track. You can also Shift-drag the pointer over each track **B**.

3. While still holding down the Shift key, right-click any of the tracks and select Synchronize **C**. The Synchronize Clips dialog appears.

 All tracks selected.

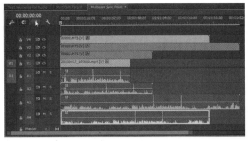

C Choose Synchronize to synchronize the tracks.

D Selecting Timecode as your synchronize point.

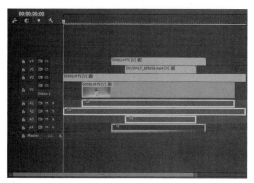

E Clips aligned by timecode.

F Adding a video track to the Source Monitor.

4. Select Timecode; you may need to enter a SMPTE timecode. If you use different hours on each camera to denote different camera angles, select the Ignore Hours check box. Click OK D.

   Premiere Pro aligns your clips on the Timeline E. To learn about using markers for sync in the nested sequence method, continue to the next task; otherwise, skip to the task "To nest a synchronized sequence."

To sync clips with markers via the nested sequence method:

1. Add the video clip from the first camera angle to the Source Monitor F. You can do this by double-clicking the clip in the Project panel, or you can drag the video clip from the Project panel and drop it into the Source Monitor.

2. If you're using an In Point marker, then you need to locate the cue point at the beginning of the video clip (it's usually a slate or a simple hand clap) F. If you're using an Out Point marker, locate the cue point at the end of the video clip. If you're using a Clip marker, locate a visual or aural cue.

3. Move the Source Monitor playhead to the exact frame where the cue point occurs. Select the appropriate marker by pressing I for In Point marker, O for Out Point marker, or M for Clip marker F; you can also click the appropriate icon below the Source Monitor.

4. Repeat steps 1–3 for each multi-cam video clip.

continues on next page

5. Create a new sequence and add the multi-camera video clips to it, being careful to place each camera angle on its own video and audio track **G**.

6. Select all of the tracks by Shift-clicking the footage in each track **H**. You can also Shift-drag the pointer over each track.

7. While still holding the Shift key, right-click any of the tracks and select Synchronize **I**. The Synchronize Clips dialog opens **J**.

G Your new sequence, with discrete video and audio tracks for each source clip.

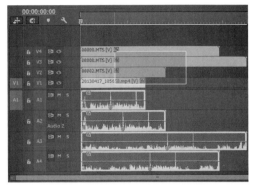

H Selecting all tracks to be synchronized.

I Select Synchronize to sync the clips.

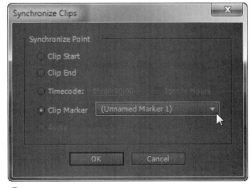

J Selecting the synchronization method.

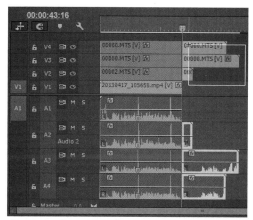

K Clips aligned by marker.

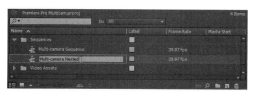

L The synchronized sequence in the Project panel.

M Choose New Sequence From Clip to create the new sequence.

N Renaming the new sequence.

O Enabling Multi-Camera.

8. Select the appropriate method, based on which marker you used in step 3, and then click OK **J**.

Premiere Pro aligns your clips on the Timeline **K**. Optionally, you can trim the starting and ending points if they don't contain any useful footage.

To nest a synchronized sequence:

1. Right-click the synchronized sequence in the Project panel **L**, and select New Sequence From Clip **M**.

2. A multi-camera nested sequence appears. Rename it "Multi-camera Nested" **N**.

3. In the multi-camera nested sequence, right-click the multi-camera track and select Multi-Camera > Enable **O**.

Producing Multi-Camera Edits

Regardless of which synchronization method you selected, the next task will have you working with the multi-camera-enabled sequence that you just created, and editing it in the Multi-Camera Monitor.

To open the Multi-Camera Monitor:

1. In the Program Monitor, click the + button. This will launch the Button Editor **A**.

2. Drag the Toggle Multi-Camera View button **A** to the Program Monitor's button toolbar (if it's not already there).

3. Drag the Multi-Camera Record On/Off Toggle button **B** to the Program Monitor's button toolbar (if it's not already there).

4. Click the Toggle Multi-Camera View button. The Multi-Camera Monitor displays a grid containing four previews and the Program Monitor. If you have more than four camera angles, Premiere Pro will increase the grid from a 2x2 grid to a 3x3 grid and beyond, as required **C**.

A Adding the Toggle Multi-Camera View button to the Program Monitor's button toolbar.

B Likewise the Multi-Camera Record On/Off Toggle button.

C The Multi-Camera Monitor in a 2x2 preview grid.

To record multi-camera edits:

1. Move the playhead to the beginning of the sequence **D**.

2. If your camera angles don't all start at the same time, you may see black in some of the windows **E**. The same goes if you have less than the total number of camera angles in a grid. If this occurs, move the playhead to a different part of the sequence and start recording there.

3. Select the desired first camera angle by using the numbers directly above the letters on your keyboard (not the numeric keypad numbers) or by clicking a camera angle in the preview grid. The selected camera angle will have a yellow box around it **F**.

   Camera angles in the multi-camera preview grid correspond to 1 in the upper-left corner, 2 in the upper-right corner, 3 in the lower-left corner, and 4 in the lower-right corner. For a grid of nine camera angles, the top row is 1–3, the middle row is 4–6, and the bottom row is 7–9.

4. Press Play ▶ or use your keyboard to start the multi-camera recording **G**. The Play icon will change to the Stop icon ■.

continues on next page

D The playhead at the beginning of the sequence: ready to record.

E A black box indicates that a clip hasn't started yet or that fewer than four camera angles were used.

F The selected first camera angle is indicated by the yellow box.

G Press the Play button to start recording.

5. Using your keyboard numbers (but not the numbers on your numeric keypad), switch camera angles when you want to make cuts. You can also click the preview window in the Multi-Camera Monitor. The angle that is currently recording will have a red box around it  .

When you stop recording, your edits will appear in the sequence, and the video clip will have cut marks at each point that you changed camera angles 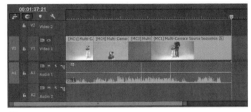 . Additionally, each clip name will be preceded by MC1, MC2, MC3, or MC4 to denote the multi-camera angle that was selected.

TIP You can re-record at any time by moving the playhead ahead of the part that you want to re-record and then recording anew.

TIP You can manually change an individual camera angle from the Timeline by right-clicking the multi-camera clip, selecting **Multi-Camera**, and then selecting the camera angle that you want to switch to. The active camera angle will be denoted by a check mark  .

TIP You can further refine your edits just as you would with single-camera video footage, including using the **Ripple Edit tool** (see Chapter 6) to adjust cut points 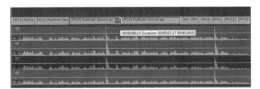 .

H The red box denotes the angle you're currently recording.

I The cut marks show where you changed camera angles. Camera angle names bear MC1–4 to denote which camera angle was selected.

J Another option for changing camera angle.

K Adjusting cut points in a multi-camera sequence with the Ripple Edit tool.

A Locating the panel menu in the upper-right corner of the Multi-Camera Monitor.

B Selecting Multi-Camera Audio Follows Video.

A Few Additional Audio Notes

Here are a few more items to consider regarding audio issues that are specific to producing videos created from multiple camera sources.

Finding the right audio mix from multiple sources

In many multi-camera video shoots, you'll want to use a single mixed-down audio track for the final edit. You can insert it at any point in the process after you've synced the video clips.

If this audio track is embedded on one of the video tracks, after synchronization you can simply turn off or delete the rest of the audio tracks and use that master audio.

If your audio still needs to be mixed down and parts were recorded on different cameras (as is usually the case when a clean soundboard feed needs to be combined with a second ambient microphone input for applause, and even with a third microphone input for stage audio that doesn't need to be amplified but still needs to be recorded for the video), you may want to keep all the audio tracks and mix down after the multi-camera edit.

The last scenario occurs when you have multiple cameras, each recording their own audio, and you need the audio to follow the video. To go this route, click the panel menu in the upper-right corner of the Multi-Camera Monitor A and select Multi-Camera Audio Follows Video B.

Dealing with mixed audio formats and right-channel stereo audio recordings

Premiere Pro now allows different audio formats to be on the same audio track. Previously, an audio track could contain only mono, stereo, or 5.1 audio.  shows two stereo tracks on the same audio track as two mono tracks.

C Mixing audio formats on the same audio track.

If you're going to use audio to synchronize your multi-camera video angles, you need to ensure that your audio is where Premiere Pro expects it to be. In the case of a two-channel recording (often called "stereo," although in many video camera recordings, it's more likely two different mono audio tracks assigned to channels 1 and 2), Premiere Pro will look for your audio on the left, or Channel 1. If this channel is empty or doesn't contain an audio recording that can be used for synchronization, you may need to remap the audio channels. Such is the case with the audio in 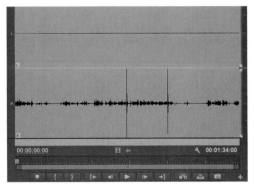, which has audio only in the right channel.

D An audio waveform showing audio only on Channel 2, or the right stereo track.

To remap right-channel-only audio:

1. Right-click the video clip that contains the audio that needs to be remapped.

2. Select Modify > Audio Channels .

E Accessing the Modify Clip dialog.

3. In the Modify Clip dialog, adjust the Source Channels so that the Right channel is pointing to Channel 1. 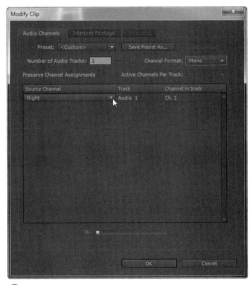 You can also change the Channel Format option from Stereo to Mono if you plan to retain only one audio track.

   You can now synchronize the multiple video clips using audio, as described in the previous tasks.

F Changing the Source Channel and Channel Format options.

Working
with Titles

Text is a critical component of many videos. You lead with the title, end with the credits, and use titles in between to introduce speakers or topics or to convey critical information.

Premiere Pro's title tool—the Titler—is exceptionally robust. Since many of my projects are text-intensive, it's a real difference-maker for me and one of the key reasons that I chose Premiere Pro as my go-to video editor years ago.

If you've ever worked with a word processor, most of the typographic concepts—like font, font size, color, and alignment—will already be familiar to you. So rather than devote valuable time to minutiae like how to change a font, I'll introduce you to Premiere Pro's title-related functionality and devote the most time to concepts that are either unique to Premiere Pro or novel to most readers.

In This Chapter

About Titles

OK, here's a quick brain dump on titles. Some of this we'll touch on in the chapter and some we won't, so listen up.

You create titles in the Titler, which has tools for adding text and for adding shapes such as circles, boxes, and lines. You can also insert logos and other digital pictures.

Once you've created your titles, Premiere Pro saves them in the Project panel. From there, you deploy them just like any other still image. You can add them to any track or stretch them to any length, and add effects and transitions.

By default, titles added to the V1 track are full-screen titles with a black background. Any space not consumed by text or other content in titles added to V2 and higher tracks is transparent, and the underlying video will show through.

Premiere Pro saves titles with your project file, not as separate files. However, you can export a title for use in other projects by clicking the title in the Project panel and choosing File > Export > Title. Titles are saved with the file extension .prtl, and you can import them into other projects.

You can also save titles into the Templates panel so you can easily reuse them in later projects. You can also set the default title, and the Templates panel contains multiple canned templates you can incorporate into your own projects.

Once you've created a title, you can open and edit it in the Titler by double-clicking it in either the Timeline or Project panel. Note that if you deploy a title more than once on the Timeline (say, as a lower-third title for a speaker), changing any one instance of that title will change all instances. Usually that's what you want, but not always.

Working with the Titler

Let's meet the Titler.

A Here's one way to create a new title.

B Choose your configuration in the New Title dialog (by default, it matches the sequence that is open in the Timeline).

To create a new title:

1. Do one of the following:
   ▸ Choose File > New > Title.
   ▸ On the bottom right of the Project panel, click the New Item button and choose Title **A**.
   ▸ Press Control/Command+T.

   Premiere Pro opens the New Title dialog, using the configuration of the sequence then open in the Timeline **B**.

2. If desired, change the parameters. Then click OK to open the new title in the Titler **C**.

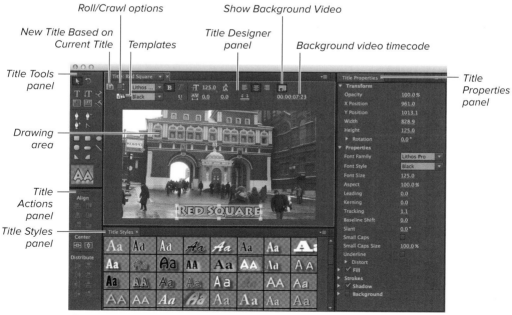

C Premiere Pro's Titler, one of its strongest features.

At the top of the Titler, the Title Designer panel contains a number of text controls for font selection, alignment, font size, and other text attributes. The drawing area is where you'll create your title.

On the top right of the Title Designer panel, the Show Background Video button 00:00:14:27 shows the video at the playhead position behind the title. Click this button to hide the video background.

On the upper left are buttons that open different dialogs. Click the New Title Based on Current Title button to create a new title based on the existing title, which you can then customize.

The Roll/Crawl button opens the dialog for configuring titles with rolls (up-and-down, like closing credits) and crawls (side-to-side, like stock tickers). The Templates button opens the Templates dialog.

The Title Tools panel contains tools to create text shapes such as rectangles, circles, ovals, and lines.

You'll configure these components in the Title Properties panel on the right. On top are transform tools that let you precisely size and position your titles and adjust rotation and opacity, and at the bottom are properties like fonts, text controls, fill, strokes, shadows, and background.

On the lower left, the Title Actions panel contains controls for aligning, centering, and distributing title components. On the bottom, the Title Styles panel contains styles that you can quickly add to title components created in the editor. The Titler has a panel menu **D** with options like Safe Title Margin and Safe Action Margin for those producing for TV.

As with most Premiere Pro components, you can drag the Titler to any size.

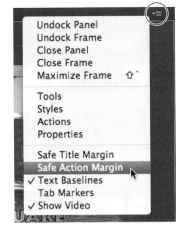

D The Titler's panel menu, where you set options like enabling the Safe Action and Safe Title margins.

TIP You can change the frame showing behind the Titler by moving the playhead in the Timeline or by dragging the background video timecode 00:00:14:27 to a new frame.

A The Templates panel.

Working with Premiere Pro's Title Templates

Premiere Pro's title templates are great design elements, and the Templates panel simplifies the reuse of titles and other functions. Note that if you downloaded your copy of Premiere Pro, you may not have the title templates (and other content). If you don't, you'll see a warning message and a link you can click to download the content.

To create a title from a template:

1. Choose New Title > Based on Template. The Templates panel opens A.

2. Click the disclosure triangles in the folders and subfolders, and click any menu to preview it A. Once you've finalized your selection, type a name in the Name field in the bottom of the panel and click OK. Premiere Pro opens the title in the Titler, where you can edit it as you wish.

To add a title to the Templates panel:

1. With the title open in the Titler, click the Templates 🖼 button **B** on the top left of the Title Designer panel, or press Control/Command+J. The Templates panel opens.

2. Click the panel menu on the upper right, and choose Import Current Title as Template **C**. The Save As dialog opens **D**.

3. Type the desired name and click OK. Premiere Pro saves the title in the Templates panel **E**.

To make a title the default title:

1. In the Templates panel, choose the target title.

2. Click the Templates panel menu and choose Set Template as Default Still **F**. Premiere Pro makes the selected template the default title, which opens whenever you create a new title.

TIP The Templates panel menu also contains controls for deleting templates and other administrative functions.

B One way to open the Templates panel.

Panel menu

C Not surprisingly, this menu option imports the current title as a template.

D Name the template, and click OK.

E The new template, ready to be crowned the default template.

Panel menu

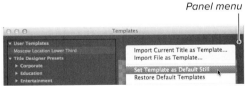
F Choose the target title, and then set it as the default in the Templates panel menu.

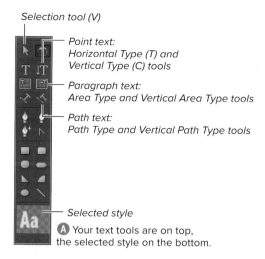

Selection tool (V)

Point text:
Horizontal Type (T) and
Vertical Type (C) tools

Paragraph text:
Area Type and Vertical Area Type tools

Path text:
Path Type and Vertical Path Type tools

Selected style

A Your text tools are on top, the selected style on the bottom.

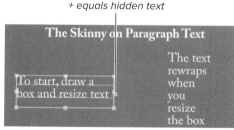

B The 4-1-1 on point text.

+ equals hidden text

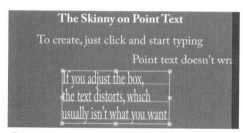

C The skinny on paragraph text.

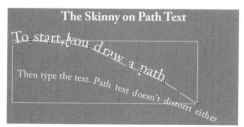

D All about path text.

Working with Text

Premiere Pro has three sets of text tools, each with horizontal and vertical controls **A**. You use each differently and for different purposes.

- Point text. Use this tool for simple one-line text strings **B**. Text inserted with this tool does not wrap when it reaches the title-safe zone, though you can change this default behavior by choosing Title > Word Wrap after creating each text string, or just press Enter/Return to start a new line of text. This style is a pain for more-complex, multiline titles, because when you resize a box, the text distorts, which usually isn't what you want.

- Paragraph text **C**. Use this tool for complex titles or text that you need to fit in a certain area. You start by drawing a box in the target area, and then you type the text and resize it to fit the box. If you later resize the box, the text rewraps and doesn't distort.

- Path text **D**. Use this tool for creating text along a path. Draw the path, and then type the text. You can resize the box without distortion.

Note that the graphics area on the bottom of the Title Actions panel shows the selected style, which Premiere Pro will apply to all text or other shapes that you create Ⓐ. As you'll learn later in this chapter, you can choose a style before you create your text, and the text will assume that style; or you can create your text and then click a style to assign that style to the existing text.

Once you've created your text, use the Selection tool ▶ Ⓔ to choose the entire bounding box in order to move the box to any location within the drawing area or to format all text within the box. Or, double-click the box to select specific text, and just format those letters.

To create text with the Horizontal or Vertical Type tool:

1. With a title open, do one of the following:

   ▸ For horizontal text, click the Horizontal Type tool .

   ▸ For vertical text, click the Vertical Type tool .

2. In the drawing area, click the location where you want to add the text. A blinking bounding box appears Ⓕ.

3. Type the desired text Ⓖ. To set the text, choose the Selection tool (V) and click outside the text you just created. If you click without choosing the Selection tool, you'll start another text string.

TIP By default, the text does not wrap. To wrap the text at the title-safe margin, choose Title > Word Wrap. Otherwise, press Enter/Return to begin a new line in the title.

TIP To move the text (or any shape), click it to make it active, and then drag to the desired location.

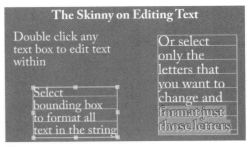

Ⓔ The basic rules of selecting, editing, and formatting text.

Ⓕ Click where you want to insert the text.

Ⓖ Then type the desired text.

TIP Resizing this text box distorts the text unless you resize proportionately. To resize proportionately, press the Shift key when you drag the bounding box.

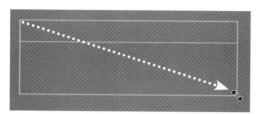

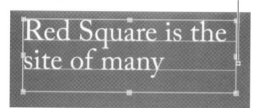

H After choosing the tool, draw your box.

Hidden text

I Then type the desired text. The plus sign indicates hidden text. Let's fix that.

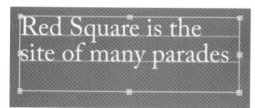

J Just drag the font size in either direction.

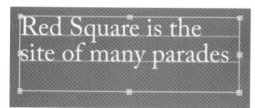

K Now it all fits.

To create text with the Area Type or Vertical Area Type tool:

1. With a title open, do one of the following:
   - ▸ For horizontal text, click the Area Type tool 🔳.
   - ▸ For vertical text, click the Vertical Area Type tool 🔳.

2. In the drawing area, drag to create a text box H.

3. Type the desired text. The text wraps automatically, and will go out of view if the text entered exceeds the capacity of the box I. A plus sign indicates hidden text.

4. To adjust font size, hover your pointer over the Font Size value in the Title Properties panel until the drag pointer 👆 appears, and then drag either way J until the text is properly sized K.

5. To set the text, choose the Selection tool (V) and click outside the text you just created. If you click without choosing the Selection tool, you'll start another text string.

TIP Resizing the text box changes the size of the box and rewraps and refits the text; the text remains the same size.

TIP For more-complicated titles (like agendas), note that you can create tab stops within an area title, which is a killer feature. Search the Adobe Help file for "Create tab stops in titles" for details on this feature.

To create text along a horizontal or vertical path:

1. With a title open, do one of the following:
   - For horizontal text, click the Path Type tool ![icon].
   - For vertical text, click the Vertical Path Type tool ![icon].

2. Click where you want the text to start, and then click additional points to create the path ![L]. Try to keep the path as smooth as possible, or you'll mess up the spacing between the letters.

3. When the path is complete, start typing. If the text exceeds the capacity of the path, it will just disappear without any indicator ![M].

4. To adjust font size, hover your pointer over the Font Size value in the Title Properties panel until the drag pointer ![icon] appears, and then drag either way ![J] until the text is properly sized ![N].

> **TIP** You can edit the path with the four tools beneath the path tools in the Title Tools panel ![O].

> **TIP** If the path is uneven, you'll have spacing issues between some letters. To address this, adjust the kerning values between the affected letters in the Title Properties panel.

> **TIP** If you are simply trying to create rotated text, you may get a better result by creating the text with a different tool and rotating the text via the Rotation adjustment in the Transform section of the Title Properties panel.

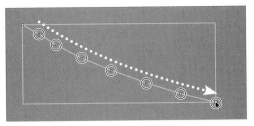

L Click multiple times along the target path.

M Then, type your text. Looks like some text is missing.

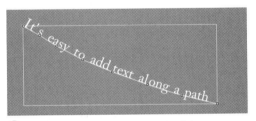

N After adjusting the font size, it's all there.

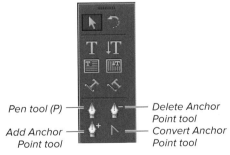

Pen tool (P) · Delete Anchor Point tool · Add Anchor Point tool · Convert Anchor Point tool

O You can use these tools to adjust the path.

Alignment controls

A Alignment controls are up top.

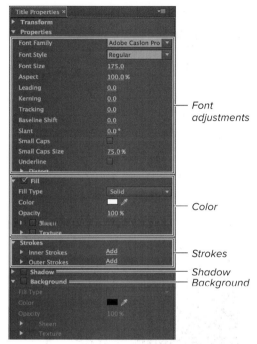

— Font adjustments

— Color

— Strokes
— Shadow
— Background

B There are four types of configurations: font, color, strokes, and shadow. Background enables a colored background for the title.

Setting Text and Shape Properties

Once you create your text, you'll want to adjust properties other than font size. You can justify the text (left, center, or right) using the controls at the top of the Title Designer panel **A**, but you'll do the heavy lifting in the Title Properties panel **B**.

In the Title Properties panel you see the following areas: font adjustments, which apply only to text; color, strokes, and shadow, which apply to text and all shapes; and background, which is a way to choose a background color or gradient for the title.

As mentioned, you adjust the entire text string by choosing the bounding box around the string, or adjust any letters within the string by choosing just them. Let's discuss these adjustments.

Text adjustments

The ways you can adjust text fonts in Premiere Pro are as follows:

- Font Family, Style, and Size. These should be familiar to you already.

- Aspect. Narrows and widens the text.

- Leading. Adjusts the spacing between lines of text.

- Kerning. Adjusts the space between characters. Particularly useful for polishing text on paths.

- Tracking. Best for adjusting the spacing of groups of letters or blocks of text.

- Baseline Shift. Adjusts the distance between the characters and the baseline (the line upon which the characters sit).

- Slant. Slants the text or shape by degrees.

continues on next page

- Small Caps. Makes selected text appear in small caps (big capital letter to start the word, then smaller caps for the remaining letters in the word).

- Small Caps Size. Adjusts the size of the small caps relative to the large initial cap.

- Underline. Not available for text on a path.

- Distort. Lets you adjust the letters along the X and Y axis.

TIP In addition to all of these adjustments, you can adjust the height and width of the text separately by using the Transform controls at the top of the Title Properties panel.

Color adjustments

The Titler also enables a range of color adjustments. This section assumes that you know your way around color selection controls.

To change text color:

1. Select the bounding box surrounding the text string that you want to adjust, or select letters within the string **C**.

2. In the Title Properties panel, choose the desired fill type from the Fill Type menu **D**. Here's a brief description of the options; most have custom options, which are detailed in the Premiere Pro Help file.

    ▸ Solid. A single color.

    ▸ Linear Gradient. Blends two colors in a linear pattern.

    ▸ Radial Gradient. Blends two colors in a radial pattern.

C Here's the text we're working with.

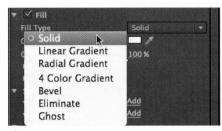

D Lots of options here.

E Configure the familiar color adjustments.

F Pretty plain now, but we'll dress it up with strokes.

▸ **4 Color Gradient.** Blends four colors from four corners together.

▸ **Bevel.** Adds a beveled edge to the background.

▸ **Eliminate.** No fill or shadow is rendered.

▸ **Ghost.** Shadow rendered, but not the fill.

3. Click the color swatch to choose a color from the Color Picker dialog, or use the eyedropper to choose a color from within the frame. I went with yellow from the color picker **E**. You can see the result in **F**.

    Let's explore some other ways to make the title more readable against the background.

Working with strokes

One of the biggest concerns with titles is contrast with the background, particularly when you're superimposing a title over moving video. Inner and outer strokes not only enhance the appearance of your titles, but also help distinguish them from the background.

Inner strokes work from the outer edge inward, and outer strokes work from the outer edge outward. You can configure up to 12 strokes on each text string or shape.

To add and configure an inner stroke:

1. In the Titler, select the text or shape. If necessary, click the disclosure triangle next to Strokes to expand that category.

2. In the Title Properties panel, click the Add button next to Inner Strokes 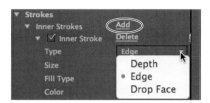. Premiere Pro adds the stroke using the default parameters.

G Adding an inner stroke.

3. In the Type menu, choose the stroke type G.

   ▸ Depth creates a stroke that looks three-dimensional.

   ▸ Edge creates a stroke around the complete edge of the shape. This is the default.

   ▸ Drop Face copies the shape and places the copy behind the original.

4. Choose the fill type and color. I'll use solid and an orange color that contrasts well with the yellow fill color.

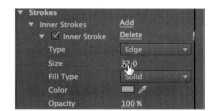

H Here is the configuration used...

5. Choose the size H of the stroke. This subjective element is best configured using the drag pointer.

6. If desired, adjust the Opacity (transparency) value.

   Here's where we are I. Let's add an outer stroke to enhance contrast with the background.

I ...to create this look. Notice that the selected orange color extends inward from the outer edge.

To add and configure an outer stroke:

1. In the Titler, select the text or shape. If necessary, click the disclosure triangle next to Strokes to expand that category.

2. In the Title Properties panel, click the Add button next to Outer Strokes J. Premiere Pro adds the stroke using the default parameters.

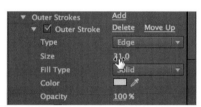

J Adding and configuring an outer stroke.

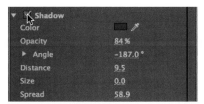

K Strokes enhance appearance and contrast with the background.

L Enabling and configuring the shadow.

M Our final title. I hope you like orange and yellow.

3. The parameters are identical to those for inner strokes. The configuration shown in **J** produces the look shown in **K**, which is distinctive and contrasts well with the background. Let's add a drop shadow and we'll be done.

TIP Strokes are one of the most powerful design elements in the Titler. For more on this feature, search the Premiere Pro Help file for "Fills, strokes, and shadows in titles."

Working with shadows

Shadows are another element that most readers are probably familiar with; they add a touch of elegance while further enhancing contrast with the background.

To add and configure drop shadows:

1. In the Titler, select the text or shape.

2. Select the Shadow check box **L**. Premiere Pro adds the shadow using the default parameters.

3. Configure the shadow's properties **L**:

   ▸ Color

   ▸ Opacity. The transparency value.

   ▸ Angle. Sets the direction of the shadow.

   ▸ Distance. Sets the distance, in pixels, between the shadow and the shape.

   ▸ Size

   ▸ Spread. Controls the blur in the shadow.

   M shows our final title. It's unique and distinctive, and should hold up well against almost any background. We've come a long way since **C**.

Working with Styles

Premiere Pro's title styles are presets with custom fonts, colors, strokes, shadows, and other elements. Premiere Pro applies styles to text, and to shapes like boxes and lines. Usually, you expect the former but not the latter. If you create a shape with unexpected colors or borders because you had a style selected, click the Caslon Pro 68 style—which is the plain, non-style style—in the upper left of the Title Styles panel.

You can save, delete, and rearrange styles, and otherwise manage and manipulate them.

To save a style:

1. In the drawing area, choose a single text string or shape with the desired configuration. I'm saving the title we configured in the last few tasks **A**.

2. Click the Title Styles panel menu and choose New Style **B**. The New Style dialog opens **C**.

3. Type the desired name and click OK **C**. Premiere Pro creates the new style and places it dead last in the Title Styles panel **D**. Let's fix that.

To move a style:

Drag it to the desired location **E**.

A Click the title element containing the style you want to save.

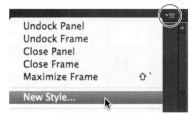

B Open the panel menu and choose New Style.

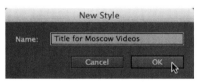

C The New Style dialog.

D The new style.

E To move a style, just drag it.

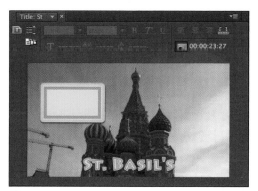

F The selected style in the Title Tools panel.

To apply a style to new content:

1. Click the desired style **E**. This loads the style in the display area in the Title Tools panel **F**.

2. All new text and shapes created with the selected style will assume its properties **G**.

To apply a style to existing content:

1. Let's fix the rectangle in **G**, which I really didn't want to apply the style to. Click the text or shape **H**.

2. Click the new style **I**. Caslon Pro 68 is the non-style style, with a plain white fill with no shadows or strokes.

G Text and shapes created with the style assume its properties.

H Click the text or shape to apply the style to.

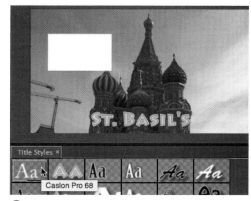

I Choose the new style. With Caslon Pro 68 applied to it, the yellow box turns white and loses the inner and outer strokes.

Creating Shapes

Premiere Pro's shapes 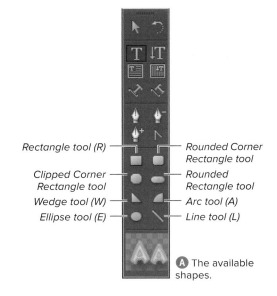 are valuable as backgrounds for text or as unique design elements. Here's how you create them.

To create shapes:

1. If desired, choose the target style.

2. Choose the shape from the Title Tools panel.

3. Move the pointer into the target position, and do one of the following:

   ▸ Drag **B** to draw without constraint **C**.

   ▸ Shift-drag to constrain the shape's aspect ratio.

   ▸ Alt/Option-drag to draw from the center.

   ▸ Alt/Option+Shift-drag to constrain the aspect ratio and draw from the center.

   ▸ Drag diagonally over the corner points to flip the shape.

   ▸ Drag across, up, or down to flip the shape horizontally or vertically as you draw.

> **TIP** To edit a shape, click it, grab one of the handles, and edit as desired. The modifier keys (Shift and Alt/Option) work the same way when you're editing.

> **TIP** To move the shape (or any text), click it to make it active, then click in the center and drag it to the desired location.

> **TIP** To flip an existing shape, use the Selection tool to drag a corner point in the direction you want it to flip.

> **TIP** To change shapes, right-click the shape and choose Graphic Type and then the new shape. Note the keyboard shortcuts for changing shapes.

Rectangle tool (R) — Rounded Corner Rectangle tool
Clipped Corner Rectangle tool — Rounded Rectangle tool
Wedge tool (W) — Arc tool (A)
Ellipse tool (E) — Line tool (L)

A The available shapes.

B I'm drawing a rectangle to place behind the St. Basil's title.

C Here it is. This will make sense after the next task.

A To make this background, I changed the white fill to gray, added a default outer stroke, and adjusted opacity to around 80. Too bad it's in front of the target.

B Note the controls for moving the object forward and backward.

C Backgrounds like this work well when the video behind the title is very dynamic.

Arranging Shapes and Text

When strokes and shadows aren't enough to distinguish your title from the video, you need a fixed background. I've created one **A**, but there's one problem: It's in front of the title. Let's fix that, and learn about adjusting the stacking order of objects in a title.

1. Choose the shape or text.

2. Right-click, and choose the desired adjustment **B**.

   ▸ **Bring to Front.** Moves the object to the top of all objects in the title.

   ▸ **Bring Forward.** Moves the object to the top of the object directly above it.

   ▸ **Send to Back C**. Moves the object to the very bottom of all objects in the title.

   ▸ **Send Backward.** Moves the object beneath the object directly beneath it.

   Premiere Pro adjusts the selected object.

Centering, Aligning, and Distributing Objects

Centering, aligning, and distributing objects in a title are simple to do via the controls in the Title Actions panel.

To center single or multiple objects:

1. In the Titler, click an object or objects in the title **A**.

2. In the Title Actions panel, click Vertical Center, Horizontal Center, or both **B**. Premiere Pro centers the objects **C**.

To align multiple objects:

1. In the Titler, choose two or more objects **D**.

2. In the Title Actions panel, choose the desired alignment **E**. Premiere Pro aligns the objects **F**.

A The title and background are off-center. I select both.

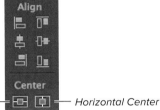

Vertical Center ——— *Horizontal Center*

B Click Vertical Center, Horizontal Center, or both. Here, I'm choosing both.

C Now both are centered.

Align

Horizontal Left ——— *Vertical Top*
Horizontal Center ——— *Vertical Center*
Horizontal Right ——— *Vertical Bottom*

E Then choose the desired alignment. I chose Horizontal Left.

D These information bits are way out of alignment. Choose them all.

F All aligned; now to fix the spacing!

G Premiere Pro distributes between the extremes, so first set the extremes.

H Then select all objects to be distributed.

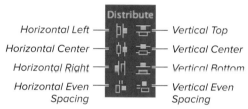

Horizontal Left — Vertical Top
Horizontal Center — Vertical Center
Horizontal Right — Vertical Bottom
Horizontal Even Spacing — Vertical Even Spacing

I Then choose the desired alignment. I chose Vertical Even Spacing.

J Aligned, distributed, and ready to go.

K Here's how I made the white background for the text.

TIP With all the objects selected, you can move them en masse by dragging or by using the arrow keys.

To distribute multiple objects:

1. In the Titler, position objects at the extremes of the distribution area G. I'm raising the top text object (using the arrow keys, so as not to disturb alignment) to spread the distribution area.

2. In the Titler, choose all objects to be distributed H.

3. In the Title Actions panel, choose the desired distribution pattern I.

4. Premiere Pro distributes the objects J.

TIP Rather than use individual backgrounds for the text in this title, I turned the entire title into a background by selecting the Background check box, choosing white, and adjusting Opacity to 50% K.

Working with Logos

Many titles contain a logo or some other graphic. They're simple to add in Premiere Pro.

To add a logo to a title and configure it:

1. In the title area, right-click and choose Graphic > Insert Graphic **A**. The Import Graphic dialog opens.

2. Navigate to and select the logo.

3. Drag the logo to the desired position **B**. With the logo selected, you can also easily resize it (press the Shift key to make the changes proportional).

4. In the Title Properties panel, click the triangle next to Transform (if necessary) to expose those controls **C**.

5. If desired, drag Opacity to the desired value **C**. The result is shown in **D**.

A Use this menu option to insert a graphic into a title.

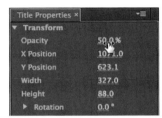

B Drag the title to the desired location. While it's selected, adjust the size as well.

C Often you'll want to adjust the opacity of the title.

D I created this title from one of Premiere Pro's templates.

Ⓐ Using the Horizontal Text Box tool to draw a text box for the rolling credit.

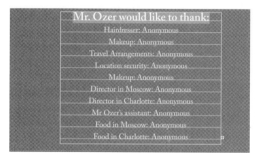

Ⓑ I hope I didn't forget anyone! The plus sign at the bottom right tells me I have hidden text.

Creating Rolls and Crawls

Rolling credits scroll downward at the end of a movie; crawls flow sideways, usually at the bottom of the frame. The duration of the title depends on the duration you set in the Timeline.

Perfecting these titles tends to be an interactive process. Note that you can have the Titler open and positioned outside the main Premiere Pro interface so you can instantly see the effects of your edits and configuration changes in the Program Monitor.

To create a rolling or crawling title:

1. Do one of the following:
   ▸ To create a rolling title, choose Title > New Title > Default Roll.
   ▸ To create a crawling title, choose Title > New Title > Default Crawl.

2. Choose a title name, and click OK.

3. Select the Horizontal Text Box tool 🖳.

4. For a rolling title, draw a large horizontal box over the frame Ⓐ. For a crawl, draw a narrow box sufficient for one line of text.

5. Add the text. It may be more efficient to produce the text in a word processor, copy it, and then paste it into the text box Ⓑ.

continues on next page

6. If some text is hidden, click the Selection tool ⬉, grab a control handle, and make the box larger **C**.

7. Format the text as desired using the options in the Title Properties panel.

8. In the upper left of the Title Designer panel, click the Roll/Crawl Options button **D**. The Roll/Crawl Options dialog opens **E**.

9. If necessary, change the title type.

10. Configure the Timing options as desired **E**:

   ▸ **Start Off Screen.** Select to make the title start out of view.

   ▸ **End Off Screen.** Select to make the title end out of view. Don't enable this if you want to close with a static "The End" fading to black.

   ▸ **Preroll.** The number of frames that play before the roll begins.

   ▸ **Ease-In.** The number of frames it takes to accelerate to full scrolling speed.

   ▸ **Ease-Out.** The number of frames it takes to decelerate to a stop.

   ▸ **Postroll.** The number of static frames at the end of the roll (that is, the static title displays for this number of frames before slowly fading to black).

11. Click OK to close the dialog **F**.

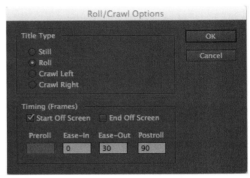

C Displaying the hidden text by dragging the text box downward.

D Opening the Roll/Crawl Options dialog.

E The settings I typically use.

F The result.

Working
with Audio

How important is the audio component of a video? Researchers have long known that lower-quality audio results in a heightened negative perception toward video quality. Often, the best thing we can do to improve the perceived quality of our videos is to devote more attention to the audio side.

Starting with a high-quality audio recording is the first step in the audio workflow. Microphone type, pick-up pattern, and placement are important considerations, as are audio recording levels and codecs, but ultimately the goal of audio acquisition is to obtain a strong signal-to-noise ratio in the audio recording. Essentially, you want the signal—the audio you're trying to capture, like a speaker or performer—to be more prominent than the noise that you don't want to hear, usually background noise.

In this chapter we'll focus on the second step in the audio workflow: editing and sweetening your audio in Premiere Pro. We'll explore volume, gain, audio effects, and Adobe Audition, a standalone sound-editing application, for more advanced audio needs.

Adjusting Volume in the Effect Controls Panel

Changes to volume affect audio amplitude, which is measured in decibels (dB). Instead of starting at zero and increasing in units, amplitude is measured by a logarithmic scale that starts at infinity (∞) and increases to a maximum of 0 dB in the digital waveform. Increasing or decreasing the volume increases the amplitude of both the signal and the noise equally.

To adjust volume in the Effect Controls panel:

1. Select the clip on the Timeline that you want to adjust the audio on **A**.

2. In the Effect Controls panel, click the disclosure triangle next to the Volume effect to reveal its controls **B**.

3. Do the same for the Channel Volume effect **C**.

   Volume affects both channels, and Channel Volume gives controls for the Left (channel 1) and Right (channel 2) channels of a stereo configuration.

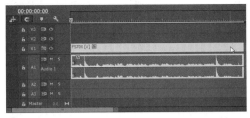

A Selecting the audio clip on the Timeline.

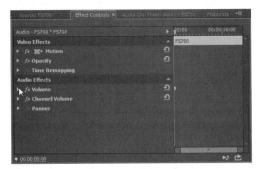

B Click the disclosure triangle to the left of Volume to reveal the Volume controls.

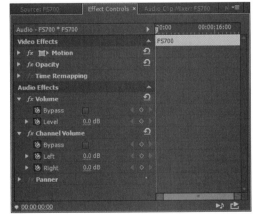

C Volume and Channel Volume controls revealed.

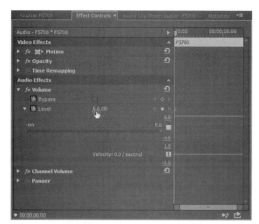

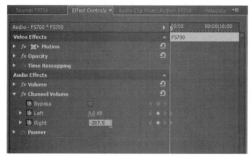

D Dragging to adjusting the audio track's level.

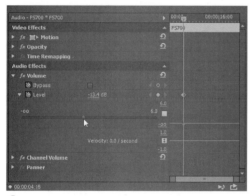

E Adjusting using the slider.

F Adjusting Right and Left channel volumes separately.

4. You can increase the volume to 6 dB and decrease it to −287.5 dB by hovering just under the level until your pointer turns into a double-headed arrow. Drag it to the right to increase the volume and to the left to decrease it **D**.

Alternatively, you can drag the slider **E**, or select the numerical value and change it.

5. To adjust the volume of the Right channel independent of the volume of the Left channel, enter different values in the Channel Volume effect **F**.

continues on next page

6. To adjust the stereo left/right balance, change the value in the Panner effect: –100 for all left, 0 for balanced, and 100 for all right 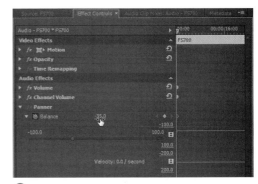.

To control the changes in volume over time in your clip, you can add keyframes on any of the effects by clicking the keyframe button ⓗ. (For more on keyframing effects, see "Animating an Effect with Keyframes" in Chapter 9.)

7. In either the Effect Controls panel Timeline or the sequence Timeline, move the playhead to where you want to enter a second keyframe, click the keyframe button ⓗ, and change the volume level as described in step 4 or 5. Or you can skip a step and directly input a numerical value ⓘ, which will add a keyframe ⓙ.

Ⓖ Adjust the Panner effect's Balance control to shift the audio balance incrementally toward the left or right channel.

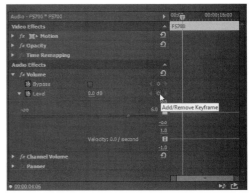

Ⓗ Add a keyframe to begin adjusting volume over time.

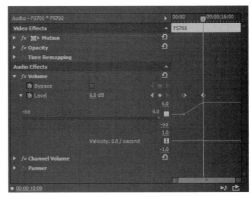

Ⓙ Adding the second keyframe.

Ⓘ Inputting a number to set the value for the keyframe.

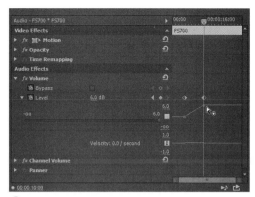

K Drag the keyframe marker up and down to further adjust the audio at that point in the Timeline.

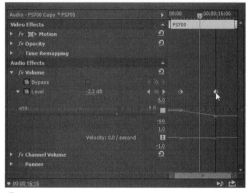

L Drag the keyframe marker in the Effect Controls Timeline to fine-tune its timing.

8. Adjust the volume as needed by dragging the keyframe marker up or down **K**.

9. Adjust the keyframe timing as desired by dragging the keyframe to the left or right **L**.

Adjusting Volume on the Timeline

In addition to adjusting the volume in the Effect Controls panel, you can adjust the volume directly on the Timeline. The audio levels are mirrored, so a change to one affects the other, and the two methods can be used interchangeably. You can adjust the overall volume levels by adjusting the volume band, or you can adjust the volume over time, such as fading the audio in or out, by adding keyframes

To adjust volume on the Timeline:

1. Hover the pointer over the volume band on the Timeline until your pointer changes to a band with two black arrows 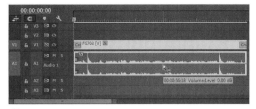 A.

2. Drag up to increase the volume B.

3. Drag down to decrease the volume C.

A The volume band pointer.

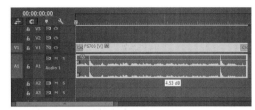

B Dragging up.

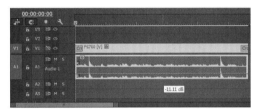

C Dragging down.

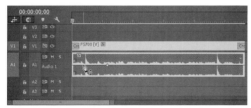

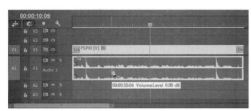

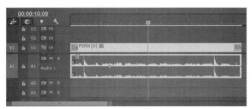

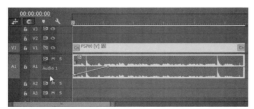

D Select the Pen tool.

E Pick a spot on which to insert a keyframe.

F Add a keyframe.

G Add the second keyframe.

H Drag it to the corner to lower the volume and create the fade-in.

To fade audio in with keyframes:

1. Select the Pen tool  **D**.

2. Select a point on the volume band **E** on which to insert a keyframe **F**.

3. Insert a second keyframe at or closer to the head of the clip **G**.

4. Drag the second keyframe into the lower-left corner of the clip **H**.

Working with Gain

On a soundboard, the gain (also called trim, sensitivity, or drive) controls the sensitivity of an input to the first stage pre-amp. It is typically the first adjustment that an audio engineer makes on the soundboard, and this same workflow applies when you edit your audio in Premiere Pro.

Adjusting audio gain

Premiere Pro offers two gain options: Set Gain To and Adjust Gain By. Both serve to increase or decrease the gain, but Set Gain To allows you to input a final gain amount in dB, whereas Adjust Gain By increases or decreases the Set Gain To amount in increments.

To set audio gain:

1. Right-click the clip on which you want to adjust gain A.

2. Select Audio Gain B. The Audio Gain dialog opens.

3. Select Set Gain To, input a gain value C, and click OK.

   Premiere Pro displays a pre-fade Peak Amplitude value at the bottom of the Audio Gain dialog C. This value does not change when gain adjustments are made, so you will need to make sure your post-fade peak amplitude does not reach the 0 dB limit. You can calculate your post-fade peak amplitude by adding the displayed Peak Amplitude to the added gain value. In this example, I entered 15 dB of gain C. When you compare the waveform in A to the one in the same track in D, you can see the increase in the audio level.

A Right-click your audio track of choice.

B Select Audio Gain.

C Set gain here, making sure not to add more gain than the negative value of the Peak Amplitude value.

D Compare the gain-adjusted waveform to the pre-adjusted track in A.

E Another approach: instead of setting the target gain, enter the adjustment from your current level.

F Compare **A**, **D**, and **F** to see your gain adjustments reflected in the waveform.

Gain vs. Volume Adjustments

Think in terms of gain being the input-level adjustment and volume being the output-level adjustment. Adjustments to both result in increased (or decreased) audio output levels, but in Premiere Pro the audio waveform increases only with adjustments to the gain, whereas the output volume, measured by the VU meters, combines the input levels and the output volume.

Increasing or decreasing the volume increases the amplitude of both the signal and the noise equally, but gain may affect louder and quieter parts differently. This is a function of the input signal-to-noise ratio.

To adjust audio gain:

1. Repeat steps 1 and 2 from the previous task.

2. In the Audio Gain dialog, select Adjust Gain By and enter a value of −3 dB **E**.

3. Note that the grayed-out Set Gain To value has decreased from 15 dB to 12 dB as a result of the −3dB value that you entered, but the Peak Amplitude value remains constant as it indicates the pre-fade peak amplitude and not the adjusted post-fade peak amplitude. Click OK.

   Notice that the waveform values in **F** are slightly lower than in **D** and higher than in **A**.

Normalizing your audio

Normalizing audio means using gain to adjust audio levels, but unlike manually setting a gain level or adjustment, normalizing analyzes an audio clip and then applies the amount of gain that will increase the waveform peak to the dB limit that you enter.

Premiere Pro offers two normalize options: Normalize Max Peaks and Normalize All Peaks. Both work the same way when applied to a single clip, but when you apply them to multiple clips you'll get different results.

Normalize Max Peaks adjusts the loudest peak over all the clips to the dB level you input and increases or decreases the rest by the same amount. Normalize All Peaks looks at the max peak in each of the selected clips and applies a varying amount of gain to each clip so that each clip's max peak matches the dB level that you input.

In this example, I'll start with two video clips that have audio recorded at different levels 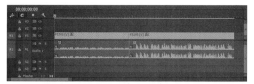.

To normalize audio:

1. Select both clips by dragging a selection over the clips or by Shift-clicking the individual clips 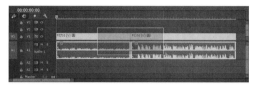.

2. Right-click any selected clip and choose Audio Gain . The Audio Gain dialog opens .

G Two clips with different audio levels—they will sound strange played sequentially if we don't normalize them.

H Selecting the two clips.

I Choose Audio Gain.

J Back in the Audio Gain dialog.

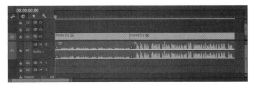

K Setting a Normalize Max Peak level.

L Both clips have higher audio levels now, but they still don't match so we've got more normalizing to do.

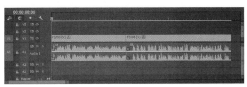

M Normalizing all peaks.

N Audio normalized across both clips.

3. Select Normalize Max Peak To and enter a value lower than 0 dB K.

   In this example I entered −3 dB. The audio waveforms increase on the audio track L as compared to the waveform shown in A. Notice that the max peak across both clips is −3 dB, but the clips still have very different audio levels.

4. Repeat steps 1 and 2, select Normalize All Peaks To, and enter a value lower than 0 dB M.

   In this example, I'm using the −3 dB level again so you can compare the clips. The audio waveforms N increase on the first clip, so now its audio peaks hit −3 dB; the second clip is unchanged (same level as in L) because its peaks were already normalized to −3 dB.

Sending Audio to Adobe Audition

Great audio is as much a function of clean and balanced audio inputs with a strong signal-to-noise ratio as it is a function of post-production effects and audio cleanup. Premiere Pro does a great job of video editing and video post- production, but sometimes video editors need to use After Effects or SpeedGrade for functionality that isn't available in Premiere Pro. The same goes for sound editing, and Adobe Audition meets that need.

In this example, we'll work with an audio clip recorded from a DSLR's internal microphone set to auto volume control and placed 12 feet away from the talent. You can't hear the audio in this book, but as you can imagine if you've captured audio under similar conditions, there is an undesirable noise floor and an unevenness to the audio levels. Both of these issues are best addressed in Audition.

To send audio to Adobe Audition:

1. Click the open track button to expand the audio waveform **A**. The track expands and displays the audio waveform **B**.

2. Hover over the lower part of the track, and drag the track down to further expand the waveform **C**.

   You can tell that there is an undesirable noise floor by examining the section to the left of the playhead **C**, where there is clearly some audio registering before the speaker starts to speak. This is best dealt with in Audition by capturing a noise print and removing that noise floor.

3. To launch Audition, right-click the clip and choose Edit Clip In Adobe Audition **D**.

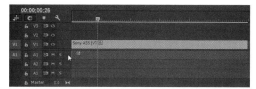

A Clicking the Open button to expand the waveform.

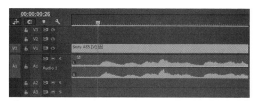

B The track expands and displays the audio waveform.

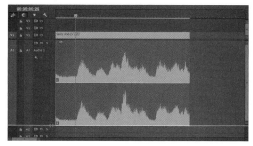

C Expanding the waveform further shows that it's too noisy to the left of the playhead, where the noise should be minimal.

D Sending the clip to Audition.

Entering the Audio Workspace

By default, the Premiere Pro workspace is set to Editing, which is optimized for video editing Ⓐ. But when you're working with audio, use the Audio workspace so that the audio tools are more prominent Ⓑ, including the Audio Mixer.

Ⓐ The (default) Editing workspace.

Ⓑ The Audio workspace.

To adjust volume in the Audio Mixer:

1. From the Premiere Pro menu ,
   choose Window > Workspace >
   Audio 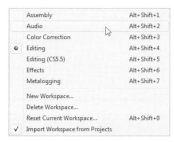 to change the layout to the
   Audio workspace. Alternatively, press
   Alt+Shift+2 (Windows) or Option+Shift+2
   (Mac OS).

   When you play back your clip, you'll
   see the audio levels in the Audio Mixer
   VU meter display both graphically and
   numerically for each individual audio
   track 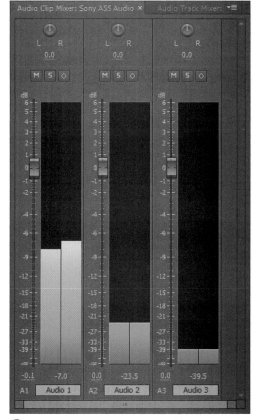.

C Accessing the
Workspace options.

D Choose
Audio to enter
the Audio
workspace.

E Audio levels represented in the Audio Mixer.

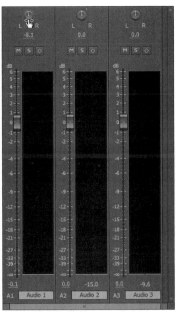

2. At the top of the window, you can adjust the pan by hovering over the L R knob until the pointer changes to a hand with a double-headed arrow **F**. Drag left to pan left, and right to pan right. A value of –100 pushes all the audio to the left; a value of 100 pushes it all to the right.

3. Mute, solo, or add keyframes by clicking the buttons below the L R knobs **G**.

4. Increase or decrease the volume by dragging the sliders up or down **H**.

5. Rename the audio track by clicking the track name and typing a new name **I**.

F Panning audio left and right.

G Mute, Solo, and Add Keyframe options.

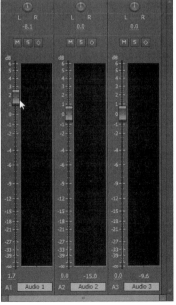

H Increase or decrease volume using the slider.

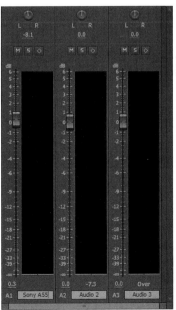

I Rename the audio track if desired.

Working with Audio Effects

Premiere Pro has more than 40 audio effects in the Effects panel. Some, like Fill Left or Fill Right, are simple effects that have no additional settings. Others feature a number of customizable parameters; EQ (short for equalization), for example, offers a five-band mid-frequency control to smooth out a sound or to emphasize or deemphasize part of an audio track.

To apply an audio effect:

1. In the Effects panel, browse the list of audio effects by toggling the Audio Effects disclosure triangle .

2. Alternatively, you can enter part or all of the name of the effect in the Effects search field and Premiere Pro will display all effects that contain the letters you type B.

(A) Premiere Pro's extensive Audio Effects palette.

(B) Searching for (and finding) EQ.

C Applying the EQ effect.

D The EQ effect is in the Effect Controls panel and ready for customizing.

3. Drag the EQ effect into the clip that you want to edit, and release **C**.

4. Open the Effect Controls panel if it's not already open, and you'll see the EQ effect there **D**.

   If this were a simple effect like Fill Left, then your work would be done, but this effect requires customization, which you'll accomplish in the next task.

To customize an audio effect:

1. In the Effect Controls panel, click the Individual Parameters disclosure triangle to view the list of controls 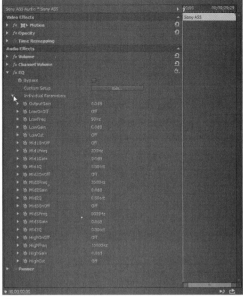.

2. Click the Edit button next to Custom Setup ❶ to launch the Clip Fx Editor ❷.

❶ Click the Individual Parameters disclosure triangle to see the EQ effect's many parameters.

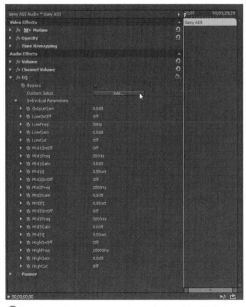

❶ Click the Edit button to launch the Clip Fx Editor.

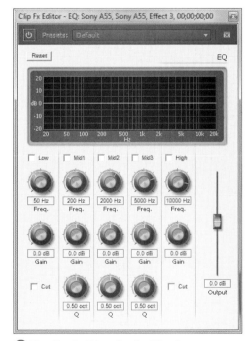

❷ The Clip Fx Editor for the EQ effect.

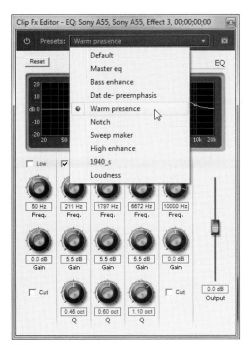

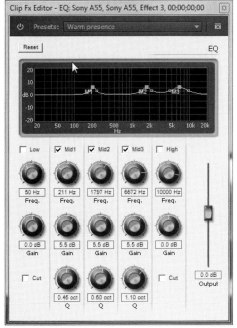

H Choosing an EQ preset.

I Our gain keyframes.

3. Select a preset EQ from the Presets menu **H**. The graphical display shows keyframes with gain levels at up to five different frequency levels **I**.

continues on next page

4. Adjust each keyframe as desired by dragging the keyframe up, down, left, or right **J**, or by adjusting the dials for Frequency (Freq.), Gain, and Q factor **K**. You can also click a numeric value and enter a different value **L**. (Q factor smooths out the slope to increase the transition.)

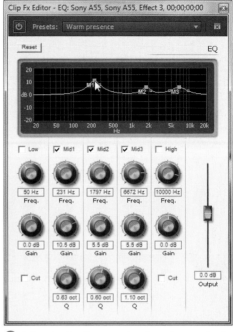

J Adjusting keyframes—the dragging method.

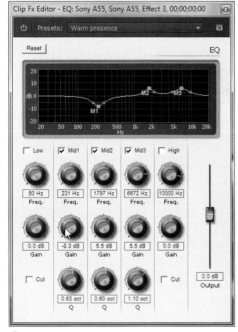

K The dial-adjustment method.

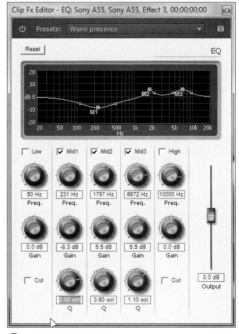

L The enter-a-numeric-value method.

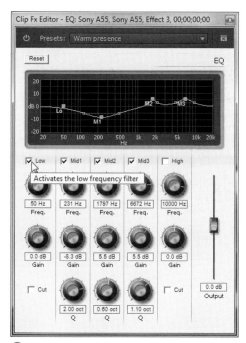

M Adding more bands.

5. To add more bands, select an additional frequency range **M**.

6. To activate the Lowpass or Highpass filter, select the Cut check box under the desired band **N**. Note that the curve changes with each adjustment.

7. Finally, increase or decrease the gain by dragging the Output slider up or down **O**.

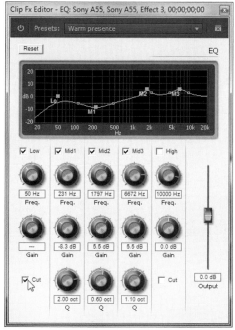

N Activating the Lowpass or Highpass filter.

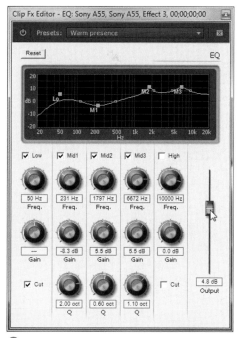

O Adjusting gain output—the slider method.

Publishing
Your Video

You've captured, trimmed, arranged, tweaked, titled, and transitioned your video project. It's not perfect (it never is), but it's time to share it with the world.

With Premiere Pro, you do the bulk of that sharing via Adobe Media Encoder, which has blossomed into an exceptionally competent, high-performance encoder that can produce for a full range of output targets, from Avid DNxHD to YouTube.

You can deploy Adobe Media Encoder presets and encode directly in Premiere Pro, which is faster than encoding with Adobe Media Encoder but locks down Premiere Pro for the duration of the encode. Or, you can send jobs from Premiere Pro to Adobe Media Encoder, where you can add multiple output targets and encode in the background. You can even encode stand-alone files or Premiere Pro sequences in Adobe Media Encoder.

We'll cover all of this in this chapter, but we'll start with a simpler and more common task: exporting still images from the Timeline.

Exporting Still Images

You'll export single frames for a variety of reasons, such as creating titles or DVD menus or sharing with your friends and colleagues. You can export from the Source Monitor or Timeline using this procedure. Premiere Pro will export frames from the Source Monitor at the resolution of the video file, and export frames from the Timeline at the resolution of the sequence.

To export a frame from Premiere Pro:

1. In the Source Monitor or Program Monitor **A**, navigate the playhead to the target frame.

2. Click the Export Frame button 📷 (at the bottom right of either monitor), or press Control/Command+E **A**. The Export Frame dialog opens **B**.

3. Customize the file name.

4. Choose a format from the Format menu **B**. JPEG is a lossy, compressed format that will produce the smallest files; PNG is a lossless format that's next-most efficient in terms of file size. Use the other formats in the menu only if the person to whom you're sending the file requests one of them.

5. Click the Browse button to choose the output path **B**.

6. Select the Import Into Project check box (partially obscured by the Format drop-down in **B**) to import the frame into your project.

7. Click OK to export the frame.

A Click the Export Frame button to export a frame from either the Source Monitor or Program Monitor.

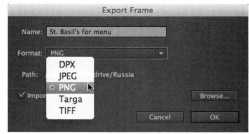

B Choose the parameters and customize the name.

A You can export a video or sequence by choosing it in the Project panel.

B But most of the time you'll probably export a sequence from the Timeline.

Exporting Media from Premiere Pro

This is where the rubber meets the road when it comes to exporting audio and video from Premiere Pro, so let's get going. Note that Premiere Pro can export clips and sequences in the Project panel, or sequences in the Timeline.

Occasionally, you'll export a file, look at the result, and ask yourself, "How did that happen? I didn't want to export that." Usually it's because you selected the wrong source before starting the process.

To open the Export Settings dialog:

1. Click the target video in the Project panel **A**, or click the sequence in either the Project panel or Timeline **B**.

2. Do one of the following:

   ▸ Press Control/Command+M

   ▸ Choose File > Export > Media

   The Export Settings dialog opens **C**.

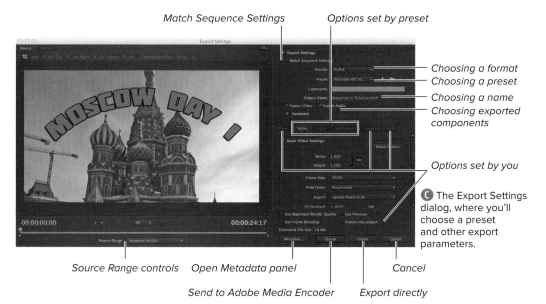

Match Sequence Settings

Options set by preset

Choosing a format

Choosing a preset

Choosing a name

Choosing exported components

Options set by you

C The Export Settings dialog, where you'll choose a preset and other export parameters.

Source Range controls   Open Metadata panel   Cancel

Send to Adobe Media Encoder   Export directly

Working in the Export Settings dialog

Typically, you work in the Export Settings dialog from the top down, starting in the Export Settings area. The Match Sequence Settings check box, which I talk about more at the end of the chapter, is a quick way to create an archival-quality version of your project. But for the purposes of this discussion, I'll assume that you will output using Premiere Pro presets, which is a good strategy for most producers.

Presets are categorized by format, so you choose the format first and then the preset. You complete work in the Export Settings dialog by choosing the output name and target folder, and then choosing to export video, audio, or both.

There are as many as six tabs beneath the Export Settings area, depending upon the preset format that you choose. The key options in three of those—Video, Audio, and Multiplexer—are determined by the preset that you choose. The others—Filters, Captions, and FTP—are (or may be) configured by you before exporting. The options at the bottom of the panel—including Use Maximum Render Quality—are also set by you before exporting. Finally, on the bottom left are Source Range controls used to choose which region of the source file to encode. I'll cover these options in the tasks.

At the bottom of the Export Settings dialog, click Metadata to open the Metadata panel and enter more information about the sequence or clip. Then click Queue to send the file to Adobe Media Encoder for encoding so you can resume working in Premiere Pro. Click Export to export directly from the Export Settings dialog (and lock yourself out of Premiere Pro for the duration). Click Cancel to close the dialog and return to Premiere Pro.

Formats and presets

Entire books have been written about file formats like those shown in ⓓ; I know because I've written four of them (but who's counting?).

When you're producing videos for others (like your webmaster, or for uploading to a service like Brightcove), the first rule is to get specific information about the required format. For example, Flash Player can play F4V, FLV, QuickTime, and H.264 files, but the authoring system your webmaster uses may support only one of the four. When in doubt, ask.

- AAC Audio. Audio compressed using the Advanced Audio Coding technology, which is the audio component of most H.264 files.

- AIFF (Audio Interchange File Format). An audio-only format predominantly used by OS X. Useful when creating audio-only output for use on a Mac.

- DNxHD MXF OP1a. Avid DNX output stored in an MXF Operational Pattern 1a format. Typically used to export for import into an Avid project, or to create a very high-quality (and high data rate) archival file from both Windows and Mac versions of Premiere Pro (ProRes is OS X only).

- DPX. Digital Picture Exchange, a format for digital intermediate and special effects work.

- F4V and FLV. Flash video using the H.264 and VP6 codecs, respectively. Use either of these only when specifically requested.

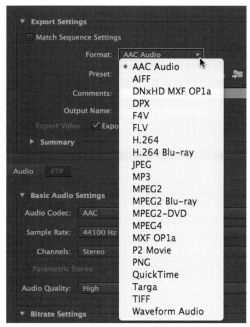

D The available formats on Adobe Media Encoder.

- H.264. The most widely used distribution codec. Presets in this category serve all mobile and set-top box platforms (like Apple TV and Roku), and encode for upload to sites like YouTube and Vimeo.

- H.264 Blu-ray. H.264 video for including in a Blu-ray disc.

- JPEG. Will create a sequence of JPEG-compressed frames.

- MP3. Will create an audio file compressed into the MP3 format.

- MPEG2. An older format mostly supplanted by H.264. May be useful when producing output for some broadcasters.

- MPEG2 Blu-ray/DVD. Use these when outputting for inclusion on Blu-ray or DVD discs.

- MPEG4. Use only for output to very old mobile devices.

- MXF OP1a. Useful for creating output for Sony's IMC and some XDCAM cameras.

- P2 Movie. Creates output compatible with P2 cards.

- PNG. Will create a sequence of PNG-compressed frames.

- QuickTime. Useful for accessing Quick-Time-based codecs, including ProRes (OS X only).

- Targa and TIFF. Will create a sequence of Targa or TIFF frames.

- Waveform Audio. Uncompressed audio output, useful when creating audio-only output for cross-platform use.

The following outputs are Windows-only:

- AVI/AVI (uncompressed). Useful for accessing AVI codecs (like some Black-Magic formats) and intermediate codecs (like Lagarith).

- BMP/GIF. Will create a sequence of BMP/GIF frames.

- Animated GIF. Exports as an animated GIF for web use.

- Windows Media. Produces Windows Media Video (WMV) output, primarily for playback on the Windows Media Player.

Working through the Export Settings tabs

Beneath the Export Settings area are six tabs that contain the bulk of the encoding configurations.

The Filters tab **E** makes available during export a Gaussian Blur filter, which helps remove noise but can noticeably blur the video. I would use this only in a total rescue situation, where the footage is so noisy that you can't publish without some level of filtering. Even then, there are better options, such as the Neat Video plug-in discussed at bit.ly/PP_Neat.

The Video tab **F** contains video-related configuration options, which vary signifi-cantly according to the selected format and preset. If you know your way around an encoding tool and are looking for set-tings like resolution, data rate, keyframe settings, H.264 profile, and level, this is the place. If you're a newbie, don't mess with these, because you could produce a file incompatible with the selected preset.

E Enable Gaussian Blur only in rescue situations.

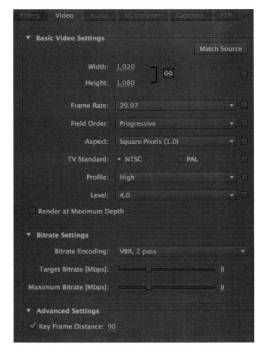

F The Video tab contains video-related encoding options.

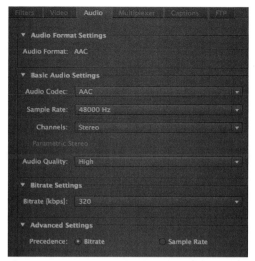

The Audio tab  contains audio-related encoding parameters and also shouldn't be messed with unless you know what you're doing. Multiplexing  refers to low-level file details like how the audio and video in the file are interleaved and is best left to the preset.

 The Audio tab contains audio-related encoding options.

Captions  options will be grayed out when your source materials have no closed captions (which is true here). I discuss the entire closed-caption workflow in Chapter 16, which is available for download from the Peachpit website.

Finally, the FTP tab  lets you automatically upload your encoded files to an FTP site. Fill in the address and your credentials, and then click the Test button to test the connection. Premiere Pro will send your file to that location once encoding is complete.

 Don't touch the Multiplexer settings unless you really know what you're doing.

 These options become available when your source footage is captioned.

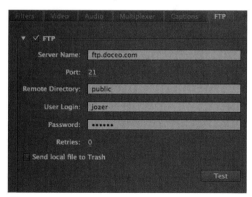

 Use these controls to upload the encoded file to an FTP site.

Final export settings

At the bottom of the Export Settings dialog are four check boxes .

- Use Maximum Render Quality. This enables a higher level of rendering that improves quality noticeably in several scenarios, including when scaling from HD to SD or with multiple-layer projects. The downside is increased rendering time for computers not equipped with a graphics card that provides GPU acceleration via the Mercury Playback Engine. If you're working on a notebook without GPU acceleration and you're in a hurry, don't enable this. If you're on a workstation with NVIDIA graphics, go for it.

- Use Frame Blending. Enable when you're changing the frame rate between the source and output.

- Use Previews. This option uses previews produced during editing to produce the final output file. This can speed rendering, but if the render format is different from the preview format, it can degrade quality. I recommend disabling this unless you're in a big hurry.

- Import into Project. Enable this to import the encoded footage back into the project.

Next, we'll work through the entire process, producing a file for uploading to YouTube. I'll start from the very beginning.

(K) The configuration options at the bottom of the Export Settings dialog.

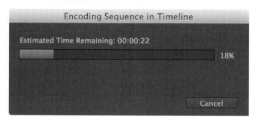

L Choosing the format and preset for uploading a
1080p file to YouTube.

M Exporting directly from Premiere Pro can
reduce rendering time by as much as 33 percent,
but you can't edit while rendering.

TIP As discussed in the "Workflows" section later in this chapter, the bitrates used in
Adobe Media Encoder's YouTube and similar
presets are very conservative. You may want
to consider boosting the data rate to achieve
higher-quality results.

To create a file for uploading to YouTube:

1. Click your target video in the Project panel A or your target sequence in either the Project panel or Timeline B.

2. Do one of the following:
   ▸ Press Control/Command+M
   ▸ Choose File > Export > Media
   The Export Settings dialog opens C.

3. Click the Format menu, and choose the H.264 format D.

4. Click the Preset menu, and choose the desired YouTube preset E.

5. Click the output name to open the Save As dialog, where you can choose a name and storage location.

6. In the Export Settings dialog, select the Export Video check box, the Export Audio check box, or both F.

7. At the bottom of the Export Settings dialog, choose the desired options:
   ▸ I enable Use Maximum Render Qual-ity for all encodes K.
   ▸ No change in frame rate, so don't enable Use Frame Blending.
   ▸ To achieve maximum quality, don't enable Use Previews.
   ▸ No need to import this back into the project, so don't enable Import into Project.

8. Do one of the following:
   ▸ Click Queue to send the encoding job to Adobe Media Encoder. We'll explore this option later in the chapter.
   ▸ Click Export to begin encoding imme-diately M.
   ▸ Click Cancel to cancel the encoding job and return to Premiere Pro.

Saving custom presets

Any time you customize a preset, you can save the preset for reuse. In the encoding that we just performed, I changed the preset by enabling Maximum Render Quality. This is now a custom preset that I can save, and the next time I apply it, I won't have to enable Maximum Render Quality.

To save a custom preset:

1. At the top right of the Export Settings dialog, click the Save Preset button **N**. The Choose Name dialog opens **O**.

2. Type the desired name **O**.

3. If you customized filter or FTP settings and wish to include them in the custom preset, select either or both check boxes **O**.

4. Click OK to save the preset **O**.

TIP Premiere Pro saves custom presets at the top of the list for that format **P**.

Exporting less than a full sequence or file

Sometimes you'll want to export less than a full file or sequence. You can accomplish this multiple ways in Premiere Pro and Adobe Media Encoder.

To export a selected area:

1. In the Source Range menu at the bottom of the Export Settings dialog, choose one of the following:

   ▶ If you marked In and Out points in the sequence, choose Sequence In/Out and skip to step 3 **Q**.

N When the Preset menu says Custom, you've changed a preset. Let's save it!

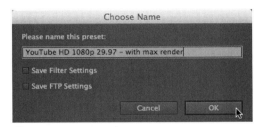

O Complete the options here, and click OK.

P Premiere Pro places custom presets at the top of the list.

Q If you haven't marked the sequence's In and Out points or Work Area, select Custom and drag the Mark In and Mark Out indicators to the desired position.

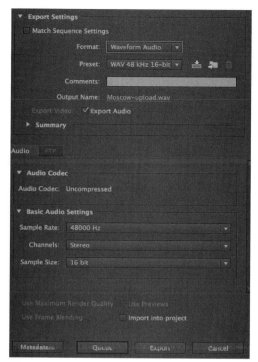

 The settings you'll use to create a Waveform file for further editing.

▸ If you set a Work Area in the sequence, choose Work Area and skip to step 3 ⓞ.

▸ To select a custom area in the selected sequence or file, choose Custom ⓞ.

2. Drag the In and Out markers to the desired location to mark the custom area ⓠ.

3. To render the file, click Queue or Export.

TIP Work Area? This book doesn't cover setting the Work Area, because marking In and Out points accomplishes the same functions and is faster and easier to do.

Exporting audio only

You can probably figure this out if you've been reading from the start of the chapter, but if you're diving in for a quick solution, you might find this task helpful.

To export an audio file:

1. Choose the appropriate format from the Format menu. Here are some suggestions:

   ▸ For distribution, choose either AAC Audio or MP3.

   ▸ For further editing, choose either AIFF or Waveform Audio ⓡ.

2. Choose the desired preset. Both AAC Audio and MP3 have at least two presets; AIFF and Waveform Audio have only a single preset ⓡ.

3. Click the output name to open the Save As dialog, where you can choose a name and storage location.

4. If desired, customize the parameters in the Audio tab ⓡ.

5. Click Export or Queue ⓡ.

About Adobe Media Encoder

Adobe Media Encoder uses the same presets that you accessed in Premiere Pro's Export Settings dialog, but it adds several critical features to the mix. First, when encoding in Adobe Media Encoder, you can be editing in Premiere Pro, which you can't when exporting via the Export Settings dialog. Adobe Media Encoder can encode standalone files, Premiere Pro sequences, and even compositions from Adobe After Effects, a nice convenience. You can load files from the File menu **A**, or you can drag and drop files.

Perhaps more importantly, Adobe Media Encoder can encode a single file to multiple outputs, which can be a great time-saver—particularly because it encodes those files in parallel (all at one time) rather than serially (one after the other). Finally, Adobe Media Encoder can set up and monitor watch folders, which are folders on a drive to which you assign a preset or presets. You or others with access to the folder can drop files into the watch folder, and Premiere Pro will automatically render the file and, if desired, transfer the encoded file to a new location via FTP. Pretty advanced stuff.

Let's take a quick tour of Adobe Media Encoder and set some preferences, and then we'll get to work encoding a single file to multiple outputs and creating a watch folder.

Touring Adobe Media Encoder

You can open Adobe Media Encoder the traditional way (supported by your operating system), or you can let it run automatically when you click Queue in the Export Settings dialog.

A You can encode disk-based files, After Effects compositions, and Premiere Pro sequences via these menu commands.

However you run the program, it has four main windows **B**. On the upper left is the Queue window, which contains the files queued for encoding. You also see the controls for starting, stopping, and pausing the queue, and for enabling the watch folders to encode automatically.

On the upper right is the Preset Browser, which contains the same presets as the Export Settings dialog, though they are in different folders. On the bottom left is the Encoding window, which shows a preview of the file being encoded; this is a nice touch, since it can alert you to problems like unexpected letterboxes and similar issues. On the bottom right is the Watch Folders window, which contains any watch folders that you've created.

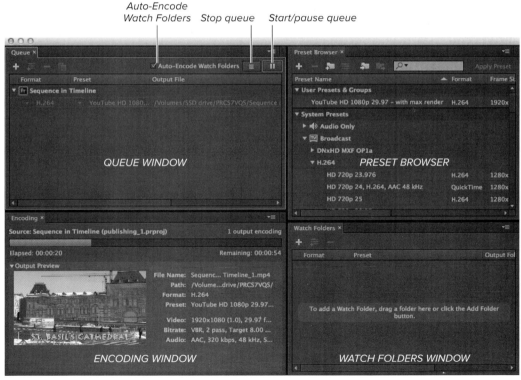

Auto-Encode Watch Folders   Stop queue   Start/pause queue

B Adobe Media Encoder.

Setting preferences

There are a few preferences that you should at least be aware of before starting serious work with Adobe Media Encoder.

To set preferences in Adobe Media Encoder:

1. Choose Edit > Preferences (Windows) or Adobe Media Encoder > Preferences (Mac OS) to open the Preferences dialog.

2. In the General tab , consider the following preferences:

   ▸ Consider selecting the "Start queue automatically when idle for" check box and setting a duration; otherwise, you'll have to manually start each queue.

   ▸ Note the ability to disable parallel encoding, which may be helpful on slower machines when you're trying to edit and encode simultaneously.

   ▸ Note the ability to specify a file location for all encoded files. Otherwise, they're stored in the same folder as the source video clip or project file.

   ▸ Note the ability to choose whether to overwrite existing files with the same name or to increment the file name.

3. When you're done configuring your options, click OK to close the Preferences dialog.

4. In the Queue window, note the Auto-Encode Watch folders check box **B**. If you want the ability to manually trigger watch folder encodes, deselect this check box.

C There are several preferences here that you need to be aware of.

D Here's how you start encoding a queue.

E To encode to a preset, drag the preset onto the queued file.

F Add as many files as you would like.

G Premiere Pro encodes the files in parallel (if you enabled that option in the preferences).

To start an encoded queue in Adobe Media Encoder:

Do one of the following:

- Click the Start Queue button **D** in the upper-right corner of the Queue window, or click the window to make it active and press Enter/Return.

- Choose File > Start Queue.

  Adobe Media Encoder starts processing the queue.

Adding presets to a queued file

As mentioned, one of the key benefits of encoding in Adobe Media Encoder is the ability to add presets to the encoded file and encode to all outputs simultaneously.

To add presets to a queued file:

1. In the Preset Browser, navigate through the folders and subfolders to find the desired presets **E**.

2. Drag the preset onto the queued file and release **E**.

3. Repeat as necessary **F**.

4. Start encoding **D**. Premiere Pro encodes the queued files to the selected outputs in parallel **G**.

Working with presets

Let's cover a couple of other important skills relating to presets in Adobe Media Encoder. The first two cover how to edit an applied preset and a preset in the Preset Browser. The latter two cover how to import and export presets.

To edit an applied preset:

In the Queue window, right-click the preset and choose Export Settings ⓗ. The Export Settings dialog opens.

To edit a preset in the Preset Browser:

In the Preset Browser, right-click the preset and choose Preset Settings ⓘ. Adobe Media Encoder opens the Preset Settings dialog ⓙ.

ⓗ You'll use this command frequently to review the configuration in the Export Settings dialog.

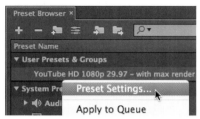

ⓘ To edit an existing preset, right-click and choose Preset Settings.

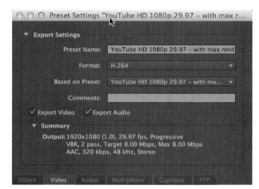

ⓙ The Preset Settings dialog (shown here truncated). It has all the configuration options available in the Export Settings dialog.

K I want to share this preset on another Mac. Note that Premiere Pro places custom presets in the User Presets & Groups folder.

L Name the preset, choose a storage location, and click Save.

M I copy the file over to the other Mac and click the Import Presets button.

N Choose the preset and click Open. Adobe Media Encoder places it in the User Presets & Groups folder **K**.

To export a preset:

1. In the Preset Browser, right-click the preset and choose Export Presets **K**. The Export Preset dialog opens **L**.

2. Name the preset and navigate to the desired storage location. Click Save **L** to save the preset, which has the file extension .epr.

To import a preset:

1. At the top of the Preset Browser, click the Import Presets 🔳 button **M**. The Import Preset dialog opens **N**.

2. Navigate to and select the preset (it will have the file extension .epr), and click Open. Adobe Media Encoder imports the preset and places it in the User Presets & Groups folder **K**.

Watch Folders

Watch folders are disk-based folders tied to presets. Anyone who can access the selected folder and drop a file in can encode the file to all selected presets.

To create a watch folder with Adobe Media Encoder:

1. To create the watch folder, do one of the following:

   ▸ In the Watch Folders window, click the Add Folder icon **A**. The Choose a Folder to Watch dialog opens. Select the watch folder, and click OK/Choose to close the dialog.

   ▸ Using Windows Explorer (Windows) or File Manager (Mac OS), drag any folder into the Watch Folders window.

2. In the Preset Browser, navigate through the folders and subfolders to find the desired presets.

3. Drag the preset onto the watch folder and release **B**. Repeat as necessary.

4. To delete any preset, right-click it and choose Remove **C**. Click Yes to confirm the deletion.

A Click the Add Folder icon to add a watch folder.

B Drag presets onto the watch folder.

C To remove a preset, right-click it and choose Remove.

Workflows

Let's spend a bit of time on workflows and workflow alternatives.

DVD and Blu-ray

You have multiple alternatives for Encore-based disc production:

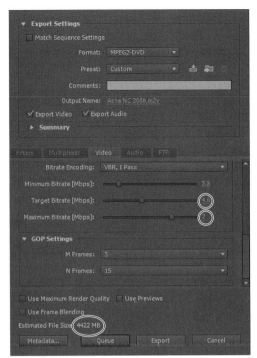

A Producing this file destined for DVD at 4.6 Mbps; the result is a file comfortably under the 4.7 GB limit.

- You can encode your files in Adobe Media Encoder using the appropriate preset. This is the simplest method, and obviously works for other DVD authoring tools as well. Depending on the length of your project and your selected media, you may have to adjust the target bitrate of the preset that you use. Adobe Media Encoder presents an estimated file size at the bottom of the panel **A**. To make this production fit on a DVD-R, which has a capacity of 4.7 GB, I had to drop the target bitrate to 4.6 Mbps, producing a video with an estimated file size of 4422 MB, or 4.42 GB.

There are two reasons I would encode at this data rate rather than trying to produce a file that's 4.6 GB or larger. First, you always want to leave a few hundred megabytes of space on the edges of the disc, which improves compatibility with older DVD players. Second, the 4422 MB is an estimate, so you want to leave some room for error. And you should never exceed the maximum bitrate of 7 Mbps; if you do, you increase the risk of poor playback on older devices. These last two issues are the same whether you encode in Encore or Adobe Media Encoder.

continues on next page

- You can send the sequence to Encore using Dynamic Link (Choose File > Adobe Dynamic Link > Send to Encore). This works well, but only when your entire production is in a single sequence, because each time you do this, Encore starts a new project. The obvious benefit of this and the next approach is that if you change the video in Premiere Pro, it automatically updates in Encore.

  Note that Encore has an Encode to Fit option. Although it's convenient to use for one-off discs, this option typically comes within a few MB of total disc capacity. If you're encoding for distribution, you may want to manually select a bitrate that produces a total file size of around 4.5 GB, which will improve compatibility with older DVD players.

- You can import sequences into Encore using Dynamic Link (File > Adobe Dynamic Link > Import Premiere Pro Sequence), which obviously works with multiple sequences. (The comments in the previous bullet point about Encore's Encode to Fit option also apply here.)

The second and third approaches are preferred.

B The Match Sequence Settings option is easy, but it's not always the best choice.

Archival workflows

When you save an archival version of your video file (as opposed to the entire project), you're preserving a file you can easily use to produce alternative outputs should an important new format come along. This is another instance where the easiest workflow may not be the best. Specifically, there's a perception that using Match Sequence Settings **B** is the best option. Unfortunately, this depends on the sequence settings.

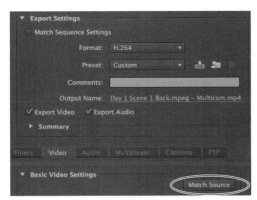

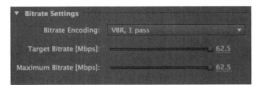

C Instead, use the H.264 codec and click the Match Source button.

D Boost the bitrate to the max.

Match Sequence Settings exports using the sequence settings and preview file format. If you choose a 1080p DSLR sequence setting, the preview file format is MPEG I-Frame, which is much less efficient than the H.264 codec initially used to capture the video.

Instead of using the Match Sequence Settings option, consider choosing the H.264 codec and then clicking the Match Source button in the Basic Video Settings area of the Export Settings dialog **C**. This ensures that the exported file matches every sequence setting but codec. Lower down in the Export Settings dialog, you can boost the data rate as high as desired **D**; more is always better, though higher bitrates obviously produce a larger file.

The highest-quality, largest-file alternative is to export using the Avid DNxHD option **E** on Windows or Mac, or using ProRes on the Mac.

E Or, if you have the space, choose an intermediate codec like Avid DNxHD (shown) or ProRes.

Uploading for UGC and OVP

UGC stands for user-generated content, which includes sites like Vimeo and YouTube. OVPs are online video platforms, and include services like Brightcove, Ooyala, and Kaltura.

I've done a lot of work on encoding for upload, most of which you can read at bit.ly/YouTube_specs, with a critical update at bit.ly/encode4UGC. The bottom line is that the higher the data rate of the encoded video, the better the result. Adobe's 1080p preset for uploading to YouTube uses a data rate of 8 Mbps. This matches the standard-quality recommendations posted by YouTube, but they recommend 50 Mbps as their highest-quality option.

Unless upload time is a significant limiter, I would encode all files destined for upload to UGC or OVP sites at the maximum data rate allowed for each preset. In the case of the aforementioned 1080p preset, I would boost the data rate to 25 Mbps .

F Consider boosting encoding for UGC and OVP to the max.

Exporting for Editing in Other Programs

If you're a Final Cut Pro or Avid Media Composer editor, Adobe offers excellent advice on how to export content and projects to these two editors in "Premiere Pro CS6 resources for Final Cut Pro and Avid Media Composer users," at http://bit.ly/switcher_pp.

Index

multiple tracks. *See also* track targeting
    extract editing for, 205
    how Premiere Pro handles, 157
    selecting, 129
    working with, 144, 146
Multiplexer tab (Export Settings dialog), 419
muting audio, 136, 137, 154, 405

N

naming
    audio tracks, 405
    bins, 84
    clips, 75
    markers, 113
    nested sequences, 361
    projects, 29
    sequences, 127
    title templates, 371, 372
navigating
    audio time units, 111
    Timeline, 149–152
    within Project panel, 73
nested sequences, 248–252
    creating on Timeline, 250
    nesting synchronized sequences, 361
    placing within nested sequence, 251
    syncing multi-camera clips via, 358–361
    using, 248–249
New After Effects Comp dialog, 67–68
New Item button, 70, 71
New Project window, 26–28
New Sequence dialog, 128, 130–132
New Title dialog, 369
noise, 418
non drop-frame timecode, 147–148
non-scan mode, 50
normalizing audio, 400–401
notebook computers, 42, 106
numeric keypad
    moving clips with, 189
    trimming from extended, 242

O

offline files
    placeholders for, 32
    working with, 34
offsetting audio, 350

online video platform (OVP) uploads, 434
opacity
    adjusting on Timeline, 266
    changing for Cross Dissolve transition, 321
    Effect Controls panel adjustments for, 262, 264
    working with fade-in, 267–268
Open Project dialog, 30
opening/closing
    Effect Controls panel, 256
    Export Settings dialog, 415
    Motion controls without Timeline, 256
    Multi-Camera Monitor, 362
    multi-camera sequence in Timeline, 354–355
    panel menus, 15
    panels, 3, 13, 14
    Preferences panel, 17
    Preview Area, 72
    projects, 30
    sequence with icon, 97
    Titler, 368, 369
orange icons, 97
Out points. *See* In/Out points
output targets
    choosing composite video, 300
    choosing sequence presets for, 126
    editing in resolution of, 262
    publishing formats for, 416–418
    selecting for archival files, 432–433
    UGC and OVP content, 434
overwrite edits
    filling gaps with lift and, 183–185
    insert edits vs., 165
    making, 165–167
    using extract with, 185–186
overwrite pointer, 165, 197
OVP (online video platform) uploads, 434

P

panel menus
    opening, 15
    Project, 70, 71
    removing transport controls in, 16
    Timeline, 137
    Titler, 370
panel tabs, 12
panels
    about, 11, 12

R

rasterization, 58

Rate Stretch tool, 245, 246–247

Razor tool, 208–210

rearrange edits, 184, 187

recording multi-camera edits, 355, 363–364

recovering crashed projects, 19

rectified waveforms, 141–142

Reference Monitor
    color correction using, 329
    illustrated, 328

reframing clips, 259–260

regular trims, 222–224

relinking files, 32, 33

remapping
    clip speed, 245, 277–278
    right-channel-only audio, 366

Remove Effects dialog, 287

removing
    clip effects, 286–287
    keyframes, 287
    time remapping, 287
    transport controls in panel menus, 16

renaming
    audio tracks, 405
    bins, 84
    clips, 75
    nested sequences, 361
    projects, 29
    sequences, 127

rendering
    Low Memory warning during, 21
    options for exported files, 420, 421, 422
    order of effects and, 285
    overview of, 7

reordering
    columns, 92
    effects, 285

replacing
    clips on Timeline, 205–207
    footage in Project panel, 207
    transitions, 315

resetting
    buttons, 16
    Effect Controls panel, 284
    keyframes, 287
    workspace, 9

resizing
    panels, 14
    Project panel, 71
    text, 374, 375

resolution
    configuring Program Monitor, 173
    editing in project, 262
    imported Photoshop content, 55
    paused, 106
    scaling HD clips for editing, 257–259
    setting Source Monitor playback, 104–106

reversing clips, 246

reverting to last saved file, 29

RGB Parade mode, 119, 337–338

ripple delete function
    about, 198
    disabling, 199
    removing Timeline gaps with, 201, 202
    when available, 202

ripple trimming
    about, 222, 225
    box color when, 225
    refining multi-camera edits with, 364
    using, 225–226, 239
    using Ripple Edit mode, 236

Roll/Crawl button (Titler), 369, 370

rolling edits
    making, 227–228
    producing split edits, 244
    slide edits vs., 231
    trimming in Rolling Edit mode, 237
    using, 222, 227

rolling titles, 389–390

rotating
    clips, 262, 263
    composited video, 302–303
    text, 376

S

safe margins
    for Program Monitor, 173
    title options for, 370
    wrapping text within, 374

safe zones
    about, 102–103
    enabling/disabling, 101

saturation, 340